The Rifle Volunteers

THE HISTORY OF THE RIFLE VOLUNTEERS

1859–1908

Ray Westlake

PICTON PUBLISHING CHIPPENHAM
1982

Photoset in 9/11 pt Times Roman
by Chippenham Typesetting, Bath Road, Chippenham, Wiltshire
Text paper supplied by Howard Smith Papers, Bristol.
Bound by Western Book Company, Maesteg.
Printed in Great Britain by Picton Print
Citadel Works, Bath Road, Chippenham, Wiltshire.

CONTENTS

To
Paul Westlake
1st Battalion
Coldstream Guards

INTRODUCTION

The intention of this work is to put on record the various rifle volunteer corps that were created as a result of the formation in 1859 of the Volunteer Force. Rifle volunteers were the infantry of the volunteer movement which also included artillery, engineers and other arms.

Listed under the counties in which they were raised and numbered are the corps that appeared in the *Monthly Army List*. Each has its formation date, location and organisation recorded. Any change in designation, disbandments and amalgamations have been noted and where known the type of person forming the unit has also been mentioned.

The location given for each corps is that of its headquarters. However, recruiting was often carried out in the surrounding area and sections of the main corps were to be found in smaller villages and towns. In cases where a corps consisted of more than one company the location given is 'Corps Headquarters'. Company HQs, if different from those of the corps, are, where known, recorded.

It will be seen that the corps of several of the smaller counties were to be included in the administrative battalions of others. The development of these units is recorded under their own county until such times that due to the consolidation of their battalion they lost their county numbers and became simply a company in the new corps. From this point subsequent changes, when known, are noted in the records of the county in which the new corps belongs. An example of this is Radnorshire whose corps were included in the 1st Herefordshire Admin. Battalion. When this battalion was consolidated as the 1st Herefordshire Corps in 1880 the 1st and 2nd Radnors became its 'I' and 'K' Companies. As part of the Herefordshire corps the Radnor Volunteers will now be considered under the Herefordshire section of the book. On occasion the names of both counties were taken into use upon consolidation. In 1880 the Clackmannanshire Admin. Battalion, which also included the corps from Kinross, was consolidated as the 1st Clackmannan and Kinross Corps. Here the post-1880 records of the last-named county will be dealt with in those of the first.

The official formation date of a corps was that on which its offer of service was accepted by the Secretary of State for War. In the vast majority of cases the letters of acceptance issued to corps cannot be traced. Instead the date of the commission issued to a corps' first officer has been used. These, in most cases, only differ from the acceptance date by a few weeks or even days.

No attempt has been made to chronicle a complete history of the volunteer rifles. Such subjects as arms, drill, etc. are far outside the scope of this work and, although included in the illustrations, badges, uniform and equipment will not be referred to.

As previously mentioned only corps recorded in the *Monthly Army List* have been included. In addition to these many were formed only to have their offer of service reach no further than the office of the Lord Lieutenant. Such units were often uniformed and even in the process of training but for various reasons did not gain official recognition.

THE INTERRUPTED DRILL.

Cartoon from
the *Boston Sunday Herald*

THE VOLUNTEER BATTALIONS

It was most probably the Duke of Wellington who was responsible for the formation in 1859 of the Volunteer Force. In a letter to Sir John Burgoyne in 1847 the Duke had made clear his concern regarding this country's national defences. He, at the age of seventy-seven did not share the general opinion of the government that the United Kingdom was safe from attack. Since the Battle of Waterloo, Britain had indeed been free from troubles in Europe. The several campaigns fought abroad were also far enough away not to render necessary the formation of additional forces to defend these shores.

The Duke, however, did not think that it was sensible to sit back in what he believed was a false sence of security. 'It was time,' he said, 'to make provisions for the defence of the country and to take all precautions against invasion.' 'I hope,' he went on, 'that the Almighty may protect me from being witness of the tragedy which I cannot persuade my contemporaries to take measures to avert.'

If, as in the days of Napoleon I, home defence was to be supplemented by volunteers, the Duke's fears were quite understandable. At the time of his letter to Sir John, only two units, as far as riflemen are concerned, were then in existence. These were the Honourable Artillery Company and the Royal Victoria Rifles who as the Duke of Cumberland's Sharpshooters had managed to survive the general disbandment of volunteers after Waterloo.

In agreement with the Duke, Captain Hans Busk of the Royal Victoria Rifles later circulated copies of his 1847 letter. Captain Busk's corps had, by 1858, dwindled to just fifty-seven effective men. As a direct result of the action taken the Victorias, by the middle of 1859, mustered no less than 800.

At the same time as Captain Busk was working on behalf of the Victorias others in the country were intent to organise a volunteer force on a national scale. A corps had already been sanctioned at Exeter in 1852 and by 1855 the formation of one in Liverpool was well under way. It was not until 1859, however, that the main serge of volunteers came forward.

At first the Government of the day were not over keen to see a volunteer force of any size created. The idea of 'amateur soldiers' was not appealing and it was also thought that the establishment of the force would interfere with the recruiting of the regular army.

The War Office finally gave way and on 12 May 1859 sanction to form volunteer corps was given. This authorisation was conveyed in a circular addressed to the Lord Lieutenants of counties who were asked to submit any plans that they might have.

Formation of volunteer corps was to be under the provisions of Act 44, George III, cap.54, dated 5 June 1804. The main provisions of the 1804 Act were summarized in the 12 May circular. These indicated that the officers' commissions should be signed by the Lord Lieutenant; that volunteers could be called out in the case of actual invasion or rebellion; while under arms members of the corps should be subject to military law and while on active service no volunteer could quit his corps.He could, however, at other times leave after giving 14 days' notice.

The next circular concerning the formation of volunteer corps was issued on 25

May. In the main, this document made clear the views of the government regarding corps. Requirements as to the standards of drill and discipline were set out and the establishment of ranges for each corps was advised. It was also suggested in the circular that rifle volunteers should be organised into companies or sub-divisions.

The 3rd War Office Circular of 1859 was issued on 13 July and again made clear the government's requirements regarding arms and training. Accompanying the Circular was a memorandum which, among other things, set out the establishment of each rifle corps. A company was to consist of not less than sixty nor more than one hundred effectives. These were to be officered by one captain, one lieutenant and one ensign. Sub-divisions were to have thirty effectives with one lieutenant and one ensign. Where several companies were raised in the same locality a battalion could be formed. The requirements here were for eight companies or of a total strength of not less than five hundred. In addition to its company officers a battalion could have a lieutenant-colonel, a major and the services of an adjutant.

It was in the memorandum of 13 July that the subject of precedence was settled. Each arm of the volunteer force was to rank more or less on the lines of the regular forces. At the time of the memorandum, rifles were to rank after artillery as these were the only arms then in existence. Within a short time, however, others were created and the precedence list read as follows; Light Horse, Artillery, Engineers, Mounted Rifles and Rifles.

The precedence of a corps within its county was indicated by the number allotted to it by the Secretary of State for War. The procedure here was that when the Lord Lieutenant received an application for the formation of a corps he would then date it and forward the offer of service on to the War Office. When the Secretary of State for War had satisfied himself that the proposed unit had fulfilled the necessary conditions he would, according to the date entered on the application by the Lord Lieutenant, allot the corps its number. The next step was to inform the corps of the acceptance by HM The Queen of its services. It is the date of the letter bearing this information that is considered to be the official formation date of a corps. As a rule these dates coincide with the precedence number assigned. However, on occasion a number was allotted but due to some special circumstances where reference had to be made to the corps because of some informality in its offer of service, the acceptance date was held up. Very soon after the acceptance of the corps and the assignment of its number the gazetting of officers was proceeded with.

Very few letters accepting the services of corps have survived and therefore the official date of formation is not known. However, as the date borne on the commission of the corps' first officer varies in the majority of cases by only a matter of weeks these are now geneally accepted.

County precedence was settled according to the date on which the first company in the county was formed. The eventual order of seniority was as follows—

1. Devonshire
2. Middlesex
3. Lancashire
4. Surrey
5. Pembrokeshire
6. Derbyshire

By the beginning of 1860 it was realised by the War Office that due to the unforeseen number of independent companies formed some kind of higher organisation was necessary. In a circular issued to Lord Lieutenants of Counties dated 24 March suggestions for companies to merge either as consolidated or administrative battalions were put forward.

A consolidated battalion, the circular explained, 'applies to a battalion whose constituent companies are drawn from the same town or city'. When such a battalion was formed the corps involved were to lose their individual numbers and continue service either as a numbered or lettered company. It was also laid down that after consolidation the new corps would thereafter be known by the number previously held by its senior company. An example of this procedure can be seen in this work in the Lanarkshire section when at the beginning of 1860 several corps formed in Glasgow, the 19th, 23rd, 24th, 28th, 36th and 41st, were united under the title of 19th Lanarkshire Rifle Volunteer Corps.

The administrative battalion in the main catered for corps situated in rural areas. In this case each battalion was designated, i.e. 1st Administrative Battalion of Shropshire Rifle Volunteers, and was allotted its own staff and headquarters. The corps included in an admin. battalion, unlike those that were consolidated, remained distinct and financially independent units and were permitted to retain their county numbers. 'The object of the formation of an Administrative Battalion' according to a memorandum dated 4 September 1860, 'is to unite the different corps composing it under one common head, to secure uniformity of drill among them, and to afford them the advantage of the instruction and assistance of an adjutant; but it is not intended to interfere with financial arrangements of the separate corps, or with the operation of the respective rules, or to compel them to meet together for battalion drill in ordinary times, except with their own consent'. In counties where there were insufficient corps to constitute a battalion these were permitted to join that of one of its neighbours. Single corps, where situated in a border area, were occasionally included in a battalion from outside of its county. Admin. Battalions were also permitted to consolidate if they chose.

Corps were designated, i.e. 1st Shropshire Rifle Volunteer Corps, and in the first regulations published for volunteers in 1861 special titles in addition to numbers were permitted. The 1861 regulations also directed that when a corps was disbanded or absorbed into a senior one, its number was to remain vacant.

By General Regulations and Instructions of 2 July 1873 the United Kingdom was divided into seventy infantry sub-districts. Each was designated as a 'Sub-District Brigade' and to it were allotted for recruiting purposes two line battalions and the militia and volunteers of a certain area. This was to be the first steps to the closer association of the volunteers with the regular forces.

Although the proposals of the committee set up in 1878 under the presidency of Viscount Bury, Parliamentry Under Secretary of State, to look into the organisation of the volunteer force did not include any material changes in its composition, consolidation of the existing administrative battalions was recommended.

During 1880 the recommendations of the committee were carried out and all remaining admin. battalions were consolidated. By the practice laid down in 1860, the corps contained within each battalion lost their independent status and became lettered companies of the new corps. The new corps also, at first, took on the number of its senior corps but in counties that had more than one unit this created a series of numbers with many blanks. By June 1880 a general re-numbering within each county had commenced and corps were numbered from one upwards. Only Suffolk, who in 1880 had its corps organised into two battal-ions, chose to retain the original numbers, 1st and 6th, adopted at the beginning of the year.

The 1881 re-organisations that formed the old Sub-districts into territorial regiments are by now too well known to repeat here. The volunteers corps, who were now to constitute 'volunteer battalions' of the new regiments were to be numbered in a separate sequence from the regulars and militia. This change in designation was carried out over a period of time, each battalion being notified in General, later Army, Orders. It was the 1st, 2nd and 3rd Somersetshire Corps who were the first to adopt the new style when under General Order 261 of October 1882 they became the 1st, 2nd and 3rd Volunteer Battalions, The Prince Albert's (Somerset Light Infantry).

The following is a list of line regiments together with the various rifle volunteer corps that provided volunteer battalions.

Royal Scots:	1st, 2nd Edinburgh, 1st, 2nd Midlothian, 1st Haddington, 1st Linlithgow, 1st Berwick.
Queen's:	2nd, 4th, 6th, 8th Surrey.
Buffs:	2nd, 5th Kent.
King's Own:	10th Lancashire.
Northumberland Fus:	1st, 2nd Northumberland, 1st Newcastle.
Royal Warwickshire:	1st, 2nd Warwick.
Royal Fusiliers:	5th, 9th, 10th, 11th, 22nd, 23rd Middlesex, 1st Tower Hamlets.
King's Liverpool:	1st, 5th, 13th, 15th, 18th, 19th Lancashire, 1st Isle of Man.
Norfolk:	1st, 2nd, 3rd, 4th Norfolk.
Lincolnshire:	1st, 2nd Lincoln.
Devonshire:	1st, 2nd, 3rd, 4th, 5th Devon.
Suffolk:	1st, 6th Suffolk, 1st, 2nd Cambridge.
Somerset LI:	1st, 2nd, 3rd Somerset.
West Yorks:	1st, 3rd, 7th Yorks West Riding.
East Yorks:	1st, 2nd Yorks East Riding.
Bedfordshire:	1st, 2nd Herts, 1st Bedford.
Leicestershire:	1st Leicester.
Yorkshire:	1st, 2nd Yorks North Riding.
Lancashire Fus:	8th, 12th, 17th Lancashire.
Royal Scots Fus:	The Galloway, 1st, 2nd Ayrshire, 1st Dumfries, 1st Roxburg and Selkirk.

Cheshire:	1st, 2nd, 3rd, 4th, 5th Cheshire.
Royal Welsh Fus:	1st Denbigh, 1st Flint and Carnarvon.
South Wales Borderers:	1st, 2nd, 3rd Monmouth, 1st Brecknock
King's Own Scottish Borderers:	1st Roxburgh and Selkirk, 1st Berwick, 1st Dumfries, The Galloway.
Cameronians:	1st, 2nd, 3rd, 4th, 7th Lanark.
Gloucestershire:	1st, 2nd Gloucester.
Worcestershire:	1st, 2nd Worcester.
East Lancs:	2nd, 3rd Lancashire.
East Surrey:	1st, 3rd, 5th, 7th Surrey.
Duke of Cornwall's:	1st, 2nd Cornwall.
Duke of Wellington's:	4th, 6th, 9th Yorks West Riding.
Border:	1st Cumberland, 1st Westmorland.
Royal Sussex:	1st, 2nd Sussex, 1st Cinque Ports.
Hampshire:	1st, 2nd, 3rd, 4th Hants, 1st Isle of Wight.
South Staffs:	1st, 3rd, 4th Stafford.
Dorsetshire:	1st Dorset.
South Lancs:	9th, 21st Lancashire.
Welsh:	1st Pembroke, 1st, 2nd, 3rd Glamorgan.
Black Watch:	1st Fife, 1st, 2nd, 3rd Forfar, 1st, 2nd Perth.
Oxfordshire LI:	1st, 2nd Oxford, 1st, 2nd Bucks.
Essex:	1st, 2nd, 3rd, 4th Essex.
Sherwood Foresters:	1st, 2nd Derby, 1st, 2nd Notts.
North Lancs:	11th, 14th Lancashire.
Northamptonshire:	1st Northampton.
Royal Berks:	1st Berks.
Royal West Kent:	1st, 3rd, 4th Kent.
Yorkshire LI:	5th Yorks West Riding.
Shropshire LI:	1st, 2nd Shropshire, 1st Hereford.
Middlesex:	3rd, 8th, 11th, 17th Middlesex.
King's Royal Rifle Corps:	1st, 2nd, 4th, 5th, 6th, 9th, 10th, 11th, 12th, 13th, 21st, 22nd, 25th, 26th, 27th Middlesex, 1st, 2nd, 3rd, 4th London.
Wiltshire:	1st, 2nd Wilts.
Manchester:	4th, 6th, 7th, 16th, 17th, 20th, 22nd Lancashire.
North Staffs:	2nd, 5th Staffords.
York and Lancaster:	2nd, 8th Yorks West Riding.
Durham LI:	1st, 2nd, 3rd, 4th, 5th Durham.
Highland LI:	5th, 6th, 8th, 9th, 10th Lanark.

Seaforth Highlanders:	1st, Elgin, 1st Inverness, 1st Ross, 1st Sutherland.
Gordon Highlanders:	1st, 2nd, 3rd, 4th Aberdeen, 1st Banff, 1st Kincardine and Aberdeen.
Cameron Highlanders:	1st Inverness.
Argyll and Sutherland:	1st Argyll, 1st Clackmannan, 1st Dumbarton, 1st, 2nd, 3rd Renfrew, 1st Stirling.
Rifle Brigade:	7th, 14th, 15th, 16th, 18th, 19th, 20th, 21st, 24th, 26th Middlesex, 1st, 2nd Tower Hamlets.

It was by no means all corps that assumed the new designations and several, whilst taking their place in their regiment's volunteer line-up, chose to retain their rifle volunteer titles. These, however, were required to change i.e. from 1st Dumbartonshire Rifle Volunteer Corps to 1st Dumbartonshire Volunteer Rifle Corps in 1891.

The higher organisation of the volunteer infantry into brigades commenced in 1888. Nineteen were created under Army Order 314 of July which were followed by a further twelve in September (Army Order 408). The number of battalions forming each brigade varied from just three in one case to seventeen in another. In 1890 (Army Orders 207 and 395) additional brigades were formed and the battalions distributed on a more even basis.

The next change affecting the Volunteer Infantry Brigades occurred in 1906 when under Army Order 130 the total was brought up to forty-four.

In 1900 and under a Special Army Order dated 2 January volunteer battalions were called upon to raise companies for active service in South Africa. For each regular battalion serving in the war one company was to be raised from its affiliated volunteers. These were to consist of 116 all ranks who in order to surmount the difficulties of the Volunteer Act had to enlist into the regular army for a period of one year or the duration of the war.

Although each volunteer was permitted to wear the designation of his volunteer battalion or corps on the shoulder strap, companies as a whole were, for example, styled 1st Volunteer Service Company, The Gordon Highlanders. A separate organisation known as the City Imperial Volunteers was also formed within the London area.

Under the Territorial and Reserve Forces Act of 1907 the Volunteer Force ceased to exist on 31 March 1908. On the following day, 1 April, the Territorial Force was born and the old volunteers invited to enlist. The change was not a popular one with the volunteers as the new system meant the re-organisation and in some cases disbandment of many of the existing companies. However the new force was soon established and the majority of battalions were to transfer on block.

The new Territorial Force battalions were, unlike those of the volunteers who had their own sequence, numbered on from the Special Reserve. The Territorial Force was redesignated as the Territorial Army in 1921 and after numerous changes in its organisation became the Territorial Army and Volunteer Reserve in 1967.

CADETS

Cadet units, which were to be formed in connection with volunteer corps or administrative battalions, were first sanctioned in the *Volunteer Regulations* of 1863. Article 279 directed that any cadet corps raised should consist of boys twelve years of age and upwards. These should be officered by gentlemen holding only honorary commissions. There were, however, numerous units formed prior to 1863. Such organisations as the Shrewsbury School Drill Company are known to have existed as early as 1860.

Cadet corps were normally organised into companies of not less than thirty boys. These were then affiliated to individual corps or admin. battalions and took precedence with them when on parade.

Recruiting of boys for cadet corps was, in the main, concentrated among the public schools of the day. However, youths from all walks of life were involved and many units were to be formed from the junior staff of factories, warehouses and large firms.

In June 1886 authority was given for the formation of cadet battalions consisting of four companies. These although linked to a line regiment were completely independent of any volunteer corps. The first of such units to find its way into the *Army List* was the 1st Cadet Battalion, The Royal Warwickshire Regiment. This battalion, together with those subsequently raised, was until 1898, placed in the list immediately after the 'Volunteer Battalion' section. For a short period they appear after the Militia Regiments of the Channel Islands but by 1899 all battalions are shown together with their respective line regiment.

The contribution made by public schools to the Volunteer Movement is well known. Not only were cadet corps formed but such schools as Eton, Harrow and Rugby provided Rifle Corps in their own right. In 1908 and upon the formation of the Territorial Force all cadet corps formed by schools were invited to join the newly-raised Officers Training Corps. The vast majority did so and from then on came under the direct authority of the War Office. At the same time all affiliations to volunteer corps, or as they were now known, Territorial Battalions, ceased. The non-school corps and those schools choosing to remain part of the Territorial Force were from 1908 listed in the *Army List* under the heading 'Cadet Companies and Corps'. This section, which appeared immediately after the OTC, was not seen after 1913 by which time all units receiving recognisition by the TF had been included with their parent battalion.

The following list gives details of the several cadet corps recorded in this work. Only those bearing distinctive titles, i.e. All Hallows School Cadet Corps or The Westerham Cadet Corps, have been included. Therefore such units formed by corps and designated simply, i.e. 1st Lancashire Rifle Volunteers Cadet Corps, have been omitted. The designations used in the right-hand column of the list are based on the post-1880 numbering.

Cadet Corps		Volunteer Corps
All Hallows School	see	3rd Devonshire
Ardingly College	see	2nd Sussex

Bath College	see	1st Somersetshire
Beaumont College	see	5th Surrey
Bedford Modern School	see	1st Bedfordshire
Berkhampstead School	see	2nd Hertfordshire
Bishop's Stortford School	see	1st Hertfordshire
Blairlodge School	see	10th Lanarkshire
Blundell's School	see	3rd Devonshire
Borden School	see	4th VB Royal West Kent, 2nd Kent
Bournemouth School	see	4th Hampshire
Bradfield College	see	1st Berkshire
Brecon Intermediate School	see	1st Brechnockshire
Bridgenorth	see	1st Shropshire
Brighton College	see	1st Sussex
Brighton Prepatory Schools	see	1st Sussex
Bristol Grammar School	see	1st Gloucestershire
British League	see	2nd Edinburgh
Bruce Castle School	see	3rd Middlesex
Brunswick House School	see	3rd Middlesex
Bury Grammar School	see	8th Lancashire
Cambridge and County School	see	1st Cambridgeshire
Chapel Works	see	2nd Forfarshire
Charterhouse School	see	4th Surrey
Chatham House College	see	2nd Kent
Cheltenham College	see	2nd Gloucestershire
Chigwell Grammar School	see	1st Essex
Christ College, Brecon	see	1st Brecknockshire
Christ College, Finchley	see	3rd Middlesex
Christ's Hospital	see	1st Sussex
Churcher's College	see	3rd Hampshire
City of London School	see	1st and 2nd London
Civil Service	see	12th Middlesex
Cookham Dean	see	1st Berkshire
Cooper's Hill College	see	1st Berkshire
Cottesmore School	see	1st Sussex
Cranbrook Grammar School	see	5th Kent
Cranleigh School	see	4th Surrey
Dane Hill School	see	2nd Kent
Denstone College	see	5th Staffordshire
Derby School	see	1st Derbyshire
Dollar Institution	see	1st Clackmannan
Dorchester County School	see	1st Dorsetshire
Dover College	see	2nd Kent
Dulwich College	see	1st Surrey
Donoon Grammar School	see	1st Argyllshire
Ealing Schools	see	8th Middlesex

Lymington	see	4th Hampshire
Magdalen College School	see	1st Oxfordshire
Maindstone Grammar School	see	1st Kent
Margate College	see	2nd Kent
Marlborough College	see	2nd Wiltshire
Mayall College	see	8th Surrey and 22nd Middlesex
Merchant Taylors' School, London	see	1st London
Merchiston Castle School	see	1st City of Edinburgh
Monkton Combe School	see	1st Somersetshire
Monmouth Grammar School	see	3rd Monmouthshire
Morgan Academy	see	1st Forfarshire
Mostyn House School	see	1st Cheshire
New Brighton High School	see	1st Cheshire
New College Schools	see	2nd Kent and 4th V.B. Royal West Kent
Norfolk County School	see	3rd Norfolk
North Berwick High School	see	1st Haddington
Nottingham High School	see	1st Nottinghamshire
Ongar Grammar School	see	1st Essex
Oundle School	see	1st Northamptonshire
Oxford Military College	see	1st Oxfordshire
Perse School	see	1st Cambridgeshire
Plymouth and Mannamead College	see	2nd Devonshire
Portsmouth Grammar School	see	3rd Hampshire
Postal Telegraph Messengers, Derby	see	1st Derbyshire
Postal Telegraph Messengers, Plymouth	see	2nd Devonshire
Proprietary School, Blackheath	see	3rd Kent
Queen Elizabeth's School, Ipswich	see	1st Suffolk
Queen Elizabeth's School, Mansfield	see	2nd Nottinghamshire
Queen Mary's School, Walsall	see	3rd Staffordshire
Quernmore School	see	3rd Kent
Reigate Grammar School	see	4th Surrey
Repton School	see	1st Derbyshire
Richmond County School	see	5th Surrey
Rossall School	see	10th Lancashire
Rugby School	see	2nd Warwickshire
St Alban's School	see	2nd Hertfordshire
St Bee's School	see	3rd V.B. Border Regt. (Cumberland)
St Edmund's School	see	2nd Kent
St John's College	see	2nd Sussex
St John's, Westminster	see	23rd Middlesex
St Lawrence College	see	2nd Kent
St Paul's College	see	1st Bucks
St Paul's School	see	2nd Middlesex
St Peter's College	see	14th Middlesex

ABERDEENSHIRE

Between 1859 and 1880 thirty-five numbered corps of rifle volunteers were raised within the County of Aberdeenshire. From almost the very beginning of the Volunteer Movement the several corps formed in the City of Aberdeen were consolidated into one unit of battalion strength. Other companies were to be included in one or other of the three administrative battalions that were created.

When the City of Aberdeen Battalion was formed in early 1860 and its companies drawn from those corps already numbered in the county list several gaps were left. Within a very short time a general renumbering throughout the county took place. Although this made for a tidier arrangement it did, however, leave future historians with the complicated task of sorting one corps from the other. Later reorganisations added to the confusion and in 1876 several corps were transferred to the care of the Kincardineshire Admin. Battalion.

In 1880 the City Corps and the three Admin. Battalions were organised into four battalions numbered 1st to 4th. It is this series of numbers that has been used in the following as headings.

1ST CORPS

As mentioned above the corps formed within the City of Aberdeen were merged into one shortly after formation. The amalgamation took place on 16 March 1860 and at first the number of the senior corps, 6th, was adopted. This was changed to 1st Corps by July.

The companies forming the new battalion were—

6th Corps: Formed on 19 November 1859.

7th Corps: Formed on 19 November 1859.

8th Corps: Formed on 26 November 1859 mainly from Aberdeen merchants.

9th Corps: Formed on 23 December 1859.

11th Corps: Formed on 13 January 1860.

12th Corps: Formed on 27 January 1860.

13th Corps: Formed on 21 January 1860 mainly from workers of the Scottish North-Eastern Railway.

The overall strength of the seven corps listed above was nine companies which upon consolidation were organised as follows—

No 1 Company late 6th Corps	No 6 Company late 11th Corps
No 2 Company late 7th Corps	No 7 Company late 13th Corps
No 3 Company late 8th Corps	No 8 Company late 12th Corps
No 4 Company late 8th Corps	No 9 Company late 12th Corps
No 5 Company late 9th Corps	

A new company was formed at Woodside just outside Aberdeen in 1870.

The title of 1st Corps was retained until 1884 when under General Order 12 of February the designation of 1st Volunteer Battalion, the Gordon Highlanders was assumed. A new company was raised from members of Aberdeen University in 1898 and in 1908 the battalion transferred to the Territorial Force as the 4th Battalion Gordons.

2ND CORPS

The 2nd Admin. Battalion of Aberdeenshire Rifle Volunteers was formed in June 1861. Headquarters were placed at Tarves and the corps included then or at some later date were—

2nd Corps: Originally formed as the 1st Corps on 15 February 1860 at Tarves. Renumbered in July 1860 and in June 1867 was divided into two corps, the 2nd with headquarters at Methlie and the 18th which remained at Tarves.

5th Corps: The 5th was renumbered as such in July 1860 having been formed as 17th Corps on 12 April at New Deer. Also at New Deer was the 19th Corps formed on 30 March 1861. According to the *London Gazette* of 19 November 1861 it would appear that the 5th and 19th were one in the same as that issue notes that the acceptance of the 19th had been cancelled due to the fact that 'the volunteers comprising that corps were identical with those of the 5th'. The 5th Corps was transferred to the 3rd Admin. Battalion in January 1862.

6th Corps: Formed as the 18th Corps at Ellon on 18 April 1860. Became 6th in July 1860.

12th Corps: The original 12th Corps was that formed in Aberdeen and eventually included in the 1st Corps formed there in early 1860. This was followed in July 1860 by a 12th Corps formed at Old Aberdeen which was to be disbanded in 1863. Yet another 12th was raised in 1864, this time at Udny and included in the 2nd Admin. Battalion. Headquarters were moved to Newmachar in 1867 and then, ten years later, to Newburgh.

13th Corps: Formed at Turriff on 8 August 1860. Did not join the battalion until 1862.

15th Corps: Formed at Fyvie on 1 October 1860. Did not join the battalion until 1862.

16th Corps: Formed at Meldrum on 2 October 1860. Did not join the battalion until 1862.

18th Corps: This was the corps created on 11 June 1867 by the division of the 2nd at Tarves.

Headquarters of the battalion were moved to Old Meldrum in 1868 and then to Aberdeen in 1877.

Consolidation as the 2nd Aberdeenshire Rifle Volunteer Corps occurred in May 1880. Headquarters remained at Aberdeen and the seven companies, which were provided in order of seniority by the former corps, were lettered 'A' to 'G'.

In February 1884 and by General Order 12 the 2nd Aberdeenshires became the 2nd Volunteer Battalion of the Gordon Highlanders. Headquarters were moved to Old Meldrum in 1899 and in April 1908 the battalion amalgamated with the 3rd VB of the regiment to form the 5th Battalion (TF). The 2nd VB providing 'D', 'E' and 'F' Companies.

3RD CORPS

The 3rd Corps of 1880 originated from the 3rd Admin. Battalion which was formed in January 1862. Headquarters were at Peterhead and the corps included then or at some later date were—

5th Corps: This corps was originally part of the 2nd Admin. Battalion and its early records are shown under the 2nd Corps section. The 5th transferred to the 3rd Admin. in January 1862.

9th Corps: Formed at Peterhead on 4 April 1860 as the 21st Corps. Was renumbered as 9th in July 1860 and in September 1875 absorbed the 24th Corps at St Fergus.

17th Corps: Formed at Old Deer on 29 October 1860.

20th Corps: Formed at Longside on 30 July 1861.

24th Corps: Formed at St Fergus on 23 December 1867. Absorbed into the 9th Corps as its No 2 Company in September 1875. A new 24th was formed at Fraserburgh on 13 November 1875.

25th Corps: Formed at New Pitsligo on 14 April 1868.

26th Corps: Formed at Cruden on 25 September 1872.

In 1868 the additional title of 'The Buchan' was granted to the battalion. This is the name given to the area of north-east Aberdeenshire extending along the coast from Ythan to Deveron, a distance of some 40 miles.

On 23 May 1880 the battalion was consolidated and as was the practice took on the number of its senior corps. The title conferred was 5th Aberdeenshire Rifle Volunteer Corps, however, this was changed to 3rd in June. The additional title (The Buchan), was retained. Headquarters of the new corps were placed at Old Deer and the nine companies were organised as follows—

'A' Company at New Dear	Late 5th Corps
'B' Company at Peterhead	Late 9th Corps
'C' Company at St Fergus	Late 9th Corps
'D' Company at Old Deer	Late 17th Corps
'E' Company at Strichen	Late 17th Corps
'F' Company at Longside	Late 20th Corps
'G' Company at Fraserburgh	Late 24th Corps
'H' Company at New Pitsligo	Late 25th Corps
'I' Company at Cruden	Late 26th Corps

Headquarters of the corps were moved to Peterhead in 1883 and in the same year those for 'H' Company moved from New Pitsligo to Fraserburgh. A new company was formed at Boddam that year and in 1884 the title of 3rd (The Buchan) Volunteer Battalion, the Gordon Highlanders was assumed and notified in General Order 12 of February.

Over the next seventeen years numerous changes were made within the battalion resulting in several amalgamations, disbandments and changes in location. In 1885 'C' Company went to Crimond and in 1888 was again moved, this time to Lonmay. 'K' moved to Peterhead that year and in 1900 the Cruden Company was disbanded. The following year 'C' Company was again involved when it was absorbed into 'E' at Strichen. Subsequently the Peterhead Company, 'K', filled the 'C' position.

Upon transfer to the Territorial Force in April 1908 the 5th Battalion, the Gordon Highlanders was formed by the amalgamation of the 2nd and 3rd VBs. The latter providing HQ and 'A', 'B', 'C', 'G' and 'H' Companies.

4TH CORPS

The 1st Admin. Battalion was formed in May 1860 with headquarters at Inverurie. The corps included then or at some later date were—

3rd Corps: Formed on 16 April 1860 as the 1st Sub-division at Cluny. Redesignated as 3rd Corps in July 1860 and in 1875 moved its headquarters to Kemnay.

4th Corps: Formed on 12 March 1860 as the 2nd Sub-division at Alford. Became 4th Corps in July 1860.

7th Corps: Formed on 6 March 1860 as the 19th Corps at Huntly. Renumbered as 7th in July 1860.

8th Corps: Formed on 9 June 1860 as the 20th Corps at Echt. Became 8th Corps in July 1860 and in 1876 was transferred to the 1st Admin. Battalion of Kincardineshire Rifle Volunteers.

10th Corps: Formed on 20 April 1860 as the 22nd Corps at Inverurie. Became 10th Corps in July 1860.

11th Corps: Formed 20 June 1860 as 23rd Corps at Kildrummy. Became 11th Corps in July 1860.

14th Corps: Formed at Tarland on 29 October 1860. Transferred to the 1st Admin. Battalion of Kincardineshire Rifle Volunteers in 1876.

19th Corps: Formed at Insch on 17 December 1867. This was the third corps to hold this number.

21st Corps: Formed at Aboyne on 22 November 1861 and also known as the 'Marquis of Huntly's Highland Rifle Volunteers'. Joined the 1st Admin. Battalion in 1862 but in 1876 was transferred to the 1st Admin. Battalion in Kincardineshire.

22nd Corps: Formed at Auchmull on 18 June 1862 joining the battalion the following year.

23rd Corps: Formed at Lumphanan on 29 March 1862. Headquarters were moved to Torphins in 1864 and in 1876 was transferred to the 1st Kincardineshire Admin. Battalion.

In 1868 headquarters of the battalion were moved to Aberdeen and as previously mentioned the 8th, 14th, 21st and 23rd Corps were all transferred to the 1st Admin. Battalion in Kincardineshire in 1876.

Consolidation as the 3rd Corps came in April 1880 followed by renumbering as 4th in June. Headquarters remained at Aberdeen and the seven companies were organised as follows—

'A' Company at Huntly   Late 7th Corps
'B' Company at Kildrummy   Late 11th Corps

'C' Company at Insch	Late 19th Corps
'D' Company at Alford	Late 4th Corps
'E' Company at Inverurie	Late 10th Corps
'F' Company at Kemnay	Late 3rd Corps
'G' Company at Auchmull	Late 22nd Corps

Redesignation as the 4th Volunteer Battalion, the Gordon Highlanders was conferred in General Order 12 of February 1884. The additional title of 'Donside Highland' was also granted in 1893. Several new companies were formed and included in the battalion. 'H' was raised at Auchmull in 1897 followed by companies at Kintore and Kildrummy in 1899. Other changes were, in 1899 when 'B' Company moved from Kildrummy to Strathdon, in 1903 when 'G' and 'H' went to Bucksburn and in 1906 when 'B' and 'C' were amalgamated as 'B' at its former home in Kildrummy.

On 1 April 1908 the 4th (Donside Highland) Volunteer Battalion and the 6th Volunteer Battalion were amalgamated to form the 6th Battalion, The Gordon Highlanders. The 4th providing 'E', 'F', 'G' and 'H' Companies.

The subsequent development of the 8th, 14th, 21st and 23rd Corps after joining the 1st Kincardineshire Admin. Battalion in 1876 will be dealt with under that county.

ANGLESEY

Three companies of rifle volunteers were raised in Anglesey during the later part of 1860. These became the 1st, 2nd and 3rd Corps and had all disappeared from the *Army List* by January 1864.

1st Corps: Formed at Amlwch on 6 November 1860. Removed from the *Army List* in December 1863.

2nd Corps: Formed at Aberffraw on 5 November 1860. Disbanded in March 1862.

3rd Corps: Formed at Menai Bridge on 2 November 1860. Disbanded in February 1862.

In 1908 the 3rd Volunteer Battalion, Royal Welsh Fusiliers, a Carnarvonshire unit, transferred to the Territorial Force as the 6th Battalion of the regiment. In addition the sub-title (Carnarvon and Anglesey) was held by the 6th which included one company at Holyhead. It is not known whether or not the Holyhead Company was a new creation of the TF in 1908 or one of the three new companies raised by the 3rd VB in 1900.

ARGYLLSHIRE

Although the numbering of the pre-1880 Argyllshire Rifle Corps reached 14th in 1868 there were in fact only twelve units raised. The 1st and 4th positions in the county were never filled or recorded in any *Army List*. With the exception of the

5th all corps eventually became part of the 1st Admin. Battalion. This was formed in July 1861 with headquarters at Oban and at first only included the 2nd, 3rd, 7th and 11th Corps. The remainder joining at some later date.

2nd Corps Formed at Inveraray on 4 May 1860.

3rd Corps: Formed at Campbeltown on 16 April 1860.

5th Corps: Formed at Mull on 6 December 1860. Disbanded in 1862.

6th Corps: Formed at Melfort on 22 April 1860. Joined the 1st Admin. Battalion in 1862 and was disbanded in 1864.

7th Corps: Formed at Dunoon on 28 March 1860.

8th Corps: Formed at Cowal on 4 June 1860. Headquarters were moved to Glendaruel in 1862 and joined the 1st Admin. Battalion in 1864.

9th Corps: Formed at Glenorchy on 12 April 1860 and was later attached to the 3rd Perthshire Rifle Volunteer Corps for drill and administration purposes. This attachment was in 1862 changed to the 2nd Perthshire Admin. Battalion. In 1865 the 9th transferred to the Argyllshire Battalion but in 1870 was disbanded having moved to Dalmally the previous year.

10th Corps: Formed at Tayvollich on 4 June 1860 from workers on the Ross Estate. Included in the 1st Admin. Battalion from 1862. The 10th Corps also had a detachment at Ardrishaig which upon disbandment of the corps in 1869 joined the 14th Corps at Kilmartin.

11th Corps: Formed at Oban on 7 July 1860. Disbanded in 1865.

12th Corps: Formed at Bridgend, Islay on 7 June 1861. Joined the 1st Admin. Battalion in 1863 and disbanded in 1865.

13th Corps: Formed at Ballachulish on 31 August 1867.

14th Corps: Formed at Kilmartin on 15 January 1868.

Headquarters of the 1st Admin. Battalion were moved to Ardrishaig in 1866 and then to Dunoon the following year. From 1873 the full title of the battalion became 1st Admin. Battalion of Argyllshire Highland Rifle Volunteers.

Upon consolidation in 1880 the battalion was redesignated as the 2nd Argyllshire (Argyllshire Highland) Rifle Volunteer Corps but after a few months was renumbered as 1st. Headquarters remained at Dunoon and the eight companies were organised as follows—

'A' Company at Inveraray	Late 2nd Corps
'B', 'C' Companies at Campbeltown	Late 3rd Corps
'D' Company at Dunoon	Late 7th Corps
'E' Company at Glendaruel	Late 8th Corps
'F', 'G' Companies at Ballachulish	Late 13th Corps
'H' Company at Kilmartin	Late 14th Corps

'G' Company moved to Southend just outside of Campbeltown in 1882 and in 1887, General Order 181 of December, the corps was redesignated as the 5th Volunteer Battalion, the Argyll and Sutherland Highlanders. New companies were raised at Carradale and Campbeltown in 1900 and in 1908 the battalion transferred to the Territorial Force as the 8th Battalion of the Argyll and Sutherland Highlanders.

In 1901 a cadet corps was formed and attached to the battalion by the Dunoon Grammar School. The school continued its affiliation after 1908.

AYRSHIRE

The 1st Admin. Battalion of Ayrshire Rifle Volunteers was formed on 27 August 1860. Headquarters were placed at Ayr and the corps included then or upon formation were as follows—

1st Corps: Formed at Kilmarnock on 14 January 1860. Absorbed the 9th Corps in 1874.

2nd Corps: Formed at Irvine on 27 December 1859.

3rd Corps: Formed at Ayr on 19 January 1860.

4th Corps: Formed at Largs on 27 February 1860.

5th Corps: Formed at Maybole on 27 February 1860.

6th Corps: Formed at Beith on 15 February 1860.

7th Corps: Formed at Saltcoats and Stevenston on 28 February 1860.

8th Corps: Formed at Colmonell on 25 May 1860. Was later disbanded and is last seen in the *Army List* for May 1878.

9th Corps: Formed at Kilmarnock on 19 May 1860. Absorbed into the 1st Corps in 1874.

10th Corps: Formed at Girvan on 22 October 1860.

11th Corps: Formed at Dalry on 4 December 1860.

12th Corps: Formed at Cumnock on 14 January 1861.

13th Corps: Formed at Sorn on 18 March 1861.

14th Corps: Formed at Ayr on 14 April 1862.

With fourteen companies under its control the battalion had become too large for comfortable management and in March 1873 it was divided into two. The 1st Admin. Battalion now consisted of the corps situated in the southern half of the county which were the 3rd, 5th, 8th, 10th, 12th, 13th and 14th. Headquarters remained at Ayr and in December 1873 the 16th Corps was formed at Newmilns and added to the battalion.

Upon consolidation in 1880 the battalion was redesignated as 3rd Corps. This, however, was changed to 1st in June and then to 2nd in September. The new corps consisted of seven companies and was organised as follows—

'A' Company at Ayr	Late 3rd Corps
'B' Company at Ayr	Late 14th Corps
'C' Company at Maybole	Late 5th Corps
'D' Company at Girvan	Late 10th Corps
'E' Company at Cumnock	Late 12th Corps

| 'F' Company at Sorn | Late 13th Corps |
| 'G' Company at Newmilns | Late 16th Corps |

When the 1st Admin. Battalion was divided in 1873 the northern portion of the county became the 2nd Admin. Battalion with headquarters at Kilmarnock. The Corps included were the 1st, 2nd, 4th, 6th, 7th, 9th and 11th. Two new companies, the 15th Corps at Darvel and the 17th at Galston, were added to the battalion upon their formation in December 1873 and October 1874 respectively.

As a battalion of eight companies the 2nd Admin. was consolidated in 1880. The original title granted in May was 1st Corps but this was changed to 2nd in June and then back to 1st in September. The organisation of the battalion went as follows—

'A' Company at Kilmarnock	Late 1st Corps
'B' Company at Irvine	Late 2nd Corps
'C' Company at Largs	Late 4th Corps
'D' Company at Beith	Late 6th Corps
'E' Company at Saltcoats	Late 7th Corps
'F' Company at Dalry	Late 11th Corps
'G' Company at Darvel	Late 15th Corps
'H' Company at Galston	Late 17th Corps

In 1883 the establishment of the 2nd Corps was brought up to equal that of the 1st when 'H' Company was raised at Troon. Also that year the headquarters of 'F' Company were moved from Sorn to Catrine.

Under General Order 181 of December 1887 the 1st and 2nd Ayrshire Rifle Volunteer Corps were redesignated as the 1st and 2nd Volunteer Battalions of the Royal Scots Fusiliers. The 1st VB increased its strength by two companies, one of which was a cyclist, when in 1900 new personnel were recruited at Kilmarnock. The 2nd also showed an increase that year by the formation of 'I' (Cyclist) Company at Ayr. Other changes to effect the 1st VB were in 1900 when the headquarters of 'C' Company moved to Stewarton and those for 'H' went to Kilmarnock. In 1901 a cadet corps was formed by Kilmarnock Academy and affiliated to the 1st VB.

Both battalions transferred to the Territorial Force in April 1908. The 1st VB formed the 4th Battalion of the Royal Scots Fusiliers while the 2nd provided the 5th. The Kilmarnock Academy Cadets did not gain recognition by the TF and were eventually disbanded on 12 January 1911.

BANFFSHIRE

Permission to form a sub-division of rifle volunteers at Macduff in Banffshire was granted in 1860. The corps, designated as 1st within the county, appeared in the *Army List* but in 1862 disappeared without having had any officers gazetted to it.

When the 1st Admin. Battalion of Banffshire Rifle Volunteers was formed on 12 August 1861 only the 2nd, 3rd and 4th Corps were then in existence and therefor included.

2nd Corps: Formed at Banff on 18 April 1860.

3rd Corps: Formed at Aberlour on 29 September 1860.

4th Corps: Formed at Keith on 2 November 1860.

In 1862 it was decided to fill the vacant position of 1st Corps left by the Macduff Sub-division. The 2nd and 3rd Corps were subsequently renumbered as 1st and 2nd and the 4th Corps, which consisted of two companies, was divided, No 1 Company becoming 3rd Corps while No 2 was made an independent unit and designated as 4th Corps. In 1866, due to a fall off in numbers, the 4th was absorbed into the 3rd.

Subsequent corps to be formed and included in the battalion were—

5th Corps: Formed at Buckie on 12 March 1863.

6th Corps: Formed at Minmore on 19 April 1867.

7th Corps: Formed at Dufftown on 1 May 1868.

In June 1880 the battalion, whose headquarters were at Keith, was consolidated as the 1st Banffshire Rifle Volunteers Corps. The six corps of the battalion then became 'A' to 'F' Companies.

In 1884 and by General Order 12 of February the title of 6th Volunteer Battalion, the Gordon Highlanders was assumed. A new company was later formed at Aberchirder and in April 1908 the 6th Battalion of the Gordon Highlanders was formed after amalgamation with the 4th VB of the regiment. The Banffshire Volunteers provided Headquarters and 'A' to 'D' Companies.

BEDFORDSHIRE

The 1st Admin. Battalion of Bedfordshire Rifle Volunteers was formed in August 1860. Headquarters were placed at Bedford and the corps included were those then in existence or subsequently raised within the county.

1st Corps: Formed at Bedford on 27 February 1860.

2nd Corps: Formed at Toddington on 1 March 1860.

3rd Corps: None formed.

4th Corps: Formed at Dunstable on 24 April 1860.

5th Corps: Formed at Ampthill on 26 April 1860.

6th Corps: Formed at Luton on 16 May 1860.

7th Corps: Formed at Biggleswade on 11 September 1860. Headquarters moved to Shefford in 1871.

8th Corps: Formed at Woburn on 18 September 1860.

9th Corps: Formed at Bedford on 16 May 1864. This corps was later disbanded and is last seen in the *Army List* for November 1872.

Before consolidation as the 1st Bedfordshire Rifle Volunteer Corps in 1880 two changes in battalion headquarters occurred, the first was in 1866 when a move was made to Toddington followed by one to Woburn in 1870. The new 1st Bedfords consisted of nine companies and was organised as follows—

'A', 'B' Companies at Bedford	Late 1st Corps
'C' Company at Toddington	Late 2nd Corps
'D' Company at Dunstable	Late 4th Corps
'E' Company at Ampthill	Late 5th Corps
'F','G' Companies at Luton	Late 6th Corps
'H' Company at Shefford	Late 7th Corps
'I' Company at Woburn	Late 8th Corps

Redesignation as the 3rd Volunteer Battalion, The Bedfordshire Regiment was notified in General Order 181 of December 1887. The establishment at this time was still nine companies but according to a feature published in the *Volunteer Service Magazine* of July 1894 these were now located at; Bedford (2), Dunstable, Ampthill, Luton (3), Shefford and Biggleswade.

A cadet corps was formed and affiliated to the battalion by the Bedford Modern School in 1900. In 1904, however, training was changed to that of Engineers and affiliation transferred to the 1st Bedfordshire RE (Vols).

Upon transfer to the Territorial Force in April 1908 the 3rd and 4th Volunteer Battalions were amalgamated as the 5th Battalion, The Bedfordshire Regiment. The former 3rd VB provided HQ and four companies while the remainder of the battalion was formed by the 4th which was located in Huntingdonshire.

BERKSHIRE

The 1st Admin. Battalion of Berkshire Rifle Volunteers was formed with headquarters at Reading in June 1860 and at first only contained the 1st to 7th Corps. The 12th joined upon its formation in 1861 and in 1863 the remaining Berkshire Corps, the 8th to 11th, are all shown in the *Army List* as part of the battalion.

1st Corps: Formed at Reading on 10 September 1859.

2nd Corps: Formed at Windsor on 27 October 1859 as the 1st Sub-division of the county. The designation of 2nd Corps was assumed on 12 January 1860 upon reaching the strength of a full company.

3rd Corps: Formed at Newbury as the 2nd Sub-division on 14 December 1859. Was later increased to a full company and appears as 3rd Corps for the first time in the *Army List* for March 1860.

4th Corps: Formed at Abingdon on 23 February 1860.

5th Corps: Formed at Maidenhead on 24 February 1860.

6th Corps: Formed at Wokingham on 14 May 1860. This corps was later disbanded and was last seen in the *Army List* for February 1865.

7th Corps: Formed at Sandhurst on 25 August 1860.

8th Corps: Formed at Faringdon on 21 September 1860.

9th Corps: Formed at Wantage on 24 October 1860.

10th Corps: Formed at Woodside on 1 March 1861. Headquarters were moved to Winkfield by July.

11th Corps: Formed at Wallingford on 13 February 1861.

12th Corps: Formed at Windsor Great Park on 9 May 1861.

The 1st Admin. Battalion was consolidated as the 1st Berkshire Rifle Volunteer Corps in 1873, appearing as such for the first time in the *Army List* for January 1874. Headquarters remained at Reading and the thirteen companies were organised as follows—

'A' 'B' 'C' Companies at Reading	Late 1st Corps
'D' Company at Windsor	Late 2nd Corps
'E' Company at Newbury	Late 3rd Corps
'F' Company at Abingdon	Late 4th Corps
'G' Company at Maidenhead	Late 5th Corps
'H' Company at Sandhurst	Late 7th Corps
'I' Company at Faringdon	Late 8th Corps
'K' Company at Wantage	Late 9th Corps
'L' Company at Winkfield	Late 10th Corps
'M' Company at Wallingford	Late 11th Corps
'N' Company at Windsor Great Park	Late 12th Corps

In a work published in 1959 to commemorate the centenary of the battalion mention of an 'O' Company being present at the Annual Camp of 1874 is made. According to the book the company was formed by the cadets of Coopers Hill College. No cadet corps is shown as having been formed at the college and the *Army List* indicates no increase in establishment at that time. Mention is also made in the history of a Mounted Infantry Company being formed in 1886.

In December 1882 the 1st Berkshire Rifle Volunteer Corps became the 1st Volunteer Battalion of the Princess Charlotte of Wales' (Berkshire Regiment). This was changed to (Royal Berkshire Regiment) after confirmation of the 'Royal' title upon the regiment in September 1885.

Three cadet units are shown in the *Army List* as being affiliated to the battalion. The first company was formed at Wellington College in 1882 which in addition to the cadet corps also provided a half company of enrolled volunteers. Members of Bradfield College had also, for some time, contributed to the battalion but it was not until 1884 that a cadet corps was shown as being formed. The last unit was at the village of Cookham Dean, three miles north of Maidenhead. This half company was raised in November 1900 and had gone from the *Army List* by July 1902.

The 1st VB transferred to the Territorial Force as the 4th Battalion of the Royal Berkshires in 1908. Both the Wellington and Bradfield Colleges joined the Officers Training Corps as part of its Junior Contingent.

BERWICK-ON-TWEED

The 1st Berwick-on-Tweed Rifle Volunteer Corps was formed on 28 March 1860 and in the following November was united with the 1st Northumberland Admin. Battalion. In June 1880 this battalion was consolidated as the 1st Northumberland and Berwick-on-Tweed Rifle Volunteers, the Berwick-on-Tweed Corps forming 'G' Company.

BERWICKSHIRE

The 1st Admin. Battalion of Berwickshire Rifle Volunteers was formed in 1863. Headquarters were placed at Duns and the corps included were the seven then in existence within the county.

1st Corps: Formed at Duns on 16 December 1859.

2nd Corps: Formed at Coldstream on 30 March 1860.

3rd Corps: Formed at Ayton on 11 May 1860.

4th Corps: Formed at Greenlaw on 24 February 1860.

5th Corps: Formed at Lauderdale on 10 April 1860.

6th Corps: Formed at Earlstoun on 5 June 1863.

7th Corps: Formed at Chirnside on 7 July 1863.

Headquarters of the battalion were, on 1 November 1876, moved from Duns to Coldstream. No further changes occurred within the battalion until April 1880 and consolidation as the 1st Berwickshire Rifle Volunteer Corps. The seven companies of the new corps were lettered 'A' to 'G' and were formed in order of seniority by the 1st to 7th Corps. Headquarters remained at Coldstream but in 1882 were moved back to the battalion's former home at Duns.

In 1881 the 1st Berwickshires joined the Royal Scots as one of its allotted 'Volunteer battalions'. They remained with the regiment until 1887 when under General Order 61 of May they were transferred to the King's Own Scottish Borderers. The position taken in the regiment's volunteer line-up was 2nd and in December the title of 2nd (Berwickshire) Volunteer Battalion was conferred in General Order 181.

The establishment of the battalion was increased to eight companies in 1891 when 'H' was formed at Duns. This was followed by 'I' Company at Ladykirk in 1900 which in 1905 was relettered as 'H' due to the disbandment of the new Duns Company. This was the last change in the structure of the battalion until 1908 when in April amalgamation with the 1st Roxburgh and Selkirk VRC as the 4th Battalion, the King's Own Scottish Borderers took place. The 2nd VB providing two companies.

BRECKNOCKSHIRE

Seven independent corps of rifle volunteers were formed within the county and included in the 1st Admin. Battalion. The battalion was formed on 30 August 1860 and its headquarters placed at Brecon.

1st Corps: Formed at Brecon on 22 August 1859.

2nd Corps: Formed at Brynmawr on 13 February 1860.

3rd Corps: Formed at Crickhowell on 25 February 1860.

4th Corps: Formed at Hay on 7 April 1860.

5th Corps: Formed at Builth on 4 June 1860.

6th Corps: Formed at Talgarth on 14 February 1861.

7th Corps: Formed at Cefn on 15 June 1878.

In the monthly *Army List* for March 1860 both the Brynmawr and Crickhowell units are shown as 2nd Corps. This is almost certainly a misprint and in the list for the following month both corps appear with their correct numbering.

In March 1880 the battalion was consolidated as the 1st Brechnockshire Rifle Volunteer Corps. Headquarters remained at Brecon and the eight company establishment was organised as follows—

'A' Company at Brecon	Late 1st Corps
'B' Company at Brynmawr	Late 2nd Corps
'C' Company at Crickhowell	Late 3rd Corps
'D' Company at Hay	Late 4th Corps
'E' Company at Builth	Late 5th Corps
'F' Company at Talgarth	Late 6th Corps
'G' Company at Cefn	Late 7th Corps
'H' Company at Brecon	Late 1st Corps

New personnel were later provided by the village of Ystradgynlais and in 1894 and 1901 respectively both Christ College, Brecon and the Brecon Intermediate School formed cadet corps.

Redesignation as the 1st (Brecknockshire) Volunteer Battalion of the South Wales Borderers was conferred in July 1885 and noted in General Order 70. This was followed in April 1908 by the transfer of the battalion to the Territorial Force as the Brecknockshire Battalion, The South Wales Borderers. Both the Christ College and Intermediate School Cadet Corps did not gain recognisition by the TF and were later disbanded.

BUCKINGHAMSHIRE

The 1st Bucks Rifle Volunteer Corps first appeared as a consolidated battalion in the *Army List* for April 1875. The new corps consisted of five companies with headquarters at Great Marlow and had been formed by the corps that previously constituted the 1st Admin. Battalion of Buckinghamshire Rifle Volunteers. Formed in July 1862 the 1st Admin. contained the 1st to 7th Corps which were joined by the 8th upon formation in 1867. Headquarters were originally placed at Aylesbury but were moved to Great Marlow in 1872.

1st Corps: Formed as the 1st Sub-division on 16 December 1859 at Great Marlow. Shown in the March 1860 *Army List* as 2nd Corps but in the following month appeared as 1st.

2nd Corps: The original 2nd Corps was raised as the 3rd Sub-division at Wycombe on 6 March 1860. Redesignated as 2nd Corps in the *Army List* for April 1860 but was not shown after that for September of the following year. A new 2nd Corps was formed on 22 November 1861. It first appeared as the 8th at High Wycombe in the November *Army*

List but was shown as 2nd in December. The High Wycombe Company was disbanded in 1872.

3rd Corps: A Buckingham Corps is first shown in the *Army List* for March 1860. It appeared as the 4th Corps and consisted of a half company only. The list for April gives the corps as 3rd and in June the officers' commissions are recorded as having been signed on 11 May 1860. In 1863 the 7th Corps was absorbed bringing the strength of the 3rd up to that of a full company.

4th Corps: Formed at Aylesbury on 11 May 1860.

5th Corps: Formed at Slough on 20 July 1860.

6th Corps: Formed as the 7th Corps at Newport Pagnell on 14 September 1860. Renumbered as 6th Corps in the *Army List* for January 1861 and is not shown again after that for June 1864 due to disbandment.

7th Corps: Formed at Winslow on 17 May 1861. Absorbed into the 3rd Corps in 1863.

8th Corps: The original 8th was formed at High Wycombe in November 1861 and is shown as such in the *Army List* for that month. Renumbered as 2nd in December. A new 8th Corps is shown at Eton College in May 1867 and the following August a cadet corps is given as being attached. Officers' commissions for both units were dated 22 January 1868.

Additional companies were later formed at High Wycombe, Buckingham and Wolverton and in 1876 a cadet corps was also provided by the St Paul's College at Stony Stratford. The latter, however, disappeared from the *Army List* in May 1883.

In 1881 the 1st Bucks joined the Oxfordshire Light Infantry as one of its alloted volunteer battalions. Although ranked as 3rd VB no change in designation was conferred and the battalion retained its volunteer rifles title until transfer to the Territorial Force in April 1908 as the Buckinghamshire Battalion, the Oxfordshire Light Infantry.

In 1878 it was decided that the Eton College elements of the battalion should be detached to form their own corps. This was done and on 15 June the first officers were gazetted to the 2nd Bucks (Eton College) Rifles Volunteer Corps. Under General Order 181 of December 1887 the corps was redesignated as the 4th (Eton College) Volunteer Battalion of the Oxfordshire Light Infantry. They once again became the 2nd (Eton College) Volunteer Rifle Corps in 1902 and in 1908 joined the Officers Training Corps as part of its Junior Division.

BUTESHIRE

Only one rifle corps was formed within the County of Buteshire and that was the company raised at Rothesay on 19 January 1860. For the first three years of its existence the 1st Buteshire was a completely independent unit and was not included in any of the local admin. battalions. In 1863, however, they were united to the 1st Admin. Battalion of Renfrewshire Rifle Volunteers. This battalion, in accordance with the 1880 re-organisations, consolidated as the 1st Renfrewshire Rifle Volunteer Corps in March of that year. The Buteshires forming 'I' Company.

CAITHNESS

Four companies of rifle volunteers were formed within the county between 1860 and 1880 and were, in 1864, or in the case of the 4th Corps, upon formation, included in the 1st Admin. Battalion of Sutherlandshire.

1st Corps: Formed at Thurso on 10 April 1860.

2nd Corps: Formed at Wick on 16 February 1861.

3rd Corps: Formed at Halkirk on 11 April 1861.

4th Corps: Formed at Watten on 25 September 1867.

In June 1880 the 1st Admin. Battalion of Sutherlandshire Rifle Volunteers was consolidated as the 1st Sutherland Corps. The establishment of the new battalion was set at ten companies four of which 'G', 'H', 'I' and 'K', were provided by the 1st to 4th Caithness Corps respectively.

CAMBRIDGESHIRE

Of the ten numbered corps formed and listed under the County of Cambridgeshire only eight were included in the two administrative battalions that were to be formed. The 1st Battalion was created on 7 December 1860 with headquarters at March and contained in it then or upon formation were the following corps—

2nd Corps: Formed at Wisbeach on 2 January 1860.

4th Corps: Formed at Whittlesea on 17 January 1860. This corps was at first known as the 1st Sub-division and appeared for the first time as 4th Corps in the *Army List* for March 1860.

5th Corps: Formed at March on 13 June 1860.

6th Corps: Formed at Ely on 11 July 1860.

7th Corps: Formed at Upwell on 7 September 1860. This company was later broken up and is last seen in the *Army List* for December 1872.

10th Corps: Formed at Soham on 28 January 1862. Was not shown in the *Army List* after October 1865.

The 2nd Admin. Battalion was not formed until November 1862 and its Cambridge headquarters indicated in the *Army List* until July 1864. The two Cambridgeshire Corps to join the battalion were—

1st Corps: Formed at Cambridge on 16 January 1860. Absorbed the 8th Corps in 1864.

8th Corps: Formed at Cambridge on 6 November 1860. Absorbed into the 1st Corps as Nos 3 and 4 Companies in 1864.

From November 1863 the 17th Essex Rifle Volunteer Corps was also included and with the 1st Cambridge formed the 2nd Admin. Battalion until 1872. In this year the battalion ceased to exist and the two corps were from then on included in the 1st Battalion.

As previously mentioned the 7th Corps was disbanded in 1872 leaving the 1st Admin. short by one company. This same year the 1st Huntingdon Corps, who had until then been attached to the 1st Hunts Light Horse Volunteers, are shown as being part of the battalion.

One of the corps to be included in the Cambridgeshire List but not in either of the 1st or 2nd Admin. Battalions was the 9th. This sub-division was in fact formed on 15 January 1861 at Newmarket in Suffolk and in the *Army List* for July 1862 is shown as being 'united' with the 1st Suffolk Admin. Battalion. The following month the 9th was removed from the Cambridgeshire list of rifle volunteers having been absorbed into the 20th Suffolk Corps at Mildenhall.

Official approval and acceptance of a corps of rifle volunteers raised within Cambridge University was received by the Vice-Chancellor in December 1859. An establishment of five companies was sanctioned and in January of the following year the first officers were gazetted to the 3rd Cambridgeshire (Cambridge University) Rifle Volunteer Corps. By March six companies were in existence all formed by university members and organised on the following basis—

> No 1 Company: Formed by Gonville and Caius, Clare, Christ's Corpus Christi, Emmanuel, Queen's, Jesus and Sidney Sussex Colleges.
>
> No 2 Company: Formed by St John's College.
>
> No 3 Company: Formed by King's, Magdalene, Peterhouse and Trinity Hall Colleges.
>
> No 4, 5, 6 Companies: Formed by Trinity College.

In 1864 personnel from St Catharine's and Pembroke Colleges were included in No 1 Company while those from Clare were transferred to No 3. The following year Sidney Sussex was also included in No 3 and in November 1867 the six companies were lettered 'A' to 'F'. At this time certain re-organisations in company structure took place resulting in the following—

> 'A' Company: Formed by St Peter's, Pembroke, Corpus Christi, Queen's, St Catharine's and Downing Colleges.
>
> 'B' Company: Formed by St John's College.
>
> 'C' Company: Formed by Clare, Gonville and Caius, Trinity Hall, King's and Sidney Sussex Colleges.
>
> 'D' Company: Formed by Jesus, Christ's, Emmanuel and Magdalene Colleges.
>
> 'E', 'F' Companies: Formed by Trinity College.

The reorganisations of 1880 saw the 1st Admin. Battalion consolidated as the 1st Cambridgeshire Rifle Volunteer Corps. The sub-title (Cambridge, Essex and Hunts) was also included in the full designation and served to indicate the inclusion in the battalion of companies from outside the county. Headquarters of the new corps were placed at Cambridge and the ten companies were organised as follows—

'A' to 'D' Companies at Cambridge	Late 1st Cambs Corps
'E' Company at Wisbeach	Late 2nd Cambs Corps
'F' Company at Whittlesea	Late 4th Cambs Corps
'G' Company at March	Late 5th Cambs Corps
'H' Company at Ely	Late 6th Cambs Corps
'I' Company at Saffron Walden	Late 17th Essex Corps
'J' Company at St Neots	Late 1st Hunts Corps

The 3rd Corps from the university was also effected by the reorganisations and were renumbered as 2nd.

Both the 1st and 2nd Corps became part of the Suffolk Regiment in 1881 and in 1887 the titles of 3rd (Cambridgeshire) and 4th (Cambridge University) Volunteer Battalions were assumed. This change was notified in General Order 181 of December.

The Hunts Company of the 3rd VB was disbanded in 1889 and in 1893–94 and due to a sudden expansion in numbers and problems with accommodation the companies of the 4th were once again reorganised.

The restructure went as follows—

'A' Company: Formed by Peterhouse, Pembroke, Queen's, Corpus Christi and St Catharine's Colleges.

'B' Company: Formed by St John's College.

'C' Company: Formed by Gonvile and Caius College.

'D' Company: Formed by Christ's, Emmanuel, Jesus and Madgalene Colleges.

'E' Company: Formed by Trinity College.

'F' Company: Formed by Clare, Trinity Hall, King's, Sidney Sussex and Selwyn Colleges.

The next change in the 4th VB occurred in 1896 when due this time to a fall off in numbers St John's became part of 'A' Company while Pembroke replaced them as 'B'. Also at this time Downing College became part of 'A' Company.

Permission to increase the establishment of the University Battalion to eight companies was granted during the early part of 1900. This required yet another regrouping of the colleges resulting in the removal of St John's from 'A' Company to form 'G' and Christ's, Magdalene, Sidney Sussex and Selwyn from 'D' and 'F' to form 'H'.

Under Army Order 56 of April 1903 His Majesty the King was graciously pleased to approve the new title of 'The Cambridge University Volunteer Rifle Corps'. This was retained until April 1908 and the transfer of the battalion to the Senior Division of the Officer Training Corps.

The title adopted by the 3rd VB upon transfer to the Territorial Force in 1908 was The Cambridgeshire Battalion, The Suffolk Regiment. The following year, however, this was changed to The Cambridgeshire Regiment.

Three cadet corps are shown in the *Army List* as being affiliated to the 3rd

(Cambridgeshire) Volunteer Battalion. Leys School of Cambridge formed a company in 1900 followed by one at Perse School, also of Cambridge, in 1905. The last formed was the Cambridge and County School in 1906 which together with Leys and Perse became part of the Junior Division of the Officers Training Corps in 1908.

CARDIGANSHIRE

Four rifle volunteer units were raised within the county during 1860. No administrative battalion was formed and the corps if attached at all either joined the battalions in Montgomeryshire or Pembrokeshire. Due to a series of disbandments and renumbering the progress of each corps can at times prove to be confusing. Two of the four units held different numbers at various times and one, the last raised, was to hold all four positions throughout its existence. With this in mind each corps has been dealt with under the heading of its location rather than number.

ABERYSTWYTH

The first corps to be formed in the county was at Aberystwyth on 12 March 1860. It first appeared in the monthly *Army List* for February 1860 as the 1st Sub-division but by the following month was shown as 1st Corps. In the *Army List* for June 1861 the corps is given as being at Talybont a town 6 miles north-east of Aberystwyth. The corps disappeared from the *Army List* in February 1864, its strength never having been above that of a half company.

Aberystwyth also provided, on 12 March 1860, the 2nd Corps of the period. This was included in the 1st Montgomeryshire Admin. Battalion in January 1864 and by June of the same year had been renumbered as 1st Corps. In 1866 and as a half company only the 1st Corps was broken up and was not seen in the *Army List* after October.

ABERBANK

Aberbank was the home of the original 3rd Corps being formed there on 12 March 1860. This sub-division was also broken up and made its last appearance in the *Army List* for May 1861.

CARDIGAN

The last corps to be formed in Cardiganshire was at Cardigan on 8 May 1860. This company was at first designated as 4th but in 1861 and due to the disappearance of the corps at Aberbank was renumbered 3rd. In June 1864 the corps is shown as being 'united' with the 1st Admin. Battalion of Pembrokeshire Rifle Volunteers and with its new number, 2nd. This had been acquired upon the redesignation of the original 2nd Corps as 1st.

The 1st position in the county list had remained vacant since the disappearance in 1866 of the Aberystwyth Corps. In 1873 the Cardigan Company took the last step up and from May appeared in the *Army List* as 1st Corps.

As previously mentioned the Cardigan Company had been united to the

Pembrokeshire Admin. Battalion. In 1880 and upon the consolidation of the battalion the 1st Cardiganshires formed 'F' Company of the 1st Pembrokeshire Rifle Volunteer Corps.

CARMARTHENSHIRE

Six companies of rifle volunteers were raised within the county during 1860 and 1861 and later included in the 1st Admin. Battalion. The battalion was formed in June 1861 and had its headquarters at Carmarthen.

1st Corps: Formed at Llandilo on 28 February 1860.

2nd Corps: Formed at Carmarthen on 20 February 1860. This corps was formed as one company but was increased to two upon amalgamation with the 6th Corps in 1872.

3rd Corps: Formed at Llandovery on 4 May 1860. Desbandment came in 1875 and the corps is last shown in the *Army List* for May of that year.

4th Corps: Formed at Llansawel on 29 May 1860. This corps was disbanded during the latter part of 1869.

5th Corps: Formed at Llanelly on 8 May 1861

6th Corps: Formed at Carmarthen on 8 May 1861. In 1872 an amalgamation between the 6th and the other Carmarthen Company, the 2nd Corps, took place. The 6th thereafter being known as No 2 Company of the 2nd Corps.

In 1875 the 1st Admin. Battalion was broken up and the corps transferred to the 1st Pembrokeshire Battalion. At this time only the 1st, 2nd, 3rd and 5th Corps were in existence. The 3rd, as mentioned above, was later disbanded but the remaining corps stayed with the Pembrokes until 1880 and the consolidation of the battalion as the 1st Pembrokeshire Rifle Volunteer Corps. This new corps consisted of ten companies of which 'G' was formed by the 1st Corps, 'H' and 'I' by the 2nd and 'K' by the 5th.

CARNARVONSHIRE

On 2 August 1860 the seven corps then in existence within the county were grouped into the 1st Admin. Battalion of Carnarvonshire Rifle Volunteers. Headquarters were at Carnarvon and the seven corps were—

1st Corps: Formed at Carnarvon on 1 March 1860, moving to Penrhyn in 1862. The corps was later broken up and made its last appearance in the *Army List* for December 1874.

2nd Corps: Formed at Carnarvon on 1 March 1860 and like the 1st Corps moved to Penrhyn in 1862. The 2nd was also broken up and was not seen after January 1877.

3rd Corps: Formed at Carnarvon on 1 March 1860.

4th Corps: Formed at Tremadoc on 1 March 1860.

5th Corps: Formed at Pwllheli on 1 March 1860. Was later disbanded and appeared for the last time in the *Army List* for January 1877. A new 5th Corps was raised at Llanberis on 5 June 1878.

6th Corps: Formed at Bangor on 3 March 1860. Disappeared from the *Army List* in October 1865.

7th Corps: Formed at Conway on 4 April 1860. Was last seen in the *Army List* for December 1866.

The Carnarvonshire Battalion was broken up in 1873 and is last seen in the *Army List* for December of that year. From then on the remaining corps, the 1st to 5th, are shown as being united to the 1st Flintshire Admin. Battalion.

In 1880 the Flintshire Battalion was consolidated as the 1st Flintshire and Carnarvonshire Rifle Volunteer Corps. The new corps consisted of ten companies of which 'G' and 'H' were formed by the 3rd Corps, 'I' by the 4th, having moved headquarters to Portmadoc, and 'K' by the 5th.

Under General Order 78 of June 1884 the 1st Flint and Carnarvon became the 2nd Volunteer Battalion of the Royal Welsh Fusiliers. By 1896 almost half the battalion, which by this time contained sixteen companies, was formed from Carnarvonshire personnel. On 26 May 1897 the establishment of the 2nd VB was reduced to eight companies when a new unit designated as 3rd VB, Royal Welsh Fusiliers was formed from the Carnarvonshire members.

Headquarters of the 3rd VB were placed at Carnarvon and the first establishment set at eight companies. In 1900 three new companies were raised but by 1904 the strength of the battalion had been reduced to nine.

It is quite probable that one of the companies raised in 1900 was recruited in Anglesey as in 1908 the title adopted by the 3rd VB upon transfer to the TF was 6th (Carnarvon and Anglesey) Battalion, The Royal Welsh Fusiliers. However, the Anglesey element of the 6th, which was located at Holyhead, may have been a newly raised unit for the Territorial Force.

CHESHIRE

Between 1859 and 1865 thirty-six numbered corps of rifle volunteers were raised in Cheshire and included in one or other of the five administrative battalions that were formed. Admin. battalions for the county are first noted in the *Army List* for June 1860, it is not until December, however, that the first four are listed together with their commanding officers. The 5th follows in January 1861 and in the April issue of the same year headquarters and the corps included in each battalion are recorded.

Headquarters of the 1st Admin. Battalion were at Birkenhead and the corps included were—

1st Corps: Formed at Birkenhead on 25 August 1859.

2nd Corps: Formed at Oxton on 30 August 1859.

3rd Corps: Formed at Wallasey on 5 September 1859.

4th Corps: Formed at Bebbington on 10 September 1859. A move to Rock Ferry is indicated in the *Army List* for March 1863 while that for October of the following year makes no mention of the corps at all. A new 4th Corps was formed at Bebbington on 5 November 1864.

11th Corps: Formed at Neston on 28 February 1860.

14th Corps: Formed at Hooton on 3 March 1860.

30th Corps: Formed at Tranmere on 30 April 1860.

34th Corps: Formed at Upton on 5 June 1861. Disbanded in 1864 and is last seen in the *Army List* for September of that year.

35th Corps: Formed at Bromborough on 25 February 1863.

The battalion was consolidated in 1880 as the 1st Cheshire Rifle Volunteer Corps. Headquarters were placed at Oxton, Birkenhead and the eight company establishment was provided in order of seniority by the former eighth corps, the headquarters of 'C' Company, late 3rd Corps, being moved from Wallasey to Egremont.

The 1st Cheshires were redesignated as the 1st Volunteer Battalion of the Cheshire Regiment by General Order 181 of December 1887. By 1900 additional companies had been raised at Birkenhead, Liscard and Heswell and in April 1908 the 1st VB transferred to the Territorial Force as the 4th Battalion, the Cheshire Regiment.

Several cadet units were formed and affiliated to the battalion, the first to appear in the *Army List* being that raised by Wirral College in 1892. Both Mostyn House School at Parkgate and the West Kirby School provided companies in 1893. The following year, however, Wirral was disbanded followed by West Kirby Park in 1900. In 1903 Liscard High School, Wallasey Grammar and the New Brighton High School all formed units. By April 1904 all three schools had disappeared from the *Army List* having had no officers appointed. Only the Mostyn House School Company survived until the 1908 reorganisations. They were, however, not recognised by the Territorial Force and later disbanded.

Chester was the headquarters of the 2nd Admin. Battalion, the corps included being—

6th Corps: Formed at Chester on 25 November 1859. Absorbed the 10th Corps as No 2 Company in June, 1860 and in 1870 was granted the additional title of 'The Earl of Chester's'.

7th Corps: Formed at Runcorn on 30 November 1859.

10th Corps: Formed at Chester on 25 February 1860. Absorbed into the 6th Corps as its No 2 Company in June 1860.

23rd Corps: The original 23rd Corps was formed at Weaverham on 15 March 1860. In the *Army List* for May 1860 the officers of the corps are shown as now forming the 19th at Stockport. A new 23rd Corps is listed at Weaverham and the officers' commissions in this case are dated 28 March 1860.

24th Corps: Formed at Frodsham on 30 March 1860.

The 16th Corps is shown in the *Army List* as being part of the battalion from June 1860 to August 1860. That for September shows the corps with the 4th Admin.

Upon consolidation in 1880 the battalion was designated as 6th Cheshire (The Earl Of Chester's) Rifle Volunteer Corps. Renumbering as 2nd, however, came after a few months. Headquarters of the 2nd remained at Chester and the nine companies were organised as follows—

'A' to 'E' Companies at Chester	Late 6th Corps
'F', 'G' Companies at Runcorn	Late 7th Corps
'H' Company at Weaverham	Late 23rd Corps
'I' Company at Frodsham	Late 24th Corps

Redesignation as the 2nd (Earl of Chester's) Volunteer Battalion, the Cheshire Regiment was notified in General Order 181 of December 1887. Two new companies were formed in 1900 and in 1908 the 2nd and 3rd Volunteer Battalions were amalgamated to form the 5th (Earl of Chester's) Battalion of the Cheshire Regiment. The 2nd VB providing headquarters and four companies.

The 5th, 8th and 27th Corps are all shown between June and August 1860 as being part of the 3rd Admin. Battalion. The *Army List* for September, however, shows them as being included in the 4th. Headquarters of the 3rd Battalion were at Altringham, moving to Knutsford in 1864. The corps included were—

12th Corps: Formed at Altringham on 1 March 1860. Absorbed the 25th Corps as No 2 Company in 1866.

15th Corps: Formed at Knutsford on 5 March 1860.

22nd Corps: The 22nd was originally formed at Northwich on 12 March 1860. In the May 1860 *Army List*, however, the officers of the company are shown as forming the 18th Corps at Stockport. A new 22nd at Northwich is shown with different officers whose commissions on this occasion are dated 26 March 1860.

25th Corps: Formed at Timperley on 2 April 1860. Absorbed into the 12th Corps as its No 2 Company in 1866.

26th Corps: Formed at Northenden on 4 April 1860. Moved to Cheadle in 1862.

28th Corps: Formed at Sale Moor on 7 April 1860.

32nd Corps: Formed at Lymm on 10 September 1860.

Redesignation as the 12th Cheshire Rifle Volunteers came in 1880 upon consolidation. By June, however, the corps had been renumbered as 3rd. Headquarters remained at Knutsford and the eight companies were organised as follows—

'A', 'B' Companies at Altringham	Late 12th Corps
'C' Company at Knutsford	Late 15th Corps
'D' Company at Northwich	Late 22nd Corps
'E' Company at Winsford	Late 22nd Corps
'F' Company at Cheadle	Late 26th Corps
'G' Company at Sale Moor	Late 28th Corps
'H' Company at Lymm	Late 32nd Corps

Redesignation as the 3rd Volunteer Battalion of the Cheshire Regiment was notified in General Order 181 of December 1887. In April 1908 the 3rd VB amalgamated with the 2nd to form the 5th (Earl of Chester's) Battalion, the Cheshire Regiment. The 3rd VB providing four companies.

The eventual components of the 4th Admin. Battalion, headquarters Stockport, were those listed below. The 5th, 8th, 16th and 27th Corps, however, were shown as part of the battalion between September 1860 and May 1861. In addition to Cheshire corps the 23rd Derbyshire was included in 1876.

9th Corps: Formed at Moottram on 10 February 1860. Was not shown in the *Army List* after February 1861.

13th Corps: Formed at Duckinfield on 20 February 1860. This corps moved to Newton in 1863, to Newton Moor near Hyde in 1868 and to Stalybridge in 1873.

17th Corps: Formed at Stockport on 10 March 1860.

18th Corps: In the *Army List* for April 1860 the first officers of the 18th, commissions dated 12 March 1860, are shown as forming the 22nd Corps at Northwich. In the *List* for the following month the 18th Corps is mentioned for the first time. It has the officers who were previously with the 22nd and the headquarters are given as being at Stockport.

19th Corps: The formation of the 19th Corps followed a pattern similar to that of the 18th. The April 1860 *List* shows the officers as with the 23rd Corps at Weaverham and the commissions dated 15 March 1860. May saw the officers with the 19th Corps at Stockport.

20th Corps: Formed at Stockport on 20 March 1860.

21st Corps: Formed at Stockport on 22 March 1860.

29th Corps: Formed at Stockport on 10 April 1860.

31st Corps: Formed at Hyde on 15 August 1860.

Upon consolidation in 1880 the battalion took the number of the senior corps, 13th, but this was changed to 4th Cheshire (Cheshire and Derby) Rifle Volunteer Corps by June. Headquarters remained at Stockport and the thirteen companies were organised as follows—

'A' to 'C' Companies at Stalybridge	Late 13th Cheshire
'D' to 'I' Companies at Stockport	Late 17th to 21st and 29th Cheshire.
'K' Company at Hyde	Late 31st Cheshire.
'L' to 'N' Companies at Glossop	Late 23rd Derby.

The 4th Cheshires joined the Cheshire Regiment in 1881 and in 1887, under General Order 181 of December, became the 4th Volunteer Battalion. The battalion became the regiment's 6th in 1908 with headquarters and seven companies in Cheshire and one in Derbyshire.

Headquarters of the 5th Admin. Battalion were placed at Congleton and the corps included were—

5th Corps: Formed at Congleton on 15 September 1859. Shown as part of the 3rd Admin. Battalion from June to August 1860 and with the 4th from September 1860 to May 1861.

8th Corps: Formed at Macclesfield on 5 January 1860. Shown as part of the 5th Admin. Battalion from June, 1861 but was previously listed as being with the 3rd and 4th at the same time as the 5th corps shown above.

16th Corps: Formed at Sandbach on 7 March 1860. Shown as part of the 2nd Admin. from June to August 1860 and the 4th from September 1860 to May 1861.

27th Corps: Formed at Wilmslow on 5 April 1860. The *Army List* records the Admin. Battalions that the corps was attached to as being the same as those for the 5th Corps.

33rd Corps: Formed at Nantwich on 5 November 1860.

36th Corps: Formed at Crewe on 20 January 1865.

When the battalion was consolidated in March 1880 as the 5th Cheshire Rifle Volunteers it was at first intended for the corps to consist of thirteen and a half companies. The former 36th Corps at Crewe was to provide the last four companies of the new corps but in fact was disbanded before the end of the year. The eventual formation of the 5th Corps was as follows—

'A' and 'B' Companies at Congleton	Late 5th Corps
'C' to 'F' Companies at Macclesfield	Late 8th Corps
'G' Company at Sandbach	Late 16th Corps
'H' Company at Wilmslow	Late 27th Corps
'I' Company at Nantwich	Late 33rd Corps

With the loss of the Crewe personnel the establishment of the corps was reduced to nine and a half companies. By October 1880 the *Army List* indicates a ten company establishment, the 10th being commanded by the former lieutenant of the 27th Wilmslow Corps.

Redesignation as the 5th Volunteer Battalion, the Cheshire Regiment was assumed in December 1887 and as the 7th Battalion (TF) in April 1908.

The 1st Cadet Battalion, the Cheshire Regiment was formed on 2 December 1901 with an establishment of four companies. Headquarters were at Northenden. The battalion transferred to the Territorial Force in 1908 gaining recognition on 29 June 1910.

CINQUE PORTS

An administrative battalion for the Cinque Ports area first appeared in the *Army List* for October 1860. The corps included were the 1st to 8th followed by the 9th in 1861. In December 1861 two battalions are listed; the 1st now contains the 1st and 9th Corps together with the 16th, 17th and 19th from the county of Sussex. The 2nd Battalion has, with the exception of the 3rd Corps who are now shown as being 'united' with the 5th Kent Admin. Battalion, the remaining Cinque Ports companies. Headquarters were placed at Hastings for the 1st Battalion and at Dover for the 2nd.

In September 1862 a 10th Corps is shown as being formed at New Romney and included in the 2nd Battalion. Two more Sussex corps, the 2nd and 4th, were added to the 1st Admin. in 1863 but in 1868 and 1870 respectively the 19th and 2nd were removed. The 20th Sussex was formed and added to the battalion in October 1870.

The Cinque Ports corps were—

1st Corps: Formed at Hastings on 17 December 1859. Later, in 1876, absorbed the 9th Corps at Rye and the 16th, 17th and 20th Sussex who were at Battle, Etchingham and Uckfield respectively.

2nd Corps: Formed as the 2nd Kent Rifle Volunteer Corps at Ramsgate on 18 September 1859. Became the 2nd Cinque Ports in April 1860.

3rd Corps: The services of a company of rifle volunteers formed in the Rye, Tenterden area, a half company each, were accepted on 1 December 1859. The corps was originally numbered as 2nd but due to the transfer of the 2nd Kent (see above) in April 1860 was restyled as 3rd. The Rye portion of the corps was later to suffer a setback when due to its commanding officer's lack of interest it began to break up. Some members were to join the 1st Cinque Ports Artillery Volunteers as Hastings while those that chose to continue service as riflemen joined the 1st Cinque Ports Rifles. In the *Army List* for September 1861 headquarters of the 3rd are now shown as being at Tenterden and in that for December the corps is given as being 'united' with the 5th Admin. Battalion of Kent Rifle Volunteers. This battalion was consolidated in 1880 as the 5th Kent Rifle Volunteers Corps, the Tenterden members forming 'G' Company.

4th Corps: Formed at Hythe on 13 February 1860 as the 1st Sub-division. Became 4th Corps in April 1860.

5th Corps: Formed at Folkestone on 30 March 1860.

6th Corps: Shown for the first time in the March 1860 *Army List* as the 3rd Sub-division at Deal. Became the 6th Corps in April of the same year but disappeared from the *List* in January 1864.

7th Corps: Formed at Margate on 22 March 1860.

8th Corps: Formed at Dover on 30 July 1860.

9th Corps: When the Rye portion of the 3rd Corps was broken up in 1861 those members who wished to continue as riflemen were transferred to the 1st Corps at Hastings and thereafter known as the Rye Sub-division. At the same time as the Rye officers were removed from the 3rd and included in the 1st (monthly *Army List* for September 1861) a 9th Corps appears as being formed at Rye. According to a booklet published in 1954 entitled *The Story of the Rye Volunteers* Rye attended the 'Great Review' at Brighton on 21 April 1862 as the 9th Corps. No officers, however, appear in the *Army List* under this heading which was removed in November 1862. Rye once again appears as providing a 9th Corps in January 1865. This time officers are listed with commissions dated 12 December 1864. This new corps was in fact formed by the Rye elements of the 1st Corps. In 1876 the Rye Volunteers once again found themselves serving as part of the 1st Corps at Hastings. This was due to the disbandment of the 9th that year.

10th Corps: A 10th Corps at New Romney is shown in the *Army List* for August 1862. No officers were appointed and the corps is not seen after April 1864. In January of the following year, however, the 10th reappears this time with officers holding commissions dated 22 December 1864.

The 2nd Admin. Battalion was broken up in 1874 and is last seen in the *Army List* for March of that year. The 2nd, 7th and 8th Corps were all absorbed into the 5th Kent Rifle Volunteer Corps while the remainder of the battalion, the 4th, 5th and 10th, joined the 4th Kent Admin. The 5th Kents were also included in the 4th Admin. Battalion which was consolidated by the end of 1874 as the 5th Kent (East Kent) Rifle Volunteers with headquarters at Canterbury.

The 1st Admin. Battalion after the inclusion of the 20th Sussex in 1870 now contained the 1st and 9th Cinque Ports and the 4th, 16th, 17th and 20th Sussex. As previously mentioned the 9th Corps at Rye became part of the 1st in 1876. At the same time the three Sussex Corps, 16th, 17th and 20th, were also absorbed bringing the strength of the 1st Corps up to five companies. Locations of the Sussex Companies were, Battle (16th Corps), Etchingham (17th Corps) and Uckfield (20th Corps).

When the 1st Admin. Battalion was consolidated as the 1st Cinque Ports (Cinque Ports and Sussex) Rifle Volunteer Corps in 1880 only the 1st Cinque Ports and 4th Sussex were at that time contained.

Headquarters of the new corps were placed at Hastings and the company disposition is given as—

'A' Company at Hastings	Late 1st Cinque Ports
'B' Company at Battle	Late 1st Cinque Ports
'C' Company at Ticehurst	Late 1st Cinque Ports
'D' Company at Lewes	Late 4th Sussex

In 1881 the 1st Cinque Ports joined the Royal Sussex Regiment as one of its allotted volunteer battalions. No change in designation, however, was assumed.

When the 1st Cinque Ports (Cinque Ports and Sussex) Corps was created in 1880 provisions for six companies were made. It was not until 1887, however, that sufficient personnel were recruited to bring the battalion up to strength. The first new company, 'E', was formed in 1885 at Rye. Next came 'F' Company at Hastings in 1887, 'G' at Crowborough and 'H' at Ore in 1890 and in 1900 'I' at Hastings and 'K' at Ore. Eastbourne College provided a cadet company in 1896.

In April 1908 the 1st Cinque Ports became the 5th (Cinque Ports) Battalion, the Royal Sussex Regiment. The Eastbourne College Cadets became part of the Junior Division of the Officers Training Corps.

CLACKMANNANSHIRE

The services of the two companies of rifle volunteers raised at Alloa in 1859 were formally accepted on 2 June 1860. These were to become the 1st Corps of the county and were followed by a company at Tillicoultry as 2nd. The services of the Tillicoultry Company were accepted on 10 March and as such would have entitled them to precedence over Alloa. The corps was in fact designated as 1st but due to the Lord-Lieutenant being absent and some confusion at his office when the applications to form corps were sent in, the numbering was reversed.

There being insufficient rifle volunteers in Clackmannanshire to form a battalion the two corps were, in 1862, included in the 1st Admin. Battalion in Stirlingshire. In 1867, however, two additional companies, No 3 (Alloa) and No 4 (Dollar), were raised by the 1st Corps. In November of the same year the 1st and 2nd were removed from the Stirlingshire Battalion and formed into the 1st Admin. Battalion of Clackmannanshire. Headquarters of the new battalion were placed at Alloa and to it were added in 1868 the 14th Stirlingshire Corps, formed that year at Alva, and in 1873 the 1st Kinross. The latter having previously been with the 1st Fifeshire Admin. Battalion.

In February 1880 the 1st Admin. Battalion of Clackmannanshire Rifle Volunteers was consolidated at the 1st Clackmannan and Kinross Rifle Volunteer Corps. Headquarters remained at Alloa and the seven companies were organised as follows—

'A' Company at Alloa	Late 1st Clackmannan Corps
'B' Company at Sauchie	Late 1st Clackmannan Corps
'C' Company at Alloa	Late 1st Clackmannan Corps
'D' Company at Dollar	Late 1st Clackmannan Corps
'E' Company at Tillicoultry	Late 2nd Clackmannan Corps
'F' Company at Alva	Late 14th Sterling Corps
'G' Company at Kinross	Late 1st Kinross Corps

In 1883 an additional company, 'H', was established at Clackmannan having been formed there as a section the previous year. A cadet company was formed and affiliated to the battalion in 1902 by the Dollar Institution.

Redesignation as the 7th (Clackmannan and Kinross) Volunteer Battalion of the Argyll and Sutherland Highlanders was notified in General Order 181 of December 1887.

In April 1908 the 4th and 7th VBs of the regiment were amalgamated to form the 7th Battalion, the Argyll and Sutherland Highlanders, the latter providing four companies, three in Clackmannanshire and one in Kinross. At the same time the Dollar Institution Cadets became part of the Junior Division of the Officers Training Corps.

CORNWALL

In the *Army List* for May 1860 two administrative battalions are noted as having been formed within the County of Cornwall. The commissions of the officers of both are dated 20 April 1860. The additional title of 'The Duke of Cornwall's' was later granted to both battalions and is shown for the first time in the *Army List* for December 1861.

Headquarters of the 1st Admin. Battalion were at Penzance and the corps included were those located in the western half of the county.

1st Corps: Formed at Penzance on 10 September 1859.

2nd Corps: Formed at Camborne on 17 October 1859.

3rd Corps: Formed at Falmouth on 28 October 1859.

7th Corps: Formed at Helston on 25 January 1860.

8th Corps: Formed at Penryn on 2 February 1860. This corps is omitted from the October 1860 *Army List* but is once again shown in that for the following month. In 1861 the 8th position is again shown as vacant the Penryn Company having been renumbered as 21st in January.

11th Corps: Formed at Truro on 13 February 1860.

12th Corps: Formed at Truro on 13 February 1860.

15th Corps: Formed at Hayle on 2 May 1860.

17th Corps: Formed at Redruth on 7 April 1860.

18th Corps: Formed at Helston on 2 June 1860. The 18th did not join the 1st Admin. Immediately upon formation but remained an independent corps until the latter part of 1861. Headquarters were moved to Trelowarren in 1864.

20th Corps: Formed at St Just in Penwith on 14 August 1860. Did not join the battalion until December 1861.

21st Corps: Formed as the 8th Corps at Penryn (see above). Joined 1st Admin. Battalion in December 1861.

Headquarters of the 2nd Admin. Battalion were at Bodmin and the corps included were those raised in the eastern portion of the county.

4th Corps: Formed at Liskeard on 13 December 1859.

5th Corps: Formed at Callington on 3 January 1860.

6th Corps: Formed at Launceston on 10 January 1860.

9th Corps: Formed at St Austell on 14 February 1860.

10th Corps: Formed at Bodmin on 24 December 1860. This corps was originally designated as the 1st Sub-division and is shown for the first time as 10th Corps in the *Army List* for March 1860.

13th Corps: Formed at Waderbridge on 7 April 1860.

14th Corps: Formed at Calstock on 15 March 1860. This Corps was later broken up and is not shown in the *Army List* after November 1860.

16th Corps: Formed at St Columb on 2 April 1860. Was not included in the 2nd Admin. until the latter part of 1863.

19th Corps: Formed at Camelford on 26 July 1860. Included in the battalion by December 1861.

22nd Corps: Formed at Saltash on 23 February 1865.

In 1880 the 1st and 2nd Admin. Battalions were respectively consolidated as the 1st and 4th Cornwall Rifle Volunteer Corps, the latter being renumbered as 2nd after a few months. The sub-title 'The Duke of Cornwall's' also formed part of the full designation of each corps. The establishment of the 1st corps was eleven companies, lettered 'A' to 'K' and were formed in order of seniority by the eleven corps of the 1st Admin. Battalion. The nine companies of the 2nd Corps were lettered 'A' tó 'I' and were also formed in order of seniority in this case by the former components of the 2nd Admin.

Headquarters of the 1st Corps were moved to Falmouth in 1881 and in 1885 redesignation as the 1st Volunteer Battalion of the Duke of Cornwall's Light Infantry was notified in General Order 106. The 2nd Corps became the 2nd Volunteer Battalion at the same time. In 1900 the 2nd VB formed a new company at Bude and two years later the headquarters of the 1st were once again moved, this time to Truro.

Upon transfer to the Territorial Force in April 1908 the 1st and 2nd VBs formed the 4th and 5th Battalions of the Duke of Cornwall's Light Infantry.

CUMBERLAND

The 1st Admin. Battalion of Cumberland Rifle Volunteers was formed in May 1860 and to it then or upon formation were added the eleven corps that were formed within the county.

1st Corps: Formed at Carlisle on 15 February 1860. By June the corps had been increased from one to two companies, the 2nd having previously been part of the 2nd Corps at Whitehaven.

2nd Corps: Formed at Whitehaven on 14 February 1860. A 2nd Company was formed on 2 March 1860 but is shown in the *Army List* for June 1860 as being part of the 1st Corps.

3rd Corps: Formed at Keswick on 15 February 1860.

4th Corps: Formed at Brampton on 24 March 1860.

5th Corps: Formed at Penrith on 5 March 1860.

6th Corps: Formed at Alston on 2 March 1860.

7th Corps: Formed at Workington on 12 April 1860.

8th Corps: Formed at Cockermouth on 24 March 1860.

9th Corps: Formed at Whitehaven on 21 May 1860. This corps was subsequently broken up and was not shown in the *Army List* after June 1863.

10th Corps: Formed at Egremont on 3 July 1860.

11th Corps: Formed at Wigton on 18 July 1860.

Battalion headquarters were originally placed at Carlisle but in 1865 were moved to Keswick. In March 1880 the battalion was consolidated as the 1st Cumberland Rifle Volunteers, a two battalion corps with thirteen companies organised as follows—

'A' 'B' 'C' Companies at Carlisle	Late 1st Corps
'D' Company at Whitehaven	Late 2nd Corps
'E' Company at Keswick	Late 3rd Corps
'F' Company at Brampton	Late 4th Corps
'G' 'H' Companies at Penrith	Late 5th Corps
'I' Company at Alston	Late 6th Corps
'K' Company at Workington	Late 7th Corps
'L' Company at Cockermouth	Late 8th Corps
'M' Company at Egremont	Late 10th Corps
'N' Company at Wigton	Late 11th Corps

In December 1887 and under General Order 181 the title of 1st (Cumberland) Volunteer Battalion of the Border Regiment was assumed. Headquarters were moved back to Carlisle in 1896 and in 1900 the companies at Whitehaven, Workington, Cockermouth, Egremont and Wigton were removed to form the 3rd (Cumberland) Volunteer Battalion.

The establishment of the new battalion, whose headquarters were placed at Workington, was set at eight companies. In addition to those drawn from the 1st VB, new personnel were found at Workington, Frizington and Aspatria. A cadet corps was formed at St Bee's School in 1904 and affiliated to the battalion.

With the formation of the Territorial Force in April 1908 the 1st VB was amalgamated with the 2nd (Westmoreland) VB of the regiment to form the 4th (Cumberland and Westmoreland) Battalion. The Cumberland personnel providing headquarters and four companies. The 3rd VB became the 5th (Cumberland) Battalion and the St Bee's Cadets went on to become part of the Junior Division of the Officers Training Corps in 1910.

DENBIGHSHIRE

The 1st Admin. Battalion of Denbighshire Rifle Volunteers was formed with headquarters at Ruabon on 10 September 1860. The corps included then or at some later date were—

1st Corps: Formed at Wrexham on 30 January 1860.

2nd Corps: Formed at Ruabon on 12 April 1860.

3rd Corps: Formed at Denbigh on 21 July 1860.

4th Corps: Formed at Gresford on 10 September 1860.

5th Corps: Formed at Gwersyllt on 10 September 1860. Was not shown as being included in the battalion until November 1861.

6th Corps: Formed at Ruthin on 20 February 1861 and shown as being part of 1st Admin. the following November.

7th Corps: Formed at Chirk on 24 August 1861. Included in battalion by November.

8th Corps: Formed at Llanrwst on 19 October 1861. Was later disbanded appearing for the last time in the *Army List* for January 1865.

9th Corps: A 9th Corps with headquarters at Wrexham appeared for the first time in the *Army List* for June 1861. It disappeared in October having had no officers appointed. A new 9th was formed at Llangollen on 6 June 1868.

In 1880 the battalion was consolidated as the 1st Denbighshire Rifle Volunteer Corps with an establishment of eight companies. Headquarters remained at Ruabon and the companies were organised as follows—

'A', 'B' Companies at Wrexham	Late 1st Corps
'C' Company at Ruabon	Late 2nd Corps
'D' Company at Denbigh	Late 3rd Corps

'E' Company at Gresford and Chirk	Late 4th and 7th Corps
'F' Company at Gwersyllt	Late 5th Corps
'G' Company at Ruthin	Late 6th Corps
'H' Company at Llangollen	Late 9th Corps

Shortly after consolidation corps headquarters were moved to Wynnstay. Redesignation as the 1st Volunteer Battalion, the Royal Welsh Fusiliers was notified under General Order 78 of June 1884 and in the following year headquarters were moved yet again, this time to Wrexham.

During 1900 three additional companies were formed increasing the establishment of the battalion to eleven. In April 1908 the 1st VB transferred to the Territorial Force as the 4th Battalion, Royal Welsh Fusiliers.

DERBYSHIRE

With headqearters at Derby the 1st Admin. Battalion of Derbyshire Rifle Volunteers was formed on 10 July 1860. The corps included then or upon subsequent formation were as follows—

1st Corps: Formed at Derby on 23 July 1859.

4th Corps: Formed at Derby on 31 December 1859.

5th Corps: Formed at Derby on 18 January 1860.

12th Corps: Formed at Butterley on 3 April 1860.

13th Corps: Formed at Belper on 14 March 1860.

15th Corps: Formed at Derby on 7 July 1860.

16th Corps: Formed at Ilkeston on 7 September 1860. Disappeared from the *Army List* in August 1863.

19th Corps: Formed at Derby on 23 April 1868. This corps was recruited mainly from the Parish of Elvaston.

20th Corps: Formed at Long Eaton on 31 July 1871 and also contained '(Trent)' in its full title.

The battalion was consolidated as the 1st Derbyshire Rifle Volunteer Corps in 1880. Headquarters remained at Derby and the twelve companies were organised as follows—

'A' Company at Derby	Late 1st Corps
'B' Company at Derby	Late 4th Corps
'C' 'D' Companies at Derby	Late 5th Corps
'E' 'F' Companies at Butterley and Condor Park	Late 12th Corps
'G' Company at Belper	Late 13th Corps
'H' 'I' Companies at Derby	Late 15th Corps
'K' Company at Derby	Late 19th Corps
'L' Company at Long Eaton	Late 20th Corps
'M' Company at Long Eaton	Late 20th and part of 13th Corps

A cadet corps is shown from 1870 as being affiliated to the 1st Admin. Battalion. It disappears from the *Army List* during 1881 but returns again in 1883. By 1895 the corps is shown as being formed by Derby School. Another cadet corps was formed by Trent College in April 1886, this, however, was later disbanded and is last seen in the *Army List* for January 1890. Next came a company formed in May 1900 by Repton School followed in December 1905 by a unit raised by the Derby GPO and known as the Postal Telegraph Messengers Cadet Corps.

Under General Order 39 of April 1887 the 1st Derbyshires became the 1st Volunteer Battalion of the Derbyshire Regiment. This title was retained until 1908 when they provided the regiment's 5th Battalion. Both the Derby and Repton Schools Cadet Corps became in 1908 contingents of the Officers Training Corps. The GPO unit continued its affiliation with the 5th Battalion.

The 3rd Admin. Battalion of the county was formed on 22 June 1860 with headquarters at Bakewell and between 1863 and 1871 also had attached to it the 1st Derbyshire Mounted Rifle Volunteer Corps. Included in the battalion were the following corps—

3rd Corps: Formed at Chesterfield on 7 January 1860.

6th Corps: Formed at Buxton on 16 February 1860. Was later disbanded and is last seen in the *Army List* for December 1861.

7th Corps: Formed at Chapel-en-le-Frith on 1 February 1860.

9th Corps: Formed at Bakewell on 28 February 1860.

11th Corps: Formed at Matlock on 17 March 1860.

17th Corps: Formed at Clay Cross on 26 January 1861.

18th Corps: Formed at Whaley Bridge on 16 March 1866.

21st Corps: Formed at Hartington on 25 May 1872.

22nd Corps: Formed at Staveley on 23 September 1874.

In 1869 the 2nd Admin. Battalion was broken up and two of its corps transferred to the 3rd. The battalion was formed in June 1860 with headquarters at Sudbury. These were moved to Ashbourne in 1864 and the corps included were—

2nd Corps: Formed at Sudbury on 6 December 1859. When the 2nd Admin. was broken up in 1869 the 2nd Corps did not transfer to the 3rd Admin. It remained independent for a while but was eventually disbanded by the end of 1869.

8th Corps: Formed at Ashbourne on 1 February 1860.

10th Corps: Formed at Wirksworth on 10 March 1860.

Upon consolidation in 1880 the battalion was originally numbered as 3rd Corps. This, however, was changed to 2nd after a few months. The establishment of the new 2nd Corps was set at ten companies wich were lettered 'A' to 'K' and provided in order of seniority by the battalion's ten corps.

In April 1887 and under General Order 39 the corps became the 2nd Volunteer Battalion of the Derbyshire Regiment. Headquarters moved to Chesterfield in 1898 and in 1900 three new companies, two at Chesterfield and one at Buxton, were raised. The battalion became the 6th Bn Sherwood Foresters in 1908.

No 14th Corps was ever formed and this position in the county list remained vacant. The last corps to be raised was on 22 January 1876 at Glossop. It was numbered 23rd and included in the 4th Admin. Battalion of the neighbouring county of Cheshire.

DEVONSHIRE

The 1st Devonshire Rifle Corps represents the senior volunteer unit in the United Kingdom, it being the first to be officially recognised by the Government. It was in 1852 that the services of the Exeter and South Devon Rifle Corps, headquarters Exeter, were offered to the Secretary of State. These were accepted and on 4 January 1853 Her Majesty Queen Victoria signed the commissions of the corps' first officers.

In 1859 the corps became the 1st Devonshire Rifle Volunteers with (Exeter and South Devon) forming part of its full title. The strength of the unit was increased when in 1860 the 24th Corps at Budleigh Salterton was absorbed and in 1863 the 1st Devonshire Engineer Volunteers were attached for drill and administration. This corps, however, was transferred in 1869 to the 1st Admin. Battalion of Gloucestershire Engineers.

The establishment of the 1st Devons soon reached eleven companies which in addition to those in Exeter also included stations at Exmouth, Crediton, Dawlish and Teignmouth. The title of the corps was changed in 1885, General Order 114, to the 1st (Exeter and South Devon) Volunteer Battalion, The Devonshire Regiment and in 1908, after amalgamation with the 3rd VB, to 4th Battalion. The Exeter School Cadet Corps, which was formed and affiliated to the battalion in 1897, was at this time transferred to the Junior Division of the Officer Training Corps.

The remaining Devonshire Rifle Corps were numbered 2nd to 28th and were, with the exception of 19th and 24th, included in one or other of the four administrative battalions that were formed. The 19th disappeared from the *Army List* in February 1861 having been formed at Okehampton on 3 March 1860 and the 24th as already mentioned was absorbed into the 1st Corps in 1860.

An admin. battalion for the county first appeared in the *Army List* for June 1860. It was designated as 1st and the corps included in it were the 2nd, 3rd and 16th. In the *List* for September 1860 there is no mention of a 1st Admin. Battalion but in its place a 2nd, 3rd, 4th and 5th are recorded. The corps formerly listed with the 1st are now with the 3rd. By April 1861 the county seems to have sorted out its admin. problems as the *Army List* for that month shows the four battalions renumbered as 1st to 4th.

Headquarters of the 1st Admin. Battalion were placed at Exeter and the corps included were—

  5th Corps: Formed at Upper Culm Vale on 22 March 1860. Headquarters were moved to Cullompton in 1862.

  8th Corps: Formed at Buckerell on 8 February 1860.

  11th Corps: Formed at Bampton on 28 February 1860.

13th Corps: Formed at Honiton on 20 February 1860.

14th Corps: Formed at Tiverton on 1 March 1860.

20th Corps: Formed at Broadhembury on 3 March 1860. Disbanded in 1875.

25th Corps: Formed at Ottery St Mary on 2 March 1860.

27th Corps: Formed at Colyton on 13 April 1861.

Attached to the battalion until their disbandment in 1878 and 1873 respectively were the 1st and 3rd Devonshire Mounted Rifle Corps.

The 1st Admin. Battalion was consolidated in 1880 as the 5th Devonshire Rifle Volunteer Corps. This was changed after a few months, however, to 3rd Corps. Headquarters remained at Exeter and the seven companies of the new corps were organised as follows—

'A' Company at Cullompton	Late 5th Corps
'B' Company at Buckerell	Late 8th Corps
'C' Company at Bampton	Late 11th Corps
'D' Company at Honiton	Late 13th Corps
'E' Company at Tiverton	Late 14th Corps
'F' Company at Ottery St Mary	Late 25th Corps
'G' Company at Colyton	Late 27th Corps

Under General Order 114 of November 1885 the 3rd Corps became the 3rd Volunteer Battalion of the Devonshire Regiment. That same year a new company was formed at Sidmouth. The next addition to the battalion came in 1900 when 'I' Company was raised at Axminster and both All Hallows School, Honiton and Blundell's School, Tiverton provided cadet corps.

Upon transfer to the Territorial Force in 1908 the 3rd VB was amalgamated with the 1st to form the 4th Battalion of the Devonshire Regiment. Both cadet units became part of the Junior Division, Officers Training Corps.

With headquarters at Plymouth the 2nd Admin. Battalion contained the following—

2nd Corps: Formed at Plymouth on 7 December 1859 and in 1874 absorbed the 16th Corps at Stonehouse.

3rd Corps: Formed at Devonport on 7 December 1859.

16th Corps: Formed at Stonehouse on 29 February 1860 and was absorbed into the 2nd Corps in 1874.

22nd Corps: Formed at Tavistock on 5 March 1860.

The 2nd Admin. Battalion was consolidated as the 2nd Corps in 1880 and was at that time also permitted to include 'Prince of Wales'' in its title. Headquarters remained at Plymouth and the companies were organised as follows—

'A' to 'F' Companies at Plymouth	Late 2nd Corps
'G' to 'I' Companies at Devonport	Late 3rd Corps
'K' 'L' Companies at Tavistock	Late 22nd Corps

The corps became the 2nd (Prince of Wales') Volunteer Battalion of the Devonshire Regiment in 1885, the change being notified in General Order 114 of that year. The establishment of the battalion was increased to twelve companies in 1900 but in 1905 a reduction was made to eight.

Several cadet units have been associated with the battalion, the first being formed in 1874 and attached to the 3rd Corps. Headquarters are given as being at Plymouth in 1883 and the corps disappeared from the *Army List* during 1885. Next came a company raised by Kelly College, Tavistock in 1894 and in 1906 the *Army List* indicates that the Postal Telegraph Messengers of Plymouth had formed a unit. The latter, however, disappeared in July 1907. The Plymouth and Mannamead College was, upon formation in 1900, affiliated to the 2nd Devonshire RGA (Vols). It later, in 1907, transferred to the 2nd (Prince of Wales') VB.

In 1908 the 2nd and 5th VBs were amalgamated to form the 5th Battalion. The Devonshire Regiment and both cadet units were transferred to the Officers Training Corps.

The corps contained within the 3rd Admin. Battalion, headquarters Barnstaple, · were as follows—

4th Corps: Formed at Ilfracombe on 3 March 1860. This corps disappeared from the *Army List* in December 1872.

6th Corps: Formed at Barnstaple on 23 February 1860.

18th Corps: Formed at Hatherleigh on 1 March 1860.

21st Corps: Formed at Bideford on 6 March 1860.

28th Corps: Formed at Lynton on 13 April 1861. This corps remained independent until inclusion in the 3rd Admin. in 1863. Disbanded in 1865. A new 28th Corps was formed at South Brent in 1868 but this was included in the 4th Admin. Battalion and was subsequently disbanded in 1875. On 8 March 1876 yet another 28th was raised this time at South Molton and like the first corps to bear that number was included in the 3rd Admin. Battalion.

Attached to the battalion until its disbandment in 1875 was the 6th Devonshire Mounted Rifles.

The battalion was originally designated as the 6th Devonshire Rifle Corps upon consolidation in 1880. This was changed to 4th Corps, however, after a few months. Headquarters remained at Barnstaple and the corps' seven companies were organised as follows—

'A' 'B' Companies at Barnstaple	Late 6th Corps
'C' Company at Hatherleigh	Late 18th Corps
'D' Company at Okehampton	Late 18th Corps
'E' Company at Bideford	Late 21st Corps
'F' Company at Torrington	Late 21st Corps
'G' Company at South Molton	Late 28th Corps

The battalion was redesignated as the 4th Volunteer Battalion of the Devonshire Regiment under General Order 114 of November 1885 and in 1908 provided the regiment's 6th Battalion.

The United Services College Cadet Corps at Westward Ho! was formed in 1900 and affiliated to the 4th VB. In 1904, however, it was moved to Harpenden and thereafter connected with the 2nd VB of the Bedfordshire Regiment.

The original headquarters of the 4th Admin. Battalion were at Totnes but from

February 1865 the *Army List* gives them as being at Newton Abbott. The corps contained within the battalion were—

9th Corps: Formed at Ashburton on 23 February 1860.

10th Corps: Formed at Newton Abbott on 27 March 1860.

17th Corps: Formed at Totnes on 3 March 1860.

23rd Corps: Formed at Chudleigh on 27 March 1860.

26th Corps: Formed at Kingsbridge on 5 July 1860.

28th Corps: Formed at South Brent on 14 October 1860. This was the second corps to bear this number and disbandment came in 1875.

Attached to the 4th Admin. were the 4th Mounted Rifles later 3rd Light Horse; the 5th Mounted Rifles later 1st Light Horse and the 7th Mounted Rifles later 2nd Light Horse. These units were disbanded in 1874, 1875 and 1874 respectively.

A cadet corps was formed and affiliated to the battalion in 1871 but this was not shown in the *Army List* after 1875.

The 4th Admin. Battalion was consolidated as the 9th Corps in 1880 but within a few months this was changed to 5th. Headquarters remained at Newton Abbott and the corps' six companies were organised as follows—

'A' Company at Ashburton	Late 9th Corps
'B' Company at Newton Abbott	Late 10th Corps
'C' Company at Totnes	Late 17th Corps
'D' Company at Chudleigh	Late 23rd Corps
'E' Company at Kingsbridge	Late 26th Corps
'F' Company at Torquay	Late 26th Corps

Redesignation as the 5th (The Hay Tor) Volunteer Battalion of the Devonshire Regiment was notified in General Order 114 of November 1885. 1908 saw the battalion amalgamated with the 2nd VB to form the regiment's 5th Battalion.

DORSETSHIRE

The following corps were all included in the 1st Admin. Battalion of Dorsetshire Rifle Volunteers. The battalion was formed on 9 May 1860 and had its headquarters at Dorchester.

1st Corps: Formed at Bridport on 22 August 1859.

2nd Corps: Formed at Wareham on 28 January 1860.

3rd Corps: Formed at Dorchester on 14 February 1860.

4th Corps: Formed at Poole on 13 February 1860.

5th Corps: Formed at Weymouth on 14 May 1860.

6th Corps: Formed at Wimborne on 14 March 1860.

7th Corps: Formed at Sherborne on 29 March 1860.

8th Corps: Formed at Blandford on 29 February 1860.

9th Corps: Formed at Shaftesbury on 10 March 1860.

10th Corps: Formed at Sturminster Newton on 10 July 1860. Towards the end of 1861 the 10th was removed from the 1st Admin. and made independent. In August 1862, however, it is once again shown in the *Army List* as being included. In the *List* for January 1877 the 12th Corps is shown as having been absorbed into the 10th. By April 1877 headquarters had been moved to Stalbridge and the additional title '(Blackmoor Vale)' adopted. Blackmoor Vale is the valley of the River Cale and is situated on the borders of Somerset and Dorset, extending south-east from Wincanton.

11th Corps: Formed at Gillingham on 7 July 1860 and was not shown as being part of 1st Admin. until August 1862.

12th Corps: Formed at Stalbridge on 7 July 1860 and included in 1st Admin. by August 1862. Absorbed into the 10th Corps at the beginning of 1877.

The battalion was consolidated in 1880 and the 1st to 11th Corps organised into eleven companies lettered 'A' to 'L' in order of their seniority. The new 1st Dorsetshire became the 1st Volunteer Battalion of the Dorsetshire Regiment under General Order 181 of December 1887 and its 4th Battalion upon transfer to the Territorial Force in April 1908.

Two schools have been associated with the battalion. Sherborne School formed a cadet corps in September 1888 which in 1908 became part of the Officers Training Corps. The County School at Dorchester provided a company in July 1893 but this disappeared from the *Army List* in January 1897.

DUMBARTONSHIRE

The following rifle volunteer corps were all formed within the county of Dumbartonshire and included in the 1st Admin. Battalion.

1st Corps: Formed at Row on 18 February 1860. Headquarters were moved to Helensburgh in January 1873. Absorbed 8th Corps in 1865.

2nd Corps: Formed at East Kilpatrick on 8 February 1860. Headquarters moved to Maryhill in 1868.

3rd Corps: Formed at Bonhill on 8 February 1860.

4th Corps: Formed at Jamestown on 8 February 1860.

5th Corps: Formed at Alexandria on 8 February 1860.

6th Corps: Formed at Dumbarton on 8 February 1860.

7th Corps: Formed at Cardross on 11 November 1859.

8th Corps : Formed at Gareloch on 16 February 1860. On 24 June 1865 the 8th was absorbed into the 1st at Row. It was, however, shown together with its three officers in the *Army List* until 1869.

9th Corps: Formed at Luss on 8 February 1860.

10th Corps: Formed at Kirkintilloch on 5 March 1860.

11th Corps: Formed at Cumbernauld on 13 June 1860.

12th Corps: Formed at Tarbet with a detachment at Arrochar on 7 March 1861. Disbanded in 1869.

13th Corps: Formed at Milngavie on 9 August 1867.

14th Corps: Formed at Clydebank on 18 May 1875.

The 1st Dumbartonshire Admin. Battalion was formed on 7 May 1860. Headquarters were placed at Balloch which on 29 April 1880 and the consolidation of the battalion as the 1st Dumbartonshire Rifle Volunteer Corps, were removed to Helensburgh. The new 1st Corps consisted of twelve companies organised as follows—

'A' Company at Helensburgh	Late 1st Corps
'B' Company at Cardross	Late 7th Corps
'C' Company at Dumbarton	Late 6th Corps
'D' Company at Bonhill	Late 3rd Corps
'E' Company at Jamestown	Late 4th Corps
'F' Company at Alexandria	Late 5th Corps
'G' Company at Clydebank	Late 14th Corps
'H' Company at Maryhill	Late 2nd Corps
'I' Company at Milngavie	Late 13th Corps
'K' Company at Kirkintilloch	Late 10th Corps
'L' Company at Cumbernauld	Late 11th Corps
'M' Company at Luss	Late 9th Corps

In 1881 the corps joined the Argyll and Sutherland Highlanders as one of its allotted volunteer battalions. Although ranked as 6th Volunteer Battalion this designation was never conferred and the 1st Dumbartons were to serve as such until redesignation as 9th Battalion, the Argyll and Sutherland Highlanders in 1908.

The disbandment of the Luss Company, 'M', occurred in January 1882 and it is of interest to mention the circumstances that brought about this event. For some time the Lieutenant-Colonel Commandant of the battalion, Henry Currie, was far from satisfied with the conduct of the company. As a kilted unit wearing blue bonnets it was the Colonel's opinion that they spoiled the appearance on parade of the rest of the battalion who were then dressed in helmets and green uniforms. On 25 August 1881 a Royal Review at Edinburgh, attended by the Queen, was to include the 1st Dumbartons. Subsequently Colonel Currie, who did not wish 'M' Company to attend, issued orders that it was to 'stay at home'. The battalion left for Edinburgh, without the Luss Company, and after taking up their positions in the parade were astonished to see it not only there but marching with another battalion. A new 'M' Company was formed in February at Renton.

Other reorganisations within the battalion were in 1884 when 'L' Company was absorbed into 'K' and a new 'L' formed at Yorker and in 1900 when 'O' (Mounted Infantry) Company was formed at Maryhill and 'Q' (Cyclist) Company at Dumbarton.

DUMFRIESHIRE

The 1st Admin. Battalion of Dumfrieshire Rifle Volunteers was formed on 4 January 1862. Battalion headquarters were placed at Dumfries and the corps included were the nine then in existence within the county.

1st Corps: Formed at Dumfries on 25 February 1860.

2nd Corps: Formed at Thornhill on 28 February 1860.

3rd Corps: Formed at Sanquhar on 28 February 1860.

4th Corps: Formed at Penpont on 29 February 1860.

5th Corps: Formed at Annan on 14 June 1860.

6th Corps: Formed at Moffat on 20 June 1860.

7th Corps: Formed at Langholm on 1 June 1860.

8th Corps: Formed at Lockerbie on 20 June 1860.

9th Corps: Formed at Lochmaben on 18 February 1861.

The battalion was consolidated as the 1st Dumfrieshire Rifle Volunteer Corps in April 1880. Headquarters remained at Dumfries and the ten company establishment was organised as follows—

'A' Company at Dumfries	Late 1st Corps
'B' Company at Dumfries	Late 1st Corps
'C' Company at Thornhill	Late 2nd Corps
'D' Company at Sanquhar	Late 3rd Corps
'E' Company at Penpont	Late 4th Corps
'F' Company at Annan	Late 5th Corps
'G' Company at Moffat	Late 6th Corps
'H' Company at Langholm	Late 7th Corps
'I' Company at Lockerbie	Late 8th Corps
'K' Company at Lochmaben	Late 9th Corps

In 1881 the 1st Dumfries joined the Royal Scots Fusiliers as one of its allotted volunteer battalions. This association continued until 1887 when under General Order 61 of May the battalion was transferred to the King's Own Scottish Borderers. Upon transfer the title of 3rd (Dumfries) Volunteer Battalion was assumed and later conferred in General Order 181 of December.

Other changes to occur within the battalion were in 1885 when 'E' Company became a section of 'C' and a new 'E' was formed at Ecclefechan and in 1888 when the headquarters of 'K' Company were removed to Canonbie.

In 1908 and upon transfer to the Territorial Force the 3rd (Dumfries) VB and the Galloway Volunteer Rifle Corps were amalgamated to form the 5th Battalion of the King's Own Scottish Borderers, the 3rd forming headquarters and four companies.

DURHAM

There were four administrative battalions formed in Durham to control the several rifle corps formed within the county. With the exception of the 2nd and

5th, which were never raised, and the 3rd, which was of sufficient strength to remain independent, all units were included. In 1880 the four battalions were consolidated and together with the 3rd Corps formed the 1st to 5th Durham Rifle Volunteers.

1ST CORPS

Formed on 1 February 1862 with headquarters at Stockton-on-Tees the 4th Admin. Battalion contained the following corps—

1st Corps: Formed at Stockton-on-Tees on 27 February 1860.

15th Corps: Formed at Darlington on 6 October 1860.

16th Corps: Formed at Castle Eden on 14 December 1860.

19th Corps: Formed at Hartlepool on 26 January 1861. This corps was disbanded in November 1872.

The above corps had until 1862 been contained within the 2nd Admin. Battalion.

In 1877 an addition was made to the battalion when the 21st Yorkshire (North Riding) Corps was included. Upon consolidation in 1880 the 4th Admin. became the 1st Durham Rifle Volunteer Corps with the additional title of (Durham and North Riding of York). Headquarters remained at Stockton-on-Tees and the companies were organised as follows—

'A' 'B' 'C' Companies at
Stockton-on-Tees   Late 1st Durham Corps
'D' 'E' Companies at Darlington   Late 15th Durham Corps
'F' Company at Castle Eden   Late 16th Durham Corps
'G' 'H' Companies at Middlesbrough   Late 21st N. Yorks Corps

The 1st Corps was redesignated as the 1st Volunteer Battalion. The Durham Light Infantry under General Order 181 of December 1887. The establishment on the battalion remained unchanged until 1900 when as a result of the war in South Africa four new companies were formed. These were located; 'I' (Stockton), 'K' (Darlington), 'L' (Middlesbrough) and 'M' (Cyclist) (Stockton).

In 1908 the 1st VB transferred to the Territorial Force as the 5th Battalion, DLI. The Middlesbrough personnel, however, joined the 4th Battalion of the Yorkshire Regiment.

2ND CORPS

The 2nd Admin. Battalion of Durham Rifle Volunteers was formed in December 1860 with headquarters at Bishop Auckland. The corps included were as follows—

4th Corps: Formed at Bishop Auckland on 24 May 1860. A 2nd Company was soon formed at Coundon and in 1865 a 3rd was added at Shildon. The latter was moved to Darlington in 1872.

12th Corps: Formed at Middleton in Teesdale on 14 July 1860. This corps was recruited mainly from employees of the London Lead Company.

17th Corps: Formed at Wolsingham on 24 November 1860 and was disbanded in 1866.

18th Corps: Formed at Shotley Bridge on 1 December 1860. The 18th was not included in the battalion until June 1861. This corps was disbanded in July 1865.

20th Corps: Formed at Stanhope on 19 February 1861.

21st Corps: This corps originated in 1860 as the 7th Yorkshire (North Riding) Rifle Volunteers. It was formed on 29 February and had its headquarters at Startforth. In 1863 the 7th were attached to the 4th Durham Admin. Battalion. This took place in November and in the following month the corps was moved to Barnard Castle, redesignated as the 21st Durham and from then on linked to the 2nd Admin. Battalion.

In addition to the above the 2nd Admin. also included the 15th and from June 1861 the 1st, 16th and 19th Corps. These units were, however, transferred to the 4th Admin. Battalion upon its formation in February 1862.

Upon consolidation in March 1880 the battalion took on the number of its senior corps which was 4th. In June, however, the county's numbering was reorganised and the title of 2nd Corps allotted. The new corps consisted of six companies with headquarters at Bishop Auckland.

'A' Company at Bishop Auckland   Late 4th Corps
'B' Company at Coundon   Late 4th Corps
'C' Company at Darlington   Late 4th Corps
'D' Company at Middleton in Teesdale   Late 12th Corps
'E' Company at Stanhope   Late 20th Corps
'F' Company at Barnard Castle   Late 21st Corps

In 1883 'D' Company was moved from Darlington to Woodland and in March 1886 two new companies, 'G' and 'H' were formed at Spennymoor. The following year, and under General Order 181 of December, the 2nd Corps became the 2nd Volunteer Battalion, The Durham Light Infantry.

The Middleton in Teesdale Company was disbanded in 1899 and in its place a new 'D' formed at Crook. In 1900 the establishment was increased by a further three companies when in May a cyclist company, 'I', was formed at Bishop Auckland and in November 'K' and 'L' were formed at Consett. 'C' Company was to move yet again, this time to Shildon, in 1903.

The 2nd VB transferred to the Territorial Force in 1908 and provided the 6th Battalion of the Durham Light Infantry.

3RD CORPS

The 3rd Durham Rifle Volunteer Corps was formed in Sunderland on 6 March 1860 and in 1867 was permitted to include (The Sunderland) as part of its full title. By 1862 five companies had been formed.

Redesignation as the 3rd (Sunderland) Volunteer Battalion of the Durham Light Infantry was notified in General Order 181 of December 1887. A new company was formed in 1900 and in 1908 the 3rd VB became the 7th Battalion, DLI.

4TH CORPS

The original headquarters of the 1st Admin. Battalion were in Durham but these were moved in 1862 to Chester le Street. Formed in October 1860 the battalion contained the following corps—

7th Corps: Formed at Durham on 24 March 1860.

10th Corps: Formed at Beamish on 12 May 1860.

11th Corps: Formed at Chester le Street on 5 June 1860.

13th Corps: Formed at Birtley on 17 August 1860. A 2nd company was later formed at Washington.

14th Corps: Formed at Felling on 31 October 1860.

Upon consolidation in May 1880 the battalion initially took on the number of its senior corps the 7th. However, after a few months the designation 4th Durham Rifle Volunteer Corps was assumed. The reorganisation went as follows—

'A' 'B' 'C' Companies at Durham	Late 7th Corps
'D' Company at Beamish	Late 10th Corps
'E' Company at Chester le Street	Late 11th Corps
'F' Company at Birtley	Late 13th Corps
'G' Company at Washington	Late 13th Corps
'H' 'I' 'K' Companies at Felling	Late 14th Corps

In 1887 and under General Order 181 of December, the 4th Corps became the 4th Volunteer Battalion, The Durham Light Infantry. Headquarters were moved to Durham in March 1890 and in 1892 'K' Company at Felling was disbanded and in its place a new 'K' raised at Stanley. In 1896 the remaining Felling Companies, 'H' and 'I', were amalgamated as 'H'. The 'I' position was then taken up by a new company raised at Sacriston. The following year the headquarters of 'H' Company were moved to Houghton-le-Spring and at the same time the Felling personnel were withdrawn from the battalion and transferred to the 5th VB DLI as its 'L' Company.

In October 1900 the last of the 4th VBs companies was raised when the battalion's cyclists were grouped together as 'L' Company with headquarters at Stanley.

The battalion transferred to the Territorial Force in 1908 as the 8th Bn DLI 'C' Company, however, continued service as part of the Durham University Contingent of the Officers Training Corps.

5TH CORPS

The 3rd Admin. Battalion of Durham was formed with headquarters at Gateshead in May 1861. Only three corps were included and they were the following—

6th Corps: Formed at South Shields on 20 March 1860. This corps was converted to artillery in December 1863 and absorbed into the 3rd Durham Artillery Volunteer Corps. A new 6th Corps was formed in the South Shields area on 8 August 1867. Its headquarters were given in the *Army List* as being at Tyne Docks.

8th Corps: Formed at Gateshead on 14 March 1860.

9th Corps: Formed at Blaydon on 3 May 1860. Moved to Blaydon Burn in 1862. No 2 Company formed at Winlaton in 1864.

The battalion was consolidated in February 1880 as the 6th Durham Rifle Volunteer Corps. This was changed by November, however, to 5th Corps. Headquarters remained at Gateshead and the corps' eight companies were organised as follows—

'A' 'B' 'C' Companies at Gateshead   Late 8th Corps
'D' 'E' 'F' Companies at South Shields Late 6th Corps
'G' Company at Blaydon Burn   Late 9th Corps
'H' Company at Winlaton   Late 9th Corps

In 1887 and under General Order 181 of December the 5th Corps became the 5th Volunteer Battalion of the Durham Light Infantry. By 1887 an additional two companies had been raised and the battalion reorganised as follows—

'A' 'B' 'C' 'D' Companies at Gateshead
'E' 'F' 'G' Companies at South Shields
'H' Company at Blaydon
'I' 'K' Companies at Winlaton

Further additions were made when in 1897 'L' Company was formed at Felling followed by 'M' (Cyclist) at Blaydon in 1900. This brought the battalion's establishment up to twelve companies which in 1908 transferred to the Territorial Force as the 9th DLI.

EDINBURGH (CITY)

From the very beginning it was intended to group all companies of rifle volunteers formed within the City of Edinburgh into one regiment. This was to be known as the 1st City of Edinburgh Rifle Volunteer Corps which by the end of 1860 consisted of twenty-two companies divided into two battalions. All companies were numbered within the corps and in addition held sub-titles which served to indicate the trades and professions of its members. Companies of highlanders were also formed as well as units composed of university students, Freemasons and even a company of total abstainers. Formation dates of the original companies are as follows—

31 August 1859	No 1 (Advocates)
31 August 1859	No 2 (Citizens)
31 August 1859	No 3 (Writers to the Signet)
31 August 1859	No 4 (Edinburgh University)
31 August 1859	No 5 (Solicitors before the Supreme Court)
31 August 1859	No 6 (Accountants)
31 August 1859	No 7 (Bankers)
31 August 1859	No 8 (1st Artisans)
31 August 1859	No 9 (2nd Artisans)
31 August 1859	1st (Highland)
7 October 1859	No 10 (Civil Service)
7 December 1859	No 11 (3rd Artisans)

7 December 1859	No 12 (Freemasons)
7 December 1859	No 13 (4th Artisans)
8 December 1859	No 14 (2nd Citizens)
21 December 1859	No 15 (1st Merchants)
29 February 1860	No 16 (Total Abstainers)
11 May 1860	No 17 (2nd Merchants)
18 May 1860	2nd (Highland)
25 May 1860	No 18 (High Constables)
23 July 1860	3rd (Highland)
8 November 1860	No 19 (5th Artisans)

The next company of rifle volunteers to be formed within the city was by the employees of Messrs W. D. Young's ironworks at Fountainbridge. This company consisted of highlanders and was raised on 3 May 1862. Contrary to the practice of placing all City of Edinburgh volunteers into the one regiment the Fountainbridge Company were constituted as a separate corps and designated as the 2nd City of Edinburgh Rifle Volunteers. They were, however, attached to the 1st Corps for drill and administrative purposes. Two additional companies were formed on 23 February 1867 which together with the 1st were absorbed into the 1st Corps as its 4th, 5th and 6th (Highland) Companies.

The subsidiary title of 'The Queen's City of Edinburgh Rifle Volunteer Brigade' was conferred upon the regiment in 1865. In 1868 the 1st and 3rd Companies were disbanded and their places taken by a 7th (Highland) Company, formed on 27 December 1867 and a No 20 Company which was formed on 19 March 1869. At this time the regiment was still divided into two battalions which contained the following companies—

1st Battalion: 2, 4, 5, 6, 7, 10, 18 and the 1st to 7th Highland.
2nd Battalion: 8, 9, 11, 12, 13, 14, 15, 16, 17, 19 and 20.

The Queen's Edinburghs joined the Royal Scots in 1881, providing two of its volunteer battalions. In April 1888 (Army Order 144) the new title of Queen's Rifle Volunteer Brigade, The Royal Scots was conferred. The companies then dropped their old numbers and titles for letters and the brigade was divided into three battalions organised as follows—

1st Battalion	2nd Battalion	3rd Battalion
'A' Company Late No 2	'A' Company Late No 8	'A' Company Late No 4
'B' Company Late No 5	'B' Company Late No 9	'B' Company Late No 17
'C' Company Late No 6	'C' Company Late No 11	'C' Company Late No 19
'D' Company Late No 7	'D' Company Late No 12	'D' Company Late No 20
'E' Company Late No 10	'E' Company Late No 13	'E' Company Late 4th H
'F' Company Late No 18	'F' Company Late No 14	'F' Company Late 5th H
'G' Company Late 1st H	'G' Company Late No 15	'G' Company Late 6th H
'H' Company Late 2nd H	'H' Company Late No 16	'H' Company Late 7th H
'I' Company Late 3rd H		

An 'I' Company for the 3rd Battalion was formed in the Parish of Colinton in 1900 and in the same year a Cyclist Company was raised and attached to Brigade Headquarters. On 24 July 1900 a complete battalion of highlanders was formed and designated as the Highland Battalion of the Brigade. The following year, however, the highlanders were constituted as an independent unit and styled as the 9th (Highlanders) Volunteer Battalion, The Royal Scots.

Two cadet units have been associated with the brigade. The first was formed in December 1886 and by 1900 is shown in the monthly *Army List* as being found by boys of the Merchiston Castle School in Edinburgh. The second unit was that formed by the George Watson's Boys College in October 1905.

In 1908 the brigade became the 4th and 5th (Queen's Edinburgh Rifles) Battalions of the Royal Scots. 'A' Company of the 3rd Battalion, the former No 4 University Company, became part of the Edinburgh University Contingent of the Officers Training Corps. Both cadet companies also transferred to the OTC.

The 9th (Highlanders) Volunteer Battalion became the 7th (Highlanders) Battalion of the regiment.

As previously mentioned the No 16 Company of the Queen's City of Edinburgh Rifle Volunteer Brigade consisted entirely of total abstainers. These volunteers were all men who had signed the pledge of total abstinence and members of the British Temperance League.

In 1867 it was decided by John Hope, the founder of the company, that an independent corps formed again of total abstainers could be contrived. Many members of the No 16 Company agreed to transfer to such a unit and on 27 May 1867 the new abstainers corps was formed. Designated as the 3rd Edinburgh Rifle Volunteers the corps had an establishment of two companies. Back in 1861 a company of boys known as the British League Cadets were formed and affiliated to the No 16 Company. This association was continued with the 3rd Corps until 1892 when the company disappeared from the *Army List*.

From formation the 3rd Corps was attached to the Queen's Edinburgh for drill and administration. Additional companies were added in 1868, 1872 and 1877 and in 1882 the corps was detached from the 1st and made independent.

Redesignation as the 2nd Edinburgh came in 1880 and as the 4th Volunteer Battalion of the Royal Scots in 1888. The latter being notified in Army Order 144 of April. In 1900 the establishment of the battalion was increased to seven companies when 'G' was formed at Portobello. 'H' Company was also formed that year and was found by members of the Church of Scotland Teachers Training College. The battalion transferred to the Territorial Force in April 1908 as the 6th Battalion, The Royal Scots.

ELGIN

The 1st Admin. Battalion of Elgin Rifle Volunteers was formed on 4 May 1860. Headquarters were placed at Elgin and the corps included were those in existence or subsequently formed within the Elgin area.

1st Corps: Formed at Forres on 3 January 1860.

2nd Corps: Formed at Elgin on 31 January 1860.

3rd Corps: Formed at Elgin on 20 February 1860.

4th Corps: Formed at Rothes on 28 May 1860.

5th Corps: Formed at Fochabers on 10 April 1861.

6th Corps: Formed at Carr Bridge on 26 August 1861. Headquarters moved to Abernethy in 1878.

7th Corps: Formed at Lhanbryde on 15 April 1863. Headquarters were moved to Urquhart in May 1863 and at the same time an additional half company was formed at Pluscarden. The sub-title '(Duff)' was also held by the corps.

8th Corps: Formed at Garmouth on 2 December 1867.

9th Corps: Formed at Grantown on 9 January 1871.

The 1st Elgin Mounted Rifles was attached to the battalion from 1869 until disbandment in November 1871.

The 1st Elgin Rifle Volunteer Corps was formed in 1880 by the consolidation of the 1st Admin. Battalion. Establishment was set at ten and a half companies organised as follows—

'A' Company at Forres	Late 1st Corps
'B' Company at Elgin	Late 2nd Corps
'C' Company at Elgin	Late 3rd Corps
'D' Company at Rothes	Late 4th Corps
'E' Company at Fochabers	Late 5th Corps
'F' Company at Abernethy	Late 6th Corps
'G' Company at Urquhart	Late 7th Corps
'H' Company at Forres	Late 1st Corps
'I' Company at Garmouth	Late 8th Corps
'K' Company at Grantown	Late 9th Corps

The half company was at Pluscarden and provided by the 7th Corps.

The 1st Elgin joined the Seaforth Highlanders in 1881 and in 1887 became the 3rd (Morayshire) Volunteer Battalion of the regiment. This change was notified in General Order 181 of December. Ten years later the half company at Pluscarden was constituted as a full company and designated 'L'. Headquarters, however, was moved to Alves in 1904. The following year 'G' Company moved to Lhanbryde and in 1908 the battalion transferred to the Territorial Force as the 6th Bn Seaforth Highlanders.

ESSEX

As a result of the 1880 reorganisations the various admin. battalions and independent Essex corps were grouped into four units.

1ST CORPS

The 3rd Admin. Battalion of Essex Rifle Volunteers was formed with headquarters in Ilford on 6 July 1861. The corps included were as follows—

1st Corps: Formed at Romford on 16 February 1860.

2nd Corps: Formed at Ilford on 12 August 1859 and was shown in the *Army List* as 3rd Corps until February 1860. Companies were later formed at Barking and Walthamston.

3rd Corps: Formed as 4th Corps at Brentwood on 12 October 1859. First shown as 3rd in February 1860. Absorbed the 21st Corps in 1872.

7th Corps: Formed at Rochford on 8 March 1860. Disappeared from the *Army List* in February 1877.

15th Corps: Formed as the 16th Corps at Hornchurch on 11 June 1860. Appeared in the *Army List* as 15th from November 1860.

18th Corps: Formed at Chipping Ongar on 4 December 1860.

19th Corps: Formed at Epping on 22 September 1860. Disappeared from the *Army List* in November 1872.

21st Corps: Formed at Brentwood on 24 September 1860 and absorbed into the 3rd Corps in 1872.

24th Corps: Formed at Woodford on 10 April 1861. Disbanded in 1872.

Of the above the 1st, 2nd, 3rd and 7th Corps were previously with the 1st Admin. Battalion.

Upon consolidation in 1880 the battalion took on the numbers of 1st Corps. As can be seen from the above the battalion contained the senior corps of the county. Headquarters were placed at Ilford and the corps' eight companies were organised as follows—

'A' 'B' Companies at Romford	Late 1st Corps
'C' Company at Ilford	Late 2nd Corps
'D' Company at Barking	Late 2nd Corps
'E' Company at Walthamstow	Late 2nd Corps
'F' Company at Brentwood	Late 3rd Corps
'G' Company at Chipping Ongar	Late 18th Corps
'H' Company at Hornchurch	Late 15th Corps

Under General Order 14 of February 1883 the 1st Essex became the 1st Volunteer Battalion of the Essex Regiment. Headquarters were moved back to Brentwood in 1890.

Two additional companies were formed in 1896 followed by four more in 1900. Several cadet units have also been associated with the battalion. The first was formed at Ongar Grammar School in 1865 and attached to the old 3rd Admin. Next came a company provided by Forest School in Walthamstow. This was formed in May 1883. In 1900 Chigwell Grammar School raised a company and three years later a unit at Loughton and Buckhurst Hill appeared.

Upon transfer to the Territorial Force in 1908 the 1st VB became the 4th Battalion, Essex Regiment. Both Forest and Chigwell Schools transferred to the Junior Division, Officers Training Corps while the remaining cadets continued service with the 4th Battalion.

2ND CORPS

The 2nd Corps of 1880 was created out of the 1st Admin. Battalion which was formed with headquarters at Colchester in June 1860. At first the 1st, 2nd, 3rd and 7th Corps were included but in July 1861 these were transferred to the 3rd Admin.

The remaining corps were—

4th Corps: Formed at Chelmsford on 8 November 1859 and was shown in the *Army List* until January 1860 as the 5th Corps.

6th Corps: Formed as the 1st Sub-division at Colchester on 8 September 1859. Redesignated as 6th Corps in December.

10th Corps: Formed as the 1st Sub-division at Witham on 30 December 1859. Appeared for the first time as 10th Corps in the *Army List* for March 1860.

11th Corps: Formed at Dunmow on 21 March 1860 and was disbanded in 1863.

12th Corps: Formed at Braintree on 6 March 1860.

13th Corps: Formed at Dedham on 8 March 1860 and from October 1861 included (Stour Valley) in its title. Disappeared from the *Army List* in December 1870.

14th Corps: Formed as the 15th Corps at Manningtree on 17 May 1860. Was first shown as 14th in November 1860 but disappeared from the *Army List* in June 1862.

16th Corps: Formed at Great Bentley on 10 September 1860. Disbanded in 1875.

20th Corps: Formed at Haverhill on 27 December 1860. Disbanded in 1871.

23rd Corps: Formed at Maldon on 13 November 1860.

Headquarters of the battalion were moved to Chelmsford in February 1862 but upon consolidation these were changed to Braintree. The battalion was at first numbered as 4th Corps but after a few months it was redesignated as 2nd. The new corps consisted of eight companies which were organised as follows—

'A' 'B' Companies at Chelmsford	Late 4th Corps
'C' 'D' Companies at Colchester	Late 6th Corps
'E' Company at Witham	Late 10th Corps
'F' Company at Braintree	Late 12th Corps
'G' Company at Maldon	Late 23rd Corps
'H' Company at Walton on the Naze	Late 23rd Corps

The corps became the 2nd Volunteer Battalion, The Essex Regiment by General Order 14 of February 1883 and in 1895 moved its headquarters to Colchester. Two new companies were formed in 1900.

A cadet corps was formed and affiliated to the 1st Admin. Battalion in 1872 but this disappeared from the *Army List* in October 1880. A new company based at Felstead School is shown from May 1883 and in 1904 the King Edward VI School Cadet Corps was formed at Chelmsford.

In 1908 the 2nd VB became the 5th Battalion, Essex Regiment. Both cadet units remained attached.

3RD CORPS

The 2nd Admin. Battalion of Essex Rifle Volunteers was formed with headquarters at Plaistow on 19 June 1860. The corps included were the 5th and 9th which were joined in 1864 by the 8th. Formed at Stratford on 6 March 1860, the 8th Corps was disbanded in 1865. In 1866 the 2nd Admin. Battalion ceased to exist and its corps made independent.

The 5th Corps was formed at Plaistow on 30 January 1860. In the reorganisation of 1880 it at first received the title of 4th Essex Rifle Volunteer Corps but this was changed to 3rd after a few months. Battalion headquarters were moved to West Ham in 1885.

In 1900 the establishment of the battalion, which had been redesignated as 3rd VB The Essex Regiment in 1883, was increased to thirteen companies. These were joined by a cadet corps in 1907.

The 3rd VB became the 6th Battalion of the Essex Regiment in April 1908.

4TH CORPS

As previously mentioned the 9th Corps formed part of the 2nd Admin. Battalion until 1866. The 9th was formed at Silvertown on 1 February 1860 and in 1880 was redesignated as the 2nd Corps. This was changed, however, to 4th after a short time.

In 1883 and under General Order 14 of February, the corps was re-styled yet again, this time as 4th Volunteer Battalion, The Essex Regiment.

In 1900 headquarters were moved to Leyton and that same year the establishment increased to eleven companies. The battalion became the 7th Bn Essex Regiment in 1908.

Other rifle corps to be raised in Essex were: the 3rd which appeared in the September 1859 *Army List* as having been formed at Cranbrooke but was not seen again after October. The 17th Corps was formed at Saffron Walden on 23 October 1860 and from November 1863 was included in the 2nd Admin. Battalion of Cambridgeshire Rifle Volunteers. This battalion was broken up in 1872 and its corps transferred to the county's 1st Admin. Battalion. Upon consolidation in 1880 the 1st Admin. Battalion of Cambridgeshire became the 1st Cambridgeshire Corps with the 17th Essex as its 'I' Company. Also outside of the county was the 22nd Corps. This was formed at Waltham Abbey on 27 November 1860 and in 1862 was united to the 2nd Hertfordshire Admin. Battalion. This battalion became its county's 1st Corps in 1880 retaining the 22nd Essex as 'H' Company.

FIFESHIRE

The 1st Admin. Battalion of Fifeshire Rifle Volunteers was formed with headquarters at St Andrew's on 21 September 1860. The corps included were the following—

1st Corps: Formed at Dumfermline on 25 February 1860.

2nd Corps: Formed at Cupar on 6 March 1860.

3rd Corps: Formed at Kilconquhar on 25 April 1860. Headquarters were moved by 1861 to East Anstruther.

4th Corps: Formed at Colinsburgh on 20 April 1860.

5th Corps: Formed at St Andrew's on 23 April 1860.

6th Corps: Formed at Strathleven on 25 August 1860. In 1872 headquarters were moved to Leslie and at the same time a second company was formed at Falkland.

7th Corps: Formed at Kirkcaldy on 23 April 1860.

8th Corps: Formed at Auchterderran on 20 April 1860. Headquarters moved to Lochgelly in 1862.

9th Corps: Formed at Newburgh on 28 July 1860.

In June 1861 the 1st Kinross Rifle Volunteer Corps was added to the battalion but this was transferred to the 1st Clackmannan Admin. Battalion in 1873.

The battalion was consolidated as the 1st Fifeshire Rifle Volunteers in 1880. Headquarters remained at St Andrew's and the twelve companies were organised as follows—

'A' Company at Dumfermline	Late 1st Corps
'B' Company at Dumfermline	Late 1st Corps
'C' Company at Cuper	Late 2nd Corps
'D' Company at Cuper	Late 2nd Corps
'E' Company at East Anstruther	Late 3rd Corps
'F' Company at Colinsburgh	Late 4th Corps
'G' Company at St Andrew's	Late 5th Corps
'H' Company at Leslie	Late 6th Corps
'I' Company at Falkland	Late 6th Corps
'K' Company at Kirkcaldy	Late 7th Corps
'L' Company at Lockgelly	Late 8th Corps
'M' Company at Newburgh	Late 9th Corps

Redesignation as the 6th (Fifeshire) Volunteer Battalion of the Black Watch was notified in General Order 181 of December 1887. In 1900 both 'C' and 'D' Companies moved to Kirkcaldy while 'K' went to Cupar. 'O' (Cyclist) Company was formed at Dumfermline in January 1901 and in 1906 'F' moved to Leven.

The 6th VB transferred to the Territorial Force in April 1908, forming the 7th Battalion, The Black Watch.

FLINTSHIRE

Six numbered corps were raised within the county and included in the 1st Admin. Battalion. Formed in August 1860 the battalion had its first headquarters at Rhyl. These were moved to Holywell in 1863 but in 1874 a return was made to Rhyl. In 1873 the 1st Carnarvonshire Admin. Battalion was broken up and its corps, the 1st to 5th, transferred to Flintshire. The 1st Carnarvonshire Corps was disbanded in 1874 followed by the 2nd and 5th in 1877. A new 5th was, however, raised in 1878.

The Flintshire corps were—

1st Corps: Formed at Mold on 27 March 1860.

2nd Corps: Formed at Hawarden on 1 June 1860.

3rd Corps: A 3rd Corps with headquarters at Rhyl was first shown in the *Army List* for May 1860. Four officers were appointed but the first of these was not commissioned until 25 June 1861.

4th Corps: Formed at Holywell on 29 June 1860.

5th Corps: Formed at Flint on 3 February 1863.

6th Corps: Formed at Caergwle on 27 November 1872.

In 1880 the battalion was consolidated as the 1st Flintshire and Carnarvonshire Rifle Volunteer Corps. Headquarters remained at Rhyl and the ten companies were organised as follows—

'A' Company at Mold	Late 1st Flintshire Corps
'B' Company at Hawarden	Late 2nd Flintshire Corps
'C' Company at Rhyl	Late 3rd Flintshire Corps
'D' Company at Holywell	Late 4th Flintshire Corps
'E' Company at Flint	Late 5th Flintshire Corps
'F' Company at Caergwle	Late 6th Flintshire Corps
'G' Company at Carnarvon	Late 3rd Carnarvonshire Corps
'H' Company at Carnarvon	Late 3rd Carnarvonshire Corps
'I' Company at Portmadoc	Late 4th Carnarvonshire Corps
'K' Company at Llanberis	Late 5th Carnarvonshire Corps

Under General Order 78 of June 1884 the corps was redesignated as the 2nd Volunteer Battalion of the Royal Welsh Fusiliers. Recruiting went well and by 1896 the establishment of the battalion stood at sixteen companies. On 26 May 1897 this was reduced to eight when the Carnarvonshire personnel were withdrawn to form the 3rd Volunteer Battalion of the regiment. That same year headquarters were moved to Hawarden.

On 1 April 1908 the 2nd VB transferred to the Territorial Force as the 5th Battalion, Royal Welsh Fusiliers, providing headquarters and seven companies.

FORFARSHIRE

The 1st Forfar (Dundee) Rifle Volunteer Corps was formed on 15 November 1859 with an establishment of five companies. By April 1860 eight companies had been raised all within the Dundee area. The 10th and 14th Corps were also provided by Dundee Volunteers but these units were independent of the 1st Corps and only attached between 1861 and 1868. On 1 February 1879 a cadet corps was formed in Dundee and is shown in the *Army List* as being affiliated to the 1st Corps. This company was later disbanded, however, and is last seen in the *Army List* for September 1888.

Redesignation as the 1st (Dundee) Volunteer Battalion, The Black Watch was notified in General Order 181 of December 1887. The sub-title was later changed to (City of Dundee) and appears for the first time in the *Army List* during 1891.

Two additional companies, one of which was a cyclist, were formed in 1900 and on 13 June a new cadet company was provided by the Morgan Academy of Dundee.

The battalion transferred to the Territorial Force in April 1908 as the 4th Battalion, The Black Watch. The Morgan Academy Cadets were not recognised by the TF and were disbanded on 9 February 1909.

The Forfarshire corps outside the Dundee area were in May 1861 formed into two Admin. Battalions. The 1st Battalion consisted of the corps formed in the eastern part of the county and included the 3rd, 5th and 7th which were joined upon formation by the 13th. Headquarters were placed at Montrose. The corps included in the 2nd or Western Battalion, headquarters Forfar, were the 2nd, 8th, 9th, 11th and 12th joined by the 15th in 1865.

2nd Corps: Formed at Forfar on 15 November 1859.

3rd Corps: Formed at Arbroath on 15 November 1859. A second company was added in May 1860 which had previously existed as the 4th Corps for a few weeks.

5th Corps: Formed at Montrose on 15 November 1859.

7th Corps: Formed at Brechin on 26 March 1860.

8th Corps: Formed at Newtyle on 4 April 1860. From 1872 this corps appears in the *Army List* with the additional title '(Wharncliffe)'.

9th Corps: Formed at Glamis on 8 May 1860.

11th Corps: Formed at Tannadice on 8 October 1860. Disbanded in 1869.

12th Corps: Formed at Kirriemuir on 17 September 1860.

13th Corps: Formed at Friockheim on 4 June 1861.

15th Corps: Formed at Cortachy on 16 August 1865. Disbanded in 1872.

All the above, with the exception of the 11th and 15th who were disbanded and the 8th that had the additional '(Wharncliffe)', from January 1877 are shown in the *Army List* with their headquarters as part of the official title i.e. '(Forfar)', '(Arbroath)', etc.

In 1874 headquarters of the 1st Battalion were moved to Friockheim by Arbroath. Later the same year the 2nd Battalion, who were now down to just the 2nd, 8th, 9th and 12th Corps, was absorbed into the 1st. Upon the amalgamation of the two battalions the new title of 1st Admin. Battalion of Forfarshire or Angus Rifle Volunteers was assumed. This, however, was not shown in the *Army List* until 1877.

The battalion was consolidated in 1880 as the 2nd Forfar (Forfarshire or Angus) Rifle Volunteer Corps. The sub-title changed to (Angus) in 1883. Headquarters remained at Friockheim by Arbroath and the fourteen companies were organised as follows—

'A' 'B' Companies at Forfar	Late 2nd Corps
'C' to 'F' Companies at Arbroath	Late 3rd Corps
'G' 'H' Companies at Montrose	Late 5th Corps
'I' 'K' Companies at Brechin	Late 7th Corps
'L' Company at Newtyle	Late 8th Corps
'M' Company at Glamis	Late 9th Corps
'N' Company at Kirriemuir	Late 12th Corps
'O' Company at Froickheim	Late 13th Corps

Redesignation as the 2nd (Angus) Volunteer Battalion, the Black Watch was assumed under General Order 181 of 1887 and the same year battalion headquarters were moved to Arbroath. In 1894 'F' Company was disbanded and 'L' and 'M' amalgamated as 'K'. The companies were then rearranged as follows—

'A' Company late 'A'	'G' Company late 'H'
'B' Company late 'B'	'H' Company late 'I'

'C' Company late 'C'	'I' Company late 'K'
'D' Company late 'D'	'K' Company late 'L' 'M'
'E' Company late 'E'	'L' Company late 'N'
'F' Company late 'G'	'M' Company late 'O'

On 10 January 1907 a cadet corps was formed and affiliated to the battalion by the Chapel Works at Montrose.

In April 1908 the battalion transferred to the Territorial Force as the 5th Battalion, the Black Watch. Headquarters and six companies of the new battalion were provided by the 2nd VB while the remaining two were supplied by the 3rd (Dundee Highland) Volunteer Battalion of the regiment. The Chapel Works cadets were not recognised by the Territorial Force and were eventually disbanded on 26 March 1909.

As previously mentioned the 10th and 14th Corps were formed at Dundee and remained independent of the 1st Corps except for a period of attachment between 1861 and 1868.

The 10th Corps was formed on 10 April 1860 followed by the 14th on 14 June 1861. In September 1868 an amalgamation between the two corps took place and a new 10th Corps of four companies was formed. The additional title of 'Dundee Highland' was also added at this time. From the *Army List* it would seem that the original idea was to place the 10th and 14th into an Admin. Battalion of their own. A 3rd (Dundee Highland) Admin. Battalion containing the two corps is in fact shown for one month only, September 1868.

Redesignation as the 3rd Forfar (Dundee Highland) Rifle Volunteer Corps was made in 1880 and as the 3rd (Dundee Highland) Volunteer Battalion of the Black Watch in 1887 (General Order 181 of December).

The battalion provided two companies of the 5th Battalion, Black Watch upon transfer to the Territorial Force in April 1908.

A 4th Corps existed in Arbroath for a short time in 1860 which became the No 2 Company of the 3rd Corps after a few weeks. No 6th Corps was raised.

GALLOWAY

Galloway is the district of South West Scotland comprising the Counties of Wigtown and Kirkcudbright. The rifle volunteer corps formed within those areas were in 1860 grouped together under the title of The Galloway Admin. Battalion and in 1880 consolidated as the Galloway Rifle Volunteer Corps.

Details of the two counties involved have been dealt with under the relevant section. Those for the Galloway Rifle Volunteer Corps have been included in Wigtownshire.

GLAMORGANSHIRE

The 1st Admin. Battalion of Glamorgan Rifle Volunteers was formed in March 1861 and its headquarters are given as being at Margam, Taibach. The following corps were included:

1st Corps: Formed at Margam on 12 October 1859.

4th Corps: Headquarters of the 4th Corps, formed 12 October 1859, were at first given in the *Army List* as being at Taibach. They appear as being at Swansea from January 1860. The corps was to remain independent until 1872 when it was attached to the 3rd Corps. By the end of 1873, however, it had transferred to the 1st Admin. Battalion.

5th Corps: Formed at Penllergaer on 12 October 1859. Became part of the 1st Admin. in 1861 but in 1864 was attached to the 3rd Corps. This corps was later disbanded and is last seen in the *Army List* for December 1873.

6th Corps: Formed at Swansea on 10 December 1859. Disbanded in 1872.

7th Corps: Formed at Taibach on 3 January 1860. The *Army List*, however, gives the headquarters of the corps as being at Swansea until July 1860.

9th Corps: Formed at Baglan on 17 February 1860. Headquarters moved to Cwm Avon in 1861.

11th Corps: Formed at Bridgend on 14 February 1860.

15th Corps: Formed at Neath on 14 February 1860.

17th Corps: Formed at Cadoxton on 2 June 1860. Disbanded in 1873.

18th Corps: Formed at Cowbridge on 25 June 1860.

In March 1880 the battalion was consolidated as the 1st Glamorganshire Rifle Volunteer Corps. Headquarters remained at Margam, Taibach and the corps' twelve companies were organised as follows—

'A' 'B' Companies at Margam	Late 1st Corps
'C' 'D' 'E' Companies at Swansea	Late 4th Corps
'F' 'G' Companies at Taibach	Late 7th Corps
'H' Company at Cwm Avon	Late 9th Corps
'I' Company at Bridgend	Late 11th Corps
'K' 'L' Companies at Neath	Late 15th Corps
'M' Company at Cowbridge	Late 18th Corps

Headquarters of the corps moved to Bridgend in 1896 and in 1887 the title 2nd (Glamorgan) Volunteer Battalion, The Welsh Regiment was conferred in General Order 181 of December. The sub-title, however, was not shown in the *Army List* after December 1888.

In 1905 three of the battalion's companies were transferred to the 3rd Corps at Swansea. In their place the personnel from around the Cardiff area were absorbed from the 3rd VB. This was to bring the establishment of the battalion up to fourteen companies with headquarters at Cardiff.

In 1908 the bulk of the 2nd VB were converted to artillery and provided the 1st (later 2nd) Welsh Brigade, RFA. Some members joined the Glamorgan Battery of the RHA and a small portion provided a nucleus for the 7th (Cyclist) Battalion of the Welsh Regiment.

With headquarters at Dowlais near Merthyr Tydfil the 2nd Admin. Battalion was formed in March 1861. The corps included in this battalion were—

2nd Corps: Formed at Dowlais on 12 October 1859. The 1st Glamorgan Engineer Volunteers were attached to this corps until transfer to the 2nd Admin. in 1864.

8th Corps: Formed at Aberdare on 14 December 1859. Headquarters were moved to Mountain Ash in 1876.

10th Corps: Formed at Cardiff on 13 January 1860.

12th Corps: Formed at Merthyr Tydfil on 7 February 1860.

13th Corps: Formed at Llandaff on 7 February 1860. Headquarters were moved to Taff's Well in 1876.

14th Corps: Formed at Aberdare on 14 February 1860.

16th Corps: Formed at Cardiff on 18 January 1860. Many members of this corps were employed at the Bute Docks and in 1869 (Bute) was permitted to be included in its title.

19th Corps: Formed at Newbridge on 23 May 1861.

20th Corps: Formed at Hirwain on 11 September 1878.

The 1st Glamorganshire Engineer Volunteers were attached to the battalion in 1864 until their disbandment in 1871.

Headquarters of the 2nd Admin. were moved to Cardeff in 1872 and in 1880 the battalion was consolidated as the 2nd Glamorganshire Rifle Volunteer Corps. Headquarters remained at Cardiff and the corps' twenty-two companies were organised as follows—

'A' 'B' Companies at Dowlais	Late 2nd Corps
'C' 'D' 'E' Companies at Mountain Ash	Late 8th Corps
'F' 'G' Companies at Cardiff	Late 10th Corps
'H' 'I' 'K' 'L' Companies at Merthyr Tydfil	Late 12th Corps
'M' 'N' Companies at Taff's Well	Late 13th Corps
'O' 'P' Companies at Aberdare	Late 14th Corps
'Q' to 'U' Companies at Cardiff	Late 16th Corps
'V' Company at Pontypridd	Late 19th Corps
'W' Company at Hirwain	Late 20th Corps

Under General Order 181 of December 1887 the 2nd Corps became the 3rd (Glamorgan) Volunteer Battalion of the Welsh Regiment. The sub-title was later removed and was last seen in the *Army List* for February 1891.

By 1900 the establishment of the battalion stood at twenty-four companies which in 1905 were reduced to fifteen due to the transfer of the personnel from around the Cardiff area to the 2nd Volunteer Battalion. From 1905 battalion headquarters were at Pontypridd.

A cadet corps was formed at Cardiff in 1889 but this was not shown in the *Army List* after August 1892.

The 3rd VB became the 5th Battalion of the Welsh Regiment in 1908.

The 3rd Corps of the county was formed at Swansea on 12 October 1859 and was to remain as such until transfer to the Territorial Force in 1908 as the 6th

Battalion, Welsh Regiment. The corps had in fact served as this regiment's 4th Volunteer Battalion since 1881 but this title was never assumed.

By 1900 the establishment of the 3rd Glamorgan stood at nine companies. This was increased to twelve when in 1905 the Swansea personnel of the 2nd VB Welsh Regiment were transferred.

GLOUCESTERSHIRE

The first officers was commissioned into the City of Bristol Rifle Volunteer Corps on 13 September 1859. By June 1860 ten companies had been sanctioned and the corps had been designated as the 1st Gloucestershire (City of Bristol) Rifle Volunteers. This title was changed under General Order 63 of May 1883 to that of 1st (City of Bristol) Volunteer Battalion, The Gloucestershire Regiment. The Bristol Grammar School provided a cadet company for the corps in 1900.

In 1908 the battalion became the 4th Bn of the Gloucestershire Regiment and the Bristol Grammar School cadets part of the Junior Division of the Officers Training Corps.

In June 1860 the *Army List* indicates that one admin. battalion, designated as 2nd, had been formed with all corps other than the 1st included. In the *List* for April 1861 there are two battalions recorded. Of these the 2nd is given as having its headquarters at Cheltenham and containing the 7th, 10th, 13th and 14th Corps. By *London Gazette* notice dated 16 October 1860 these corps were noted as having amalgamated but this direction was cancelled in that for 11 December. From February 1861 the four corps appear in the *Army List* as forming a 3rd Admin. Battalion. In January 1864 the 2nd Admin. Battalion disappeared from the *Army List* and its corps subsequently transferred to the 1st.

Headquarters of the 1st Admin. Battalion were in Gloucester. Attached to the battalion were, in 1863, the 1st Gloucestershire Light Horse and in 1864 the 1st Gloucestershire Engineers. By December 1864 the engineers had been transferred and in 1867 the mounted volunteers were disbanded.

2nd Corps: Formed with headquarters at Gloucester Dock on 21 October 1859.

3rd Corps: Formen at Gloucester on 21 October 1859.

4th Corps: Formed at Stroud on 5 September 1859. This corps disappeared from the *Army List* in August 1861.

5th Corps: Formed at Stroud on 6 September 1859. Absorbed the 6th Corps in 1865.

6th Corps: Formed at Stroud on 7 September 1859. Absorbed into the 5th Corps in 1865.

7th Corps: Formed at Cheltenham on 20 September 1859. Disbanded in September 1864.

8th Corps: Formed as the 1st Sub-division at Tewksbury on 6 December 1859. Appeared for the first time as 8th Corps in the *Army List* for March 1860. Disbanded in 1877.

9th Corps: Formed at Cirencester on 13 February 1860.

10th Corps: Formed at Cheltenham on 1 March 1860.

11th Corps: Formed at Dursley on 9 March 1860.

12th Corps: Formed at Forest of Dean on 21 April 1860.

13th Corps: Formed at Cheltenham on 23 March 1860. Disbanded in 1874.

14th Corps: Formed at Cheltenham on 3 July 1860. Disbanded is September 1864.

15th Corps: Formed at Stow-in-the-Wold on 3 December 1860.

16th Corps: Formed at Moreton-in-the-March on 23 November 1860. Headquarters moved to Campden in 1862.

The 1st Admin. Battalion was consolidated as the 2nd Gloucestershire Rifle Volunteer Corps in 1880. Headquarters remained at Gloucester and the corps' ten companies were organised as follows—

'A' Company at Gloucester Dock	Late 2nd Corps
'B' Company at Gloucester	Late 3rd Corps
'C' Company at Stroud	Late 5th Corps
'D' Company at Cirencester	Late 9th Corps
'E' Company at Cheltenham	Late 10th Corps
'F' Company at Dursley	Late 11th Corps
'G' Company at Coleford	Late 12th Corps
'H' Company at Newnham	Late 12th Corps
'I' Company at Stow-on-the-Wold	Late 15th Corps
'K' Company at Campden	Late 16th Corps

The corps became the 2nd Volunteer Battalion of the Gloucestershire Regiment in 1883 the change being notified in General Order 63 of that year. The Regiment's 5th Battalion was provided upon transfer to the Territorial Force in 1908.

A cadet corps is first shown as being affiliated to the 1st Admin. Battalion in 1867 and in 1883 this same unit is given as being formed by Cheltenham College. The college transferred its affiliation in 1889 to the 1st Gloucestershire Engineer Corps but was again associated with the battalion from 1904. In 1908 the college became part of the Junior Division of the Officer Training Corps.

Other cadet units to be linked with the battalion were the Gloucester County School Company which was formed at Hempstead in 1889 and the Cirencester Cadet Corps which was formed in 1896. Both were disbanded in 1891 and 1897 respectively.

On 24 July 1900 a 3rd Volunteer Battalion was raised for the Gloucestershire Regiment. Headquarters were placed at Bristol and its eight companies all recruited from that area. The 3rd VB became the regiment's 6th Battalion in 1908.

HADDINGTONSHIRE

Haddington was the headquarters of the 1st Admin. Battalion of Haddingtonshire Rifle Volunteers formed in August 1860. The original components were the 1st to 5th Corps but a 6th and 7th were also included upon formation.

1st Corps: Formed at Haddington on 19 January 1860.

2nd Corps: Formed at Gifford on 20 January 1860 mainly from workers on Lord Tweeddale's Estate. Disbanded in 1874.

3rd Corps: Formed at Haddington on 21 January 1860.

4th Corps: Formed at Aberlady on 17 March 1860. This company was raised mainly from workers on Lord Wemyss's Estate.

5th Corps: Formed at East Linton on 7 April 1860.

6th Corps: Formed at Dunglass on 27 August 1861. Headquarters moved to West Barns in 1873.

7th Corps: Formed at North Berwick on 21 July 1868.

The battalion was consolidated in 1880 as the 1st Haddington Rifle Volunteer Corps. Headquarters remained at Haddington and the six companies were organised as follows—

'A' Company at Haddington	Late 1st Corps
'B' Company at Haddington	Late 3rd Corps
'C' Company at Aberlady	Late 4th Corps
'D' Company at East Linton	Late 5th Corps
'E' Company at West Barns	Late 6th Corps
'F' Company at North Berwick	Late 7th Corps

Shortly after consolidation 'E' Company, which since formation as 6th Corps in 1861 had only the strength of a sub-division, was absorbed into 'D'. A new 'E' together with a section at Prestonpans being formed in 1881.

Redesignation as the 7th Volunteer Battalion, The Royal Scots was notified in Army Order 144 of 1888. In April 1906 'C' Company was absorbed into 'A' and the section at Prestonpans was increased to a full company and lettered 'C'.

On 20 February 1901 the first officers were gazetted into the North Berwick High School Cadet Corps. This company was affiliated to the 7th VB and was later joined by the Haddington Cadet Corps upon its formation in 1906.

In 1908 the battalion was amalgamated with the 6th VB of the regiment to form the 8th Battalion, Royal Scots. The 7th providing headquarters and four companies. Both cadet units continued their affiliation with the 8th and were eventually recognised by the Territorial Force in June 1910.

HAMPSHIRE

With the exception of the 2nd, 3rd, 10th, 14th and 19th the several rifle corps then in existence within the county of Hampshire were, in December 1860, divided up into three administrative battalions. In January 1865 a 4th Admin. Battalion was formed and the *Army List* for that month shows it to contain the above corps. During 1868 the 3rd Admin. Battalion, whose headquarters were at Fareham, was broken up and its corps dispersed as follows: 8th, 21st to the 1st Admin. and the 7th, 12th, 17th, and 20th to the 2nd. One corps not to be included in the transfer was the 22nd. This company had been formed at Bishop's Waltham on 13 September 1860 and had been part of the 3rd Admin. until disbandment in 1865. In 1880 the remaining three battalions were consolidated into three corps. A 4th was later formed out of the 2nd.

1ST CORPS

The 1st Corps of 1880 was formed by the consolidation of the 1st Admin. Battalion. With headquarters at Winchester the battalion contained the following corps—

1st Corps: Formed at Winchester on 18 October 1859.

8th Corps: Formed at Botley on 14 May 1860. Headquarters were moved to Bitterne by July.

11th Corps: The services of the 11th Corps were accepted on 24 March 1860. Headquarters were at Romsey.

13th Corps: Formed at Andover the services of the 13th Corps were accepted on 5 May 1860.

15th Corps: The first headquarters of the 15th Corps, whose services were accepted on 30 May 1860, were at Yateley. A move was made to Hartley Wintney in 1870.

16th Corps: The services of the 16th Corps were accepted on 14 June 1860. Headquarters were at Alresford.

18th Corps: Headquarters of the 18th, whose services were acepted on 31 July 1860, were at Basingstoke. This corps was disbanded in 1864.

21st Corps: The services of the 21st, headquarters Alton, were accepted on 10 August 1860.

24th Corps: This corps was formed on 21 December 1874 from the senior members and staff of Winchester College.

25th Corps: Formed at Basingstoke on 9 June 1875.

The 1st Hampshire Light Horse, later Mounted Rifles, was attached to the 3rd Admin. Battalion from 1861. This attachment was, in 1868, transferred to the 1st. The 1st Hants. MRVC was disbanded in 1878.

Upon consolidation the strength of the battalion stood at ten companies. These were organised as follows—

'A' 'B' Companies at Winchester	Late 1st Corps
'C' Company at Botley	Late 8th Corps
'D' Company at Romsey	Late 11th Corps
'E' Company at Andover	Late 13th Corps
'F' Company at Hartley Wintney	Late 15th Corps
'G' Company at Alresford	Late 16th Corps
'H' Company at Alton	Late 21st Corps
'I' Company at Winchester	Late 24th Corps
'K' Company at Basingstoke	Late 25th Corps

On 22 March 1884 a new company 'L', was sanctioned and was to be formed by St Mary's College, Winchester. This was followed in 1889 by 'M' Company which was raised from the Aldershot section of 'H'. In 1892 a new company was formed at Stockbridge. This was designated as 'J' and according to the history of the Royal Hampshire Regiment became as ASC Company in 1903. By 1900 the establishment of the battalion stood at eighteen companies, of which five had been formed as a result of the war in South Africa.

As previously mentioned the 24th Corps, later 'I' Company, was formed from members of Winchester College. The College had for many years been associated with the battalion and in 1870 provided a company of cadets.

Under General Order 91 of September 1885 the 1st Hants became known as the 1st Volunteer Battalion, The Hampshire Regiment and in 1908 provided that regiment's 4th Battalion. Also in 1908 both the Winchester College Company and cadet corps became part of the Junior Division, Officers Training Corps.

2ND CORPS

Headquarters of the 4th Admin. Battalion were, according to the January 1865 *Army List*, situated in Southampton. In that for March, however, Lyndhurst is recorded. The corps included in the 4th were as follows—

2nd Corps: Formed at Southampton on 24 February 1860.

3rd Corps: Formed at Lymington on 30 December 1859 and attached to the 2nd Corps from 1863 until joining the 4th Admin.

10th Corps: Formed at Christchurch on 9 March 1860. Attached to the 2nd Corps from 1863 until 1865.

14th Corps: Formed at Lyndhurst on 16 June 1860. Attached to the 2nd Corps from 1863 until 1865.

19th Corps: Formed at Bournemouth on 18 August 1860 and attached to the 2nd Corps from 1863 until 1865.

Also attached to the 2nd Corps above and later the Admin. was the 1st Hants Engineer Volunteers and the 2nd Hants Light Horse. The former was, in 1870, transferred to the 2nd Tower Hamlets Engineers while the latter was disbanded in 1864.

Battalion headquarters are once again shown as being in Southampton from January 1873.

Upon consolidation in 1880 the 4th Admin. became the 2nd Hampshire Rifle Volunteer Corps. Headquarters remained at Southampton and the corps' nine companies were organised as follows—

'A' 'B' 'C' 'D' Companies at Southampton	Late 2nd Corps
'E' Company at Lymington	Late 3rd Corps
'F' Company at Christchurch	Late 10th Corps
'G' Company at Lyndhurst	Late 14th Corps
'H' 'I' Companies at Bournemouth	Late 19th Corps

By 1883 the establishment of the corps had reached twelve companies but in 1885 this was reduced to eight when part of the corps was detached to form the 4th Hampshire Rifle Volunteers. According to the regimental history of the Royal Hampshire Regiment the companies removed were those at Bournemouth, Christchurch, Lymington and Ringwood. This would suggest that one of the Bournemouth Companies, 'H' or 'I' had been lost and its place taken by one at Ringwood.

Also in 1885 the corps took on the title of 2nd Volunteer Battalion, The Hampshire Regiment. This change was notified in General Order 91 of September. One new company was raised in 1900 and in 1908 the 2nd VB became the 5th Battalion of the Hampshire Regiment.

3RD CORPS

The 3rd Corps was derived from the 2nd Admin. Battalion headquarters of which were at Portsmouth. Included in the battalion were the following corps—

4th Corps: Formed at Havant on 3 February 1860.

5th Corps: Formed at Portsmouth on 18 February 1860. This was a strong unit and from July 1861 was also known as the 'Portsmouth Rifle Volunteer Corps'.

6th Corps: Formed at Gosport on 9 March 1860.

7th Corps: Formed at Fareham on 14 May 1860.

12th Corps: Formed at Petersfield on 18 May 1860.

17th Corps: Formed at Titchfield on 29 August 1860. This corps was disbanded in 1874.

20th Corps: Formed at Wickham on 27 July 1860. Disbanded in 1874.

23rd Corps: Formed at Cosham on 29 November 1860. Headquarters were moved to Portchester in 1869.

Upon consolidation the new corps took on the number of its senior corps, 4th. After a few months, however, this was changed to 3rd. The 3rd had eleven companies which were organised as follows—

'A' 'B' 'C' 'D' E' Companies at Portsmouth	Late 5th Corps
'F' 'G' Companies at Gosport	Late 6th Corps
'H' Company at Havant	Late 4th Corps
'I' Company at Petersfield	Late 12th Corps
'K' Company at Fareham	Late 7th Corps
'L' Company at Portchester	Late 23rd Corps

A new company was added in 1884 and in 1897 a cadet corps was provided by the Portsmouth Grammar School. In 1900 an additional six companies were raised followed in 1905 by another cadet corps at Churchers College, Petersfield.

The 3rd Corps was redesignated as the 3rd Volunteer Battalion, The Hampshire Regiment in 1885, General Order 91 of September. In 1893 HRH The Duke of Connaught was made Hon Colonel of the battalion and from that year the title became 3rd (Duke of Connaught's Own) Volunteer Battalion.

The battalion became the 6th Hampshires in 1908 and its cadet corps became part of the Junior Division, Officers Training Corps.

4TH CORPS

The 4th Corps was formed in April 1885 from the Bournemouth, Christchurch, Lymington and Ringwood Companies of the 2nd Corps. Headquarters were placed at Bournemouth and the establishment set at six companies. By 1900 this had increased to eleven and one company, which was mounted on Forest ponies, was known as the New Forest Scouts.

Shortly after formation the 4th Corps was redesignated as the 4th Volunteer Battalion, The Hampshire Regiment. In 1908 they became the regiment's 7th Battalion.

Two cadet units have been associated with the 4th VB. The first was formed in 1903 by Bournemouth School and in 1908 transferred to the Officers Training Corps. In 1905 a company was formed at Lymington which after 1908 continued its affiliation to the 7th Battalion.

HAVERFORDWEST

The first company of rifle volunteers to be raised in the Borough of Haverfordwest, Pembrokeshire was formed on 4 February 1860. Designated as the 1st Haverfordwest Rifle Volunteers the corps was united to the 1st Pembrokeshire Admin. Battalion in 1862. Upon consolidation of that battalion in 1880 the corps became 'B', 'C' and 'D' Companies of the 1st Pembrokeshire Rifle Volunteer Corps.

HEREFORDSHIRE

The 1st Admin. Battalion of Herefordshire Rifle Volunteers was formed with headquarters at Hereford on 20 February 1861. Included in the battalion were the eight rifle corps then in existence within the county.

1st Corps: Formed at Hereford on 10 April 1860.

2nd Corps: Formed at Ross on 27 March 1860.

3rd Corps: Formed at Ledbury on 27 March 1860.

4th Corps: Formed at Bromyard on 15 May 1860.

5th Corps: Formed at South Archenfield on 15 May 1860. Disappeared from the *Army List* in January 1873.

6th Corps: Formed at Leominster on 6 May 1860.

7th Corps: Formed at Kington on 18 May 1860.

8th Corps: Formed at Hereford on 27 September 1860. This corps consisted entirely of members from a lodge of Oddfellows.

From 1864 the 1st, 2nd and 3rd Radmorshire Rifle Corps were shown in the *Army List* as being part of the 1st Herefordshire Admin. Battalion. The 3rd Corps, however, disappeared from the *Army List* in 1872.

In 1880 the battalion was consolidated as the 1st Herefordshire (Hereford and Radnor) Rifle Volunteer Corps. Headquarters remained at Hereford and the ten and a half company establishment was organised as follows—

'A' Company at Hereford	Late 1st Hereford Corps
'B' Company at Ross	Late 2nd Hereford Corps
'C' Company at Ledbury	Late 3rd Hereford Corps
'D' Company at Bromyard	Late 4th Hereford Corps
'E' Company at Ross	Late 2nd Hereford Corps
'F' Company at Leominster	Late 6th Hereford Corps
'G' Company at Kington	Late 7th Hereford Corps
'H' Company at Hereford	Late 8th Hereford Corps

| 'I' Company at Presteigne | Late 1st Radnor Corps |
| 'K' Company at Rhayader | Late 2nd Radnor Corps |

The half company was provided by the 8th Corps at Hereford.

Shortly after joining the King's (Shropshire Light Infantry) in 1881 'E' Company, the former No 2 Company of the 2nd Corps, was merged with 'B'. In December 1887 other volunteer elements of the King's, the 1st and 2nd Shropshire Rifle Corps, assumed the titles of 1st and 2nd Volunteer Battalions. The Herefords, however, did not take on the new designation and although ranked as 3rd VB continued to serve under their volunteer corps title.

The strength of the battalion was once again brought up to ten and a half companies when in 1889 a new 'E' Company was formed at Weobley. Also in 1889 a Bearer Company was formed at Hereford to serve the Welsh Border Infantry Brigade. This company was, as no permission had been granted to increase the establishment of the battalion, designated as part of 'A' Company.

In 1905 several changes in organisation took place. 'L' Company was formed at Hereford from members of the Cyclist Section created there in 1888 and 'M' was formed at Ruardean. An amalgamation between 'I' and 'G' Companies reduced the strength of the battalion and the Bearer Company became a separate unit designated as the Welsh Border Brigade Company RAMC(V).

In 1902 the Hereford Cathedral School applied to the War Office for permission to form a cadet corps. This was granted in December and on 28 March 1903 the school's first officers received their commissions. The corps was affiliated to the 1st Herefords and had an establishment of one company.

On 1 April 1908 the title conferred upon the 1st Herefords was 'The Herefordshire Battalion, The King's (Shropshire Light Infantry)' but after four months this was changed to '1st Battalion, The Herefordshire Regiment'. The Cadet Corps became part of the Junior Division of the Officers Training Corps.

HERTFORDSHIRE

During the period 1859–76 fourteen numbered corps of rifle volunteers were formed in the county of Hertfordshire.

1st Corps: Formed at Hertford on 22 November 1859.

2nd Corps: Formed at Watford on 5 January 1860.

3rd Corps: Formed at St Albans on 5 March 1860.

4th Corps: Formed at Ashridge on 1 March 1860.

5th Corps: Formed at Hemel Hempstead on 10 March 1860.

6th Corps: Formed at Bishop's Stortford on 20 March 1860.

7th Corps: Formed at Great Berkhampstead on 13 March 1860. Absorbed the 8th Corps in 1866.

8th Corps: Formed at Tring on 20 April 1860. Absorbed into the 7th Corps in 1866.

9th Corps: Formed at Ware on 13 June 1860.

10th Corps: Formed at Royston on 25 June 1860.

11th Corps: Formed at Cheshunt on 25 August 1860. Disbanded in 1870.

12th Corps: Formed at Hitchin on 15 September 1860. Disbanded in 1867.

13th Corps: Formed at Watton on 8 September 1864. Disbanded in 1868.

14th Corps: Formed at Welwyn on 13 September 1876. A 2nd Company was formed the following year at Hitchin.

All the above were to be included in one or other of the two administrative battalions that were formed by the county in October 1860. Headquarters of the 1st Battalion were placed at Little Gaddesden, Great Berkhampstead and the corps included were the 2nd, 3rd, 4th, 5th, 7th and 8th. Included in the 2nd Battalion, headquarters Hertford, were the 1st, 6th, 9th, 10th, 11th and 12th Corps. In 1862 the 22nd Essex Rifle Volunteers at Waltham Abbey was added to the battalion as was the 13th and 14th Herts upon their formation in 1864 and 1876 respectively.

Consolidation for both battalions came in 1880. However, the seniority of the two units was reversed resulting in the 1st Admin. becoming the 2nd Hertfordshire Rifle Volunteer Corps while the 2nd became the 1st with the additional title of (Herts and Essex)

Headquarters of the new 1st Corps were at Hertford and the eight company establishment was organised as follows—

'A' 'B' Companies at Hertford	Late 1st Herts Corps
'C' Company at Bishop's Stortford	Late 6th Herts Corps
'D' Company at Ware	Late 9th Herts Corps
'E' Company at Royston	Late 10th Herts Corps
'F' Company at Welwyn	Late 14th Herts Corps
'G' Company at Hitchin	Late 14th Herts Corps
'H' Company at Waltham Abbey	Late 22nd Essex Corps

Headquarters of the 2nd Corps were at Little Gaddesden, Great Berkhampstead and the five company establishment was organised as follows—

'A' Company at Watford	Late 2nd Corps
'B' Company at St Albans	Late 3rd Corps
'C' Company at Ashridge	Late 4th Corps
'D' Company at Hemel Hempstead	Late 5th Corps
'E' Company at Great Berkhampstead	Late 7th Corps

The 1st Hertfordshire Rifle Volunteer Corps was redesignated as the 1st (Hertfordshire) Volunteer Battalion, The Bedfordshire Regiment by General Order 181 of December 1887. A new company, 'I' at Hoddesdon, was formed in 1900 bringing the establishment of the battalion up to nine companies.

The five company establishment of the 2nd Corps was increased when in 1883 'F' Company was formed at Tring. This new company was in fact formed from the Tring detachment of 'E' Company which was originally raised as the 8th Corps in 1860. The title of 2nd (Hertfordshire) Volunteer Battalion, the Bedfordshire Regiment was assumed in December 1887 and like the 1st VB was notified in General Order 181 of that year. 'G' Company was formed at Watford in 1892.

Upon transfer to the Territorial Force in April 1908 the 1st and 2nd Volunteer Battalions were amalgamated. Parts of both went to form a nucleus for the 1st and

2nd Hertfordshire Batteries of the Royal Field Artillery but the main body were to form the Hertfordshire Battalion, The Bedfordshire Regiment. This was not a popular title and after a few months the Hertfordshires were redesignated as 1st Battalion, The Hertfordshire Regiment.

Three cadet units have been associated with the 1st Volunteer Battalion all of which transferred to the Junior Division of the Officers Training Corps in 1908. Haileybury College formed a corps in 1886 followed by companies at the Bishop's Stortford and Hertford Grammar Schools in 1906.

The Berkhampstead and St Albans Schools Cadet Corps, formed 1891 and 1903 respectively, were both affiliated to the 2nd Volunteer Battalion until transfer to the Junior Division, Officers Training Corps in 1908. Another company, the United Services College, joined the battalion in May 1904. The college was originally located at Westward Ho! in Devonshire and had, since formation of its cadet corps in 1900, been affiliated to the 4th VB Devonshire Regiment. The transfer to the 2nd VB Bedfords came about as a result of a move by the college to new premises at Harpenden. Yet another move came in March 1907 when the college went to Windsor and affiliation transferred to the 1st London Royal Engineer (Vols).

HUNTINGDONSHIRE

The 1st Corps of this county was raised with headquarters in Huntingdon on 18 April 1860. In the *Army List* for July 1861 the corps is shown as being attached to the 1st Huntingdon Light Horse Volunteers for Administration purposes. In 1872, however, they were transferred to the 1st Cambridgeshire Admin. Battalion. Headquarters were moved to St Neot's in 1876 and in 1880 the 1st Hunts became 'J' Company of the 1st Cambridgeshire Rifle Volunteer Corps.

In 1887 the 1st Cambs became the 3rd Volunteer Battalion of the Suffolk Regiment. Two years later its 'J' Company was disbanded and its personnel absorbed into the remainder to the battalion.

On 4 December 1900 the county once again provided a unit of rifle volunteers when the 4th (Hunts) Volunteer Battalion, The Bedfordshire Regiment was formed at Huntingdon. The establishment of the new battalion was at first set at eight companies but this was reduced to six after a short time. Recruiting was carried out mainly in the Huntingdon, St Ives, Fletton and St Neot's areas. In 1908 the 4th VB was amalgamated with the 3rd of same regiment. Together they formed the 5th Battalion Bedfords, the Hunts men providing four companies.

INVERNESS-SHIRE

Ten numbered corps were formed within the county and included in the 1st Admin. Battalion. The battalion was formed on 18 June 1860 with headquarters at Inverness.

1st Corps: Formed at Inverness on 18 November 1859.

2nd Corps: Formed at Fort William on 9 April 1860.

3rd Corps: Formed at Inverness on 26 March 1860.

4th Corps: Formed at Inverness on 3 May 1860.

5th Corps: Formed at Inverness on 16 July 1860.

6th Corps: Formed at Kingussie on 3 June 1861.

7th Corps: Formed at Beauly on 1 July 1861.

8th Corps: Formed at Portree on 20 July 1867.

9th Corps: Formed at Campbelltown, Ardersier on 12 November 1867.

10th Corps: Formed at Roy Bridge on 11 February 1869.

From 1864 the battalion was also shown in the *Army List* as the 'Inverness Highland'. This was also used in 1880 upon the consolidation of the 1st Admin. Battalion as the 1st Inverness-shire (Inverness Highland) Rifle Volunteer Corps. The new 1st Corps consisted of ten companies with headquarters at Inverness and was organised as follows—

'A' Company at Inverness	Late 1st Corps
'B' Company at Inverness	Late 3rd Corps
'C' Company at Inverness	Late 4th Corps
'D' Company at Inverness	Late 5th Corps
'E' Company at Fort William	Late 2nd Corps
'F' Company at Kingussie	Late 6th Corps
'G' Company at Beauly	Late 7th Corps
'H' Company at Portree	Late 8th Corps
'I' Company at Campbelltown	Late 9th Corps
'K' Company at Roy Bridge	Late 10th Corps

In 1881 the 1st Inverness joined the Seaforth Highlanders as one of its allotted volunteer battalions. They remained with the regiment until transfer to the Cameron Highlanders in February 1883. Redesignation as the 1st (Inverness Highland) Volunteer Battalion was notified in General Order 181 of December 1887 and in September 1903 the headquarters of 'K' Company was moved to Augustus. The battalion transferred to the Territorial Force in 1908 as the 4th Bn Cameron Highlanders.

ISLE OF MAN

The following rifle volunteer corps were raised on the Isle of Man—

1st Corps: Formed at Castletown on 29 September 1860. Headquarters were moved to Ballasalla in 1867. This corps was later disbanded and was last seen in the *Army List* for July 1870.

2nd Corps: Formed at Douglas on 29 September 1860. In 1873 the 2nd was attached for administration to the 15th Lancashire Rifle Volunteer Corps. This was later changed, however, to the 64th Lancs in 1877.

3rd Corps: Formed at Ramsey on 29 September 1860. The 3rd was later disbanded and appeared for the last time in the *Army List* for June 1869.

4th Corps: Formed at Crosby on 24 April 1866. Disappeared from the *Army List* in December 1870.

In October 1880 the remaining Isle of Man corps, the 2nd, was renumbered as 1st. At the same time affiliation was transferred back to the 15th Lancashire Corps but this was changed yet again, in 1884, to the 19th. In 1888 and under Army Order 81 of March the 1st Isle of Man became the 7th (Isle of Man) Volunteer Battalion, The King's (Liverpool Regiment).

When the Territorial Force was created in 1908 the Isle of Man Volunteers did not transfer. Instead they remained as the 7th (Isle of Man) Volunteer Battalion and as such continued to serve under the volunteer system. The battalion was to hold the unique distinction of being the only volunteer unit until 1914 and the introduction of the Volunteer Training Corps.

ISLE OF WIGHT

The 1st Admin. Battalion of Isle of Wight Rifle Volunteers was formed on 6 July 1860 and included the following corps—

1st Corps: Formed at Ryde on 25 January 1860. Absorbed the 3rd Corps in 1864.

2nd Corps: Formed at Newport on 14 January 1860.

3rd Corps: Formed at Ryde on 25 January 1860. Absorbed into the 1st Corps in 1864.

4th Corps: Formed at Nunwell as the 1st Sub-division on 16 February 1860. Appeared for the first time as 4th Corps in the *Army List* for March 1860.

5th Corps: Formed as the 2nd Sub-division at Ventnor on 25 February 1860. Appeared as 5th Corps for the first time in the *Army List* for March 1860.

6th Corps: Formed at Sandown on 31 March 1860. This corps was later disbanded and was last seen in the *Army List* for March 1862.

7th Corps: Formed at Cowes on 27 April 1860.

8th Corps: Formed at Freshwater on 6 July 1860. Disappeared from the *Army List* in February 1869.

In 1880 the 1st Admin. was consolidated as the 1st Isle of Wight Rifle Volunteer Corps. Headquarters remained at Newport and the eight companies were organised as follows—

'A' 'B' at Ryde	Late 1st Corps
'C' 'D' at Newport	Late 2nd Corps
'E' at Nunwell	Late 4th Corps
'F' 'G' at Ventnor	Late 5th Corps
'H' at Cowes	Late 7th Corps

Redesignation as the 5th (Isle of Wight 'Princess Beatrice's') Volunteer Battalion of the Hampshire Regiment was notified in General Order 91 of September 1885. Princess Beatrice being the wife of HRH Prince Henry of Battenberg, the battalion's first Hon Colonel.

In 1900 a new company consisting entirely of cyclists was formed at Newport and in 1908 the battalion transferred to the Territorial Force as the 8th Bn, Hampshire Regiment.

KENT

During 1880 the existing Kent rifle corps and admin. battalions were organised into five corps designated as 1st to 5th.

1ST CORPS

The 2nd Admin Battalion of Kent Rifle Volunteers was formed on 3 July 1860. Headquarters were placed at Tunbridge Wells and the corps included were as follows—

11th Corps: Formed at Farnborough on 24 January 1860 and was disbanded in November 1862.

14th Corps: Formed as the 2nd Sub-division at Tunbridge on 2 December 1859. Was first shown in the *Army List* as 14th Corps in March 1860.

17th Corps: Formed at Tunbridge Wells on 29 March 1860.

23rd Corps: Formed at Penshurst on 28 February 1860.

33rd Corps: Formed at Sevenoaks on 23 March 1860.

35th Corps: Formed at Westerham on 7 May 1860.

39th Corps: Formed at Mallins on 26 June 1860 but was transferred to the 3rd Admin. in May 1861.

Headquarters of the battalion were moved to Penshurst in 1863 to Sevenoaks in 1867 and finally back to Tunbridge in 1871.

In 1874 the 3rd Admin. Battalion of Kent Rifle Volunteers was broken up and all but one of its corps transferred to the 2nd. The 3rd had been formed in August 1860 with headquarters at Maidstone and contained the following corps—

1st Corps: Formed at Maidstone on 25 August 1859.

9th Corps: Formed at Chatham on 31 December 1859. This corps was later disbanded and was last seen in the *Army List* for November 1872.

12th Corps: Formed at Dartford on 23 February 1860 and was transferred upon break up of the 3rd Admin. in 1874 to the 1st Admin. Battalion.

15th Corps: Formed at Sutton on 15 February 1860. Headquarters were given as Sutton Valence from 1861 and in 1873 the corps was disbanded.

19th Corps: Formed at Rochester on 23 February 1860. This corps was later disbanded and was last seen in the *Army List* for December 1873.

20th Corps: Formed at Northfleet on 11 April 1860 and was disbanded in August 1868.

22nd Corps: Formed at Sheerness on 30 March 1860 and was disbanded in November 1870.

31st Corps: Formed at Leeds Castle on 23 March 1860.

38th Corps: Formed at Sheerness on 30 May 1860 and was disbanded in October.

39th Corps: Formed at Malling on 26 June 1860 and was until May 1861 included in the 2nd Admin. Battalion. Headquarters were given as West Malling from March 1862 and in August 1874 the corps disappeared from the *Army List*.

45th Corps: Formed at Rochester on 4 July 1861 and was disbanded in 1876.

The 2nd Admin. remained in the *Army List* until 1877 when in November it appeared as a consolidated battalion designated as 1st Corps. Headquarters of the new 1st Corps were placed at Tunbridge and its establishment set at eight companies. These were organised as follows—

'A' 'B' Companies at Maidstone	Late 1st Corps
'C' Company at Tunbridge	Late 14th Corps
'D' Company at Tunbridge Wells	Late 17th Corps
'E' Company at Penshurst	Late 23rd Corps
'F' Company at Leeds Castle	Late 31st Corps
'G' Company at Sevenoaks	Late 33rd Corps
'H' Company at Westerham	Late 35th Corps

In 1883 and under General Order 14 of February the 1st Corps was redesignated as the 1st Volunteer Battalion. The Queen's Own (Royal West Kent Regiment). During 1900 the establishment of the battalion was increased to eleven companies and in 1908 both the 4th and 5th Battalions of the West Kents were provided upon transfer to the Territorial Force.

Several cadet corps were formed and affiliated to the battalion. The first of these was raised by Skinner's School at Tunbridge Wells in April 1901. This was followed in 1904 by a company at Westerham and in 1906 by a unit formed at Maidstone Grammar School. In 1908 the Westerham Company continued its affiliation with the 4th Batallion while the two schools transferred to the Junior Division of the Officers Training Corps.

2ND CORPS

Formation of the 2nd Corps began in 1860 upon the formation in August of the 4th Admin. Battalion of Kent Rifle Volunteers. Headquarters of the battalion were at Canterbury and the corps included were as follows—

5th Corps: Formed at Canterbury on 1 December 1859.

6th Corps: Formed at Canterbury on 6 December 1859.

16th Corps: Formed at Sittingbourne on 15 February 1860.

24th Corps: Formed at Ash on 29 February 1860 and was disbanded in 1869.

29th Corps: Formed at Ashford on 15 March 1860.

36th Corps: Formed at Wingham on 18 May 1860.

In April 1874 the 2nd, 7th and 8th Cinque Ports Corps were amalgamated with the Kent Corps of the 4th Admin. Battalion to form a corps designated as the 5th Kent (East Kent) Rifle Volunteers. The three Cinque Ports Corps had until April 1874 been part of the 2nd Cinque Ports Admin. Battalion. Also included in this battalion were the 4th, 5th and 10th Cinque Ports Corps who together with the 5th

Kent from April 1874 constituted the 4th Kent Admin. Battalion. By the end of 1874 the 4th, 5th and 10th Cinque Ports had been absorbed into the 5th Kent which was to bring the strength of the corps up to eleven companies.

In September 1880 the 5th were renumbered as the 2nd and in 1883 redesignation as the 1st Volunteer Battalion, The Buffs (East Kent Regiment) was notified in General Order 63 of May. Headquarters of the battalion were moved from Canterbury to Dover in 1901 and in 1908 the Buff's 4th Battalion was formed upon transfer to the Territorial Force.

Associated with the battalion were several cadet corps the first of which was formed at Dane Hill School, Margate in November 1889. This company was later disbanded and was last seen in the *Army List* for May 1897. The Chatham House College Company was formed at Ramsgate in 1891 and in 1908 became part of the Junior Division of the Officers Training Corps. Also to join the OTC in 1908 were the South Eastern College, Ramsgate Cadet Corps which was formed in 1898 and redesignated as St Lawrence College in 1907, the Dover College Cadet Corps, formed 1901, St Edmund's School, Canterbury Cadet Corps, formed 1903 and Sir Roger Manwood's School, Sandwich, formed 1903. Other units to be affiliated to the battalion were the Margate College Cadets who were formed in 1892 and disbanded in 1901 and New College Schools, Herne Bay Cadet Corps which was transferred from the 4th VB Queen's Own (Royal West Kent Regiment) in 1906. This company was eventually accepted by the TF in 1911 and affiliated to the 4th Buffs.

3RD CORPS

The 1st Admin. Battalion of Kent Rifle Volunteers was formed with headquarters at Blackheath on 12 June 1860. The corps included were as follows—

3rd Corps: Formed at Lee on 7 November 1859.

4th Corps: Formed at Woolwich on 21 December 1859. This corps was removed from the battalion and attached to the 26th Corps in 1870.

7th Corps: Formed at Kidbrooke on 21 December 1859 and was disbanded in January 1869.

8th Corps: Formed at Sydenham on 22 December 1859. This corps was later disbanded and was last seen in the *Army List* for March 1871.

13th Corps: Formed as the 1st Sub-division at Greenwich on 11 November 1859. Redesignated as 13th Corps in February 1860.

18th Corps: Formed at Bromley on 26 March 1860.

21st Corps: Formed at Lewisham on 25 February 1860 and disbanded in October 1861.

25th Corps: Formed at Blackheath on 18 February 1860.

27th Corps: Formed at Deptford on 28 February 1860.

28th Corps: Formed at Charlton on 18 February 1860.

32nd Corps: Formed at Eltham on 22 March 1860 and disbanded in 1876.

34th Corps: Formed at Deptford on 23 March 1860.

In 1874 the 12th Corps which was formed at Dartford on 23 February 1860 was transferred to the 1st Admin. from the 3rd.

The battalion was consolidated as the 3rd Kent (West Kent) Rifle Volunteer Corps in April 1880. Headquarters remained at Blackheath and the corps' eleven companies were organised as follows—

'A' 'B' Companies at Lee	Late 3rd Corps
'C' 'D' Companies at Dartford	Late 12th Corps
'E' Company at Greenwich	Late 13th Corps
'F' Company at Bromley	Late 18th Corps
'G' 'H' Companies at Blackheath	Late 25th Corps
'I' Company at Deptford	Late 27th Corps
'K' Company at Charlton	Late 28th Corps
'L' Company at St John's	Late 34th Corps

The 3rd Corps was redesignated as the 2nd Volunteer Battalion, The Queen's Own (Royal West Kent Regiment) under General Order 14 of February 1883. By 1900 the strength of the battalion stood at thirteen companies and in 1908 the 20th Battalion of the London Regiment was formed upon transfer to the Territorial Force.

Affiliated to the battalion was the Proprietary School, Blackheath and Quernmore School, Bromley Cadet Corps. This unit was formed in 1900 and in 1908 became part of the Junior Division of the Officers Training Corps.

4TH CORPS

The 26th Kent Rifle Volunteer Corps, with headquarters at Royal Arsenal, Woolwich, is first seen in the *Army List* for April 1860 and is shown as a two battalion corps whose first officers commissions were dated 25 February 1860. It was at first intended to number the 2nd Battalion as the 30th Corps but they never appeared as such in any *Army List*.

By August 1860 the corps consisted of sixteen companies and had obtained permission in include (Royal Arsenal) in its full title.

In July 1864 the corps was divided. The 1st Battalion became the 21st Corps which was to fill the gap in the county list left by the Lewisham Corps in 1861, while the 2nd Battalion remained as 26th Corps. Both units retained the (Royal Arsenal) title and from January 1865 the 26th Corps is shown in the *Army List* as having its headquarters at the Royal Gun Factory Office, Woolwich.

Also formed at Woolwich was the 4th Corps which was raised on 21 December 1859. From July 1860 the 4th was included in the 1st Admin. Battalion but in 1870 was removed and attached to the 26th Corps.

The 21st and 26th were once again united when in 1870 they were merged as 26th. In 1880 yet another merger, this time with the 4th and 26th, saw the formation of the 4th Corps with headquarters at Woolwich Arsenal and an establishment of ten companies.

The 4th became the 3rd Volunteer Battalion of the Queen's Own (Royal West Kent Regiment) under General Order 14 of February 1883. In 1908 the battalion was amalgamated with the 2nd VB of the regiment to form the 20th Bn of the newly created London Regiment.

5TH CORPS

The 37th Kent Rifle Volunteer Corps was formed at Cranbrook on 6 June 1860 and soon consisted of six companies. In the *London Gazette* dated 5 April 1861 it is recorded that the 37th was to be divided and its companies formed into separate corps which were to be grouped into an admin. battalion. The battalion, which was numbered 5th, was formed the following month and the corps created by the division of the 37th were as follows—

37th Corps: Headquarters remained at Cranbrook.

38th Corps: This corps, whose headquarters were placed at Hawkhurst, filled the gap left by the Sheerness Corps which was disbanded in October 1860. The 38th was disbanded in 1872 but reformed again on 23 May 1877.

40th Corps: Headquarters were placed at Staplehurst.

41st Corps: Headquarters were placed at Gondhurst and moved to Lamberhurst in 1874.

42nd Corps: This corps, whose headquarters were at Brenchley, absorbed the 44th Corps in May 1863.

43rd Corps: Headquarters were placed at Rolvenden.

44th Corps: This corps, whose headquarters were at Lamberhurst, was absorbed into the 42nd Corps in May 1863.

Also included in the 5th Admin. Battalion, whose headquarters were placed at Cranbrook, were the 3rd Cinque Ports Corps and the 17th Sussex which had been attached to the 37th Corps since August 1860. The 17th was transferred to the 1st Cinque Ports admin. Battalion in November 1861.

The corps included in the battalion were recruited from the area known as 'The Weald' and in 1877 the additional title of (the Weald of Kent) was granted.

In 1880 the battalion was consolidated as the 37th (the Weald of Kent) Corps but this was changed to 5th after a few months. Headquarters remained at Cranbrook and the corps' seven companies were organised as follows—

'A' Company at Cranbrook	Late 37th Kent Corps
'B' Company at Hawkhurst	Late 38th Kent Corps
'C' Company at Staplehurst	Late 40th Kent Corps
'D' Company at Lamberhurst	Late 41st Kent Corps
'E' Company at Brenchley	Late 42nd Kent Corps
'F' Company at Rolvenden	Late 43rd Kent Corps
'G' Company at Tenterden	Late 3rd Cinque Ports Corps

Under General Order 63 of May 1883 the 5th Corps was redesignated as the 2nd (the Weald of Kent) Volunteer Battalion, The Buffs (East Kent Regiment). In 1908 the 2nd VB provided the regiment's 5th Battalion.

Affiliated to the 2nd VB was the Cranbrook Grammar School Cadet Corps which was formed in February 1900. This company was at first shown in the *Army List* as being attached to the 1st Cadet Battalion of the Buffs but by December 1900 had transferred to the 2nd VB. The school became part of the Junior Division of the Officers Training Corps in 1908.

No 10th Corps was recorded in the *Army List* as having been formed in Kent. A 2nd was formed at Ramsgate on 18 September 1859 but in April 1860 this became the 2nd Cinque Ports Corps.

Also formed in Kent was the 4th Volunteer Battalion, The Queen's Own (Royal West Kent Regiment). The battalion had its headquarters at Chatham and was raised on 27 April 1900. The establishment of the 4th VB was nine companies and affiliated was the Borden School Cadet Corps. Formed in October 1903 the school was located near Sittingbourne. In November 1906 The Borden School Cadet Corps was removed from the *Army List*. However, the officers formally with the corps now appear as being with The New College Schools, Herne Bay Cadets and affiliated to the 1st VB of the Buffs.

Formed on 24 October 1894 was the 1st Cadet Battalion of the Buffs (East Kent Regiment). The battalion consisted of four companies and had its first headquarters in Ramsgate. These were moved to Margate in 1903 and on 14 June 1907 the battalion was disbanded.

KINCARDINESHIRE

Included in the 1st Admin. Battalion of Kincardineshire Rifle Volunteers, formed with headquarters at Stonehaven on 14 May 1861, was the seven corps then in existence within the county. An 8th was later formed and added.

1st Corps: Formed at Fetteresso on 10 January 1860. Headquarters were moved to Stonehaven in 1867 and the corps was disbanded in October 1870.

2nd Corps: Formed at Banchory on 28 January 1860.

3rd Corps: Formed at Laurencekirk in February 1860. Was absorbed into the 5th Corps in 1873.

4th Corps: Formed at Fettercairn on 13 March 1860 and absorbed into the 5th Corps in 1871.

5th Corps: Formed at Auchinblae on 9 June 1860. Absorbed the 4th Corps in 1871 followed by the 3rd in 1873. Headquarters were moved to Laurencekirk in June 1878.

6th Corps: Formed at Netherley on 7 May 1860. Headquarters were moved to Portlethen in May 1869.

7th Corps: Formed at Durris on 13 February 1861.

8th Corps: Formed at Maryculter and Peterculter on 21 October 1869.

As the 1st Admin. was now down to five companies it was decided in 1876 to build up the battalion by drawing in corps from the neighbouring county of Aberdeenshire. On 23 February headquarters were moved to Banchory and the following corps transferred from the 1st Admin. Battalion of Aberdeenshire Rifle Volunteers, 8th, 14th, 21st and the 23rd their headquarters being at Echt, Tarland, Aboyne and Torphins respectively. By the end of 1876 a new title '1st Admin. Battalion of Kincardineshire or Deeside Highland Rifle Volunteers' had been conferred.

The title adopted in March 1880 upon consolidation of the battalion was 2nd Kincardineshire (Kincardine, or Deeside Highland) Rifle Volunteer Corps. In May 1880, however, a change to 2nd Kincardineshire and Aberdeenshire (Deeside Highland) occurred with renumbering as 1st following in June. Headquarters of the new corps remained at Banchory and the ten company establishment was organised as follows—

'A' Company at Banchory	Late 2nd Kincardine Corps
'B' Company at Laurencekirk	Late 5th Kincardine Corps
'C' Company at Portlethen	Late 6th Kincardine Corps
'D' Company at Durris	Late 7th Kincardine Corps
'E' Company at Maryculter	Late 8th Kincardine Corps
'F' Company at Echt	Late 8th Aberdeen Corps
'G' Company at Tarland	Late 14th Aberdeen Corps
'H' Company at Aboyne	Late 21st Aberdeen Corps
'I' Company at Ballater	Late 21st Aberdeen Corps
'K' Company at Torphins	Late 23rd Aberdeen Corps

In 1883 a series of company mergers and changes in location began when on 28 November 'K' Company amalgamated with 'A' and a new 'K' was formed at Stonehaven. This was followed in May 1885 by the merger of 'G' and 'H' Companies. Battalion headquarters were moved to Aberdeen in the following year and in 1887 and 1891 respectively 'E' Company moved to Peterculter and 'F' to Skene. Finally, in June 1894, battalion headquarters were moved back to Banchory.

Redesignation as the 5th (Deeside Highland) Volunteer Battalion The Gordon Highlanders was assumed in January 1884, being notified by General Order 12 of February. The battalion in turn became the 7th Battalion, Gordon Highlanders in April 1908.

KINROSS-SHIRE

The 1st and only rifle corps to be formed within the county was originally raised as one sub-division on 31 October 1860 at Kinross. It was increased to a full company in May 1861 and in June of the same year was included in the 1st Admin. Battalion of Fifeshire Rifle Volunteers.

In 1873 the 1st Kinross was transferred to the 1st Admin. Battalion of Clackmannanshire Rifles and in 1880 upon consolidation of that battalion became 'G' Company of the 1st Clackmannan and Kinross Rifle Volunteer Corps.

KIRKCUDBRIGHTSHIRE

Six independent corps of rifle volunteers were raised within the county of Kirkcudbrightshire and included in the Galloway Admin. Battalion of Rifle Volunteers from June 1860.

1st Corps: Formed at Kirkcudbright on 2 March 1860.

2nd Corps: Formed at Castle-Douglas on 2 March 1860.

3rd Corps: Formed at New Galloway on 28 March 1860.

4th Corps: Formed at Gatehouse on 19 May 1860. Was disbanded in 1866.

5th Corps: Formed at Maxwelltown on 1 June 1860.

6th Corps: Formed at Dalbeattie on 23 June 1869.

In 1880 the Galloway Admin. Battalion was consolidated and designated as the Galloway Rifle Volunteer Corps. The new corps consisted of eight companies six of which were provided by the Kirkcudbrightshire Corps while the remainder were found by the corps in Wigtownshire. The Kirkcudbrightshire Companies were—

'A' Company, late 1st Corps   'F' Company, late 5th Corps
'B' Company, late 2nd Corps   'G' Company, late 5th Corps
'E' Company, late 3rd Corps   'H' Company, late 6th Corps

Details of the Galloway Rifle Volunteer Corps have been included in the Wigtownshire section of this work.

LANARKSHIRE

The last rifle corps to be raised and numbered in Lanarkshire was that formed at Leadhills in 1875. This company received the title of 107th Lanarkshire Rifle Volunteer Corps and as such held the highest number allotted to any volunteer corps in the land.

The county was to provide the usual administrative battalions for its smaller corps. Of the seven created only one, the 3rd, was still in existence in 1880, the others all having been subject to consolidation before the reorganisations of that year. As a result the Lanarkshire rifle corps, before 1880, stood at nine corps of at least battalion strength. The consolidation of the 3rd Admin. Battalion in 1880 made this ten.

The position of 20th corps in the county was intended for a company raised by the western shipbuilding yards. Recruiting did not go well, however, and the corps was never formed. The 49th Corps was disbanded in 1862 having been formed at Lambhill on 3 May 1860. The 92nd place in the county list was set aside for a company raised at Uddingston but its offer of service was not accepted. The 97th or 'Glasgow Guards' Corps was formed on 30 July 1861 and soon consisted of four companies. These were later converted to an engineer roll and in 1863 were absorbed into the 1st Lanarkshire Engineer Volunteer Corps. The remaining Lanarkshire Corps have all been recorded below under the titles and numbers allotted in 1880.

1ST CORPS

The 1st Lanarkshire Corps was formed on 28 February 1860 by the amalgamation of the following Glasgow units—

1st Corps: Formed on 24 September 1859 with the additional title of '1st Western'.

2nd Corps: Formed by professors and students of the University of Glasgow on 24 September 1859.

9th Corps: This corps was formed on 10 October 1859 and originally consisted of members of the banking profession.

11th Corps: Formed on 4 November 1859 and also known as the '2nd Western'.

15th Corps: Also known as the 'Procurators' corps having been raised by members of the legal profession on 5 December 1859.

17th Corps: This was the 'Stockbrokers and Accountants' Corps and was formed by members of these professions on 5 December 1859.

18th Corps: Formed on 5 December 1859 by employees of Messrs Wylie & Lochhead a Glasgow firm of furnishers and undertakers.

33rd Corps: Formed in the Partick Division of Glasgow on 22 December 1859.

39th Corps: Formed on 29 December 1859 by employees of shipping companies.

50th Corps: This company was formed by newspaper employees and pressmen on 10 January 1860. Also known as '1st Press' Corps.

53rd Corps: Formed on 30 January 1860 by employees of J & W Campbell Ltd.

The following corps were also included during March and April.

63rd Corps: Formed on 15 February 1860. Members were bakers and workers in the grain and provision trades.

72nd Corps: This corps was also known as the 'Fine Arts' and was raised by jewellers, silversmiths and watch and clockmakers. Formed on 23 February 1860.

76th Corps: Formed on 26 March 1860 by men working in the wharves, stores, distilleries and saw-mills of Port Dundas.

77th Corps: Formed on 8 March 1860. This company had, for a few months previous, existed as a drill class at the university. Some members of the corps were from the university but in the main recruits were of the mercantile community. The 77th was also known as the 'City Rifle Guard' or '2nd University' Corps.

79th Corps: Formed on 29 March 1860 and also known as the '3rd Western'.

In June 1860 the corps, now of sixteen companies, was divided into two battalions of eight companies each—

1st Battalion	2nd Battalion
No 1 Company late 1st Corps	No 9 Company late 2nd Corps
No 2 Company late 9th Corps	No 10 Company late 18th Corps
No 3 Company late 11th Corps	No 11 Company late 50th Corps
No 4 Company late 15th Corps	No 12 Company late 53rd Corps
No 5 Company late 17th Corps	No 13 Company late 63rd Corps
No 6 Company late 33rd Corps	No 14 Company late 72nd Corps
No 7 Company late 39th Corps	No 15 Company late 76th Corps
No 8 Company late 79th Corps	No 16 Company late 77th Corps

In 1863 the No 11 Company was disbanded and the No 14 absorbed into No 15. The following year No 7 disappeared when it was absorbed into No 3 and the remaining companies were lettered as follows—

1st Battalion	2nd Battalion
'A' Company late No 1	'K' Company late No 9
'B' Company late No 2	'L' Company late No 10
'C' Company late No 3	'M' Company late No 12
'D' Company late No 4	'N' Company late No 13
'E' Company late No 5	'P' Company late No 15
'F' Company late No 6	'Q' Company late No 16
'G' Company late No 8	

The strength of the corps was reduced to twelve companies when in 1870 'K', the old University Company, was absorbed into 'Q'. This company was previously the 77th Corps and as already mentioned was formed, in part, from university members. A new 'K' Company was formed, together with an 'O', in 1878. In 1881 the former was re-lettered as 'I', a new 'K' formed and to bring the corps up to its original establishment of sixteen companies an additional company, designated as 'H', was created.

The 1st Lanarks joined the Cameronians (Scottish Rifles) in 1881 as one of its allotted volunteer battalions. The corps was to serve as the regiment's 1st VB but redesignation as such was never assumed. In 1908 and the transfer to the Territorial Force the 5th Battalion, Cameronians was formed. 'K' Company, however, who since 1900 had once again been formed by members of Glasgow University, became part of the Senior Division of the Officers Training Corps.

Associated with the 1st Lanarks since formation in 1902 was the High School, Glasgow Cadet Corps. Two companies were formed by the school which in 1908 transferred to the Junior Division, Officers Training Corps.

2ND CORPS

The 2nd Corps of the post-1880 period originated in May 1860 upon the formation of the 3rd Battalion of Lanarkshire Rifle Volunteers. This battalion was redesignated as the 1st Admin. in March 1861 and is shown from that date as having its headquarters at Hamilton. The corps included were—

16th Corps: Formed at Hamilton on 24 February 1860.

42nd Corps: Formed at Uddingston on 31 January 1860.

44th Corps: Formed at Blantyre on 6 February 1860 from employees of Messrs Henry Monteith & Co.

52nd Corps: Formed at Hamilton on 24 February 1860.

56th Corps: Formed at Bothwell on 23 February 1860.

57th Corps: Formed at Wishaw on 7 March 1860.

102nd Corps: Formed at Motherwell on 14 February 1867.

103rd Corps: Formed at East Kilbride on 6 June 1867.

106th Corps: Formed at Strathaven in October 1873.

Less than a month after the formation of the 106th Corps the battalion was consolidated as the 16th Lanarkshire Rifle Volunteer Corps. Headquarters remained at Hamilton and its ten companies were organised as follows—

'A' Company at Hamilton	Late 16th Corps
'B' Company at Hamilton	Late 52nd Corps
'C' Company at Uddingston	Late 42nd Corps
'D' Company at Strathaven	Late 106th Corps
'E' Company at Bothwell	Late 56th Corps
'F' 'G' Company at Wishaw	Late 57th Corps
'H' Company at Motherwell	Late 102nd Corps
'I' Company at Blantyre	Late 44th and 103rd corps
'K' Company at Motherwell	Newly-formed

Redesignation as the 2nd Corps came in 1880 and as the 2nd Volunteer Battalion, Cameronians (Scottish Rifles) in 1887 (General Order 181 of December). In 1892 'D' Company was amalgamated with 'K' and a new 'D' was formed at Larkhall. 'L' (Cyclist) Company was raised at Hamilton in 1899 when 'K' Company absorbed 'D' in 1892 its headquarters were at the same time moved to those of 'D' at Strathaven. In 1904, however, these were moved back to Motherwell.

The 2nd VB transferred to the Territorial Force in April 1908 as the 6th Battalion, Cameronians.

3RD CORPS

On 8 August 1860 the following Glasgow corps were amalgamated as the 3rd Lanarkshire Rifle Volunteers.

3rd Corps: Formed on 9 September 1859 and also known as the '1st Southern' Corps.

10th Corps: Formed on 19 October 1859. Like the 3rd Corps the 10th was raised south of the Clyde and was also known as the '2nd Southern' Corps.

14th Corps: Formed on 5 December 1859 and known as the 'South Western' Corps.

22nd Corps: Formed on 5 December 1859 by employees of Messrs Cogan's Spinning Factory.

54th Corps: Formed on 30 January 1860. Members of the 54th were all total abstainers.

82nd Corps: Formed on 11 April 1860 and like the 54th also consisted of total abstainers.

87th Corps: This corps was formed at Busby just outside of Glasgow on 18 May 1860. Its members were mostly workers from Messrs Inglis & Wakefields.

By December 1860 a new company was formed in Glasgow by workers at the Etna Foundry and before it could receive a number was merged into the 3rd Corps. Also, by 1862, the 78th 'Old Guard of Glasgow' Corps was absorbed. This company had been formed on 28 May 1860 by ex-members of the 'Napoleonic Volunteers' and included one gentleman of 88 years of age who had served with the Glasgow Light Horse of 1796.

The 3rd Lanarks became a volunteer battalion of the Cameronians (Scottish Rifles) in 1881 but although ranked as 3rd was never designated as such. The corps

26th Middlesex (Cyclist) RVC.

Band, 2nd VB Suffolk Regt *c*1907.

Band of the King's Lynn Company, 3rd VB Norfolk Regt going to camp 14 July 1906.

'A' Company (Watford), 1st (Herts) VB Bedfordshire Regt.
Photo taken on the last parade, (21 March 1908), before transfer to TF.

Band of the 4th Devonshire Rifle Volunteers

No 4 Section, Glasgow Academy Cadet Corps, 1st VB Highland Light Infantry *c*1905.

Band of the 1st Lanarkshire RVC 1899.

Cyclist, 2nd VB Worcestershire Regt *c*1906

1st VB Sherwood Foresters *c*1907.

2nd VB West Yorkshire Regt *c*1890.

1st Nottingham (Robin Hood) RVC *c*1890.

Colour-Sergeant William Ingram, 3rd
Lanarkshire RVC. The arm badges
represent awards for rifle shooting.

Corporal R. Norbury of the 2nd VB
South Lancashire Regt. Winner of the
'Beecham Cup' for Shooting 1887.

Corporal and Bandsman of the 1st
Bucks VRC *c*1904 (by courtesy of
British Rail).

1st VB Royal Sussex Regt *c*1890.

Lt-Col T. J. Long
3rd VB Royal Fusiliers c1897.

Major R. S. Doll,
VD 3rd London RVC *c*1897.

Bugler of the 4th VB South Wales
Borderers c1906.

Corporal, 2nd VB Royal Fusiliers
c1906.

3rd London RVC *c*1902.

36th Middlesex RVC *c*1876.

Sergeant and bugler, 2nd VB South Staffordshire Regt *c*1907.

Capt E. H. Rossiter, 4th VB
East Surrey Regt c1890.

Queen's Edinburgh Rifle Volunteer
Brigade c1875.

Sergeant, 1st VB South Wales
Borderers c1907

Boys of the 1st Cadet Battalion,
Queen's (Royal West Surrey Regiment)
c1890.

Corporal, 4th VB Black Watch c1902.

Sergeant, 11th Middlesex RVC c1878.

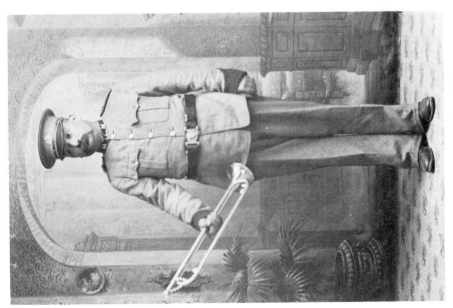

Trumpeter, 2nd VB Suffolk Regt c1907.

RV – H

Plaid brooch, 6th VB Royal Scots
*c*1888.

Silver plaid-brooch
of the 3rd Volunteer Battalion,
Gordon Highlanders.

Glengarry badge,
Perthshire Highland Corps c1880.

Other ranks' glengarry badge, 1st VB,
The King's Own Light Infantry
1883–1887.

Other ranks' glengarry badge, 1st Volunteer Battalion,
Royal Berkshire Regiment c1885.

Glengarry badge, 1st Dumbartonshire
RVC 1887–1908.

Waist-belt clasp, 15th, later
7th, Middlesex RVC, introduced 1875.

Waist-belt clasp of the 1st Bucks Rifle
Volunteer Corps.

Shoulder belt plate, 1st Bedfordshire
RVC 1878–1887.

Waist-belt 44th (Staines) Middlesex RVC 1860–1880.

Pouch-belt plate, 5th Middlesex RVC
*c*1880.

Pouch-belt plate, 4th Sutherland RVC
1860–1880.

Officers' pouch-belt plate,
22nd later 13th Middlesex RVC.

Pouch-belt plate, 3rd Middlesex RVC
*c*1880.

Shoulder title, 4th VB, East Surrey Regt
*c*1904.

Shoulder title, 5th (Irish) VB,
The King's (Liverpool Regt) *c*1904.

Shoulder title, 5th (Deeside Highland)
VB, The Gordon Highlanders *c*1904.

Shoulder title, 2nd VB, The Buffs
(East Kent Regt) *c*1904.

Shoulder title, 4th VB, The Black
Watch (Royal Highlanders) *c*1904.

Shoulder title, 7th (Isle of Man) VB,
The King's (Liverpool Regt) *c*1904.

Shoulder title, 1st (Oxford University)
VB, The Oxfordshire LI *c*1904.

Shoulder title, 3rd (Cambridgeshire)
VB, The Suffolk Regt c1904.

White metal shoulder title of
the 2nd Volunteer Battalion,
The Royal Welsh Fusiliers c1904.

Helmet-plate, 2nd Middlesex RVC
c1880

Other ranks' helmet-plate,
1st Volunteer Battalion,
Leicestershire Regt c1883.

Other ranks' helmet plate of the
1st Cambridgeshire Corps 1880–1887.

Officers' helmet plate of the
4th Caithness Corps 1879–1880.

Other ranks' helmet-plate,
5th Volunteer Battalion, The Royal
Scots c1888.

remained with the regiment and upon transfer to the Territorial Force in 1908 provided its 7th Battalion.

4TH CORPS

The 4th Lanarkshire (Glasgow 1st Northern) Corps was formed on 12 December 1859 by the amalgamation of the following corps—

4th Corps: Formed on 10 October 1859 and also known as the '1st Northern' Corps.

6th Corps: Formed on 10 October 1859.

7th Corps: Formed on 10 October 1859.

8th Corps: Formed on 10 October 1859.

12th Corps: Formed on 5 December 1859. This corps was also known as the 'North Eastern' and was raised by employees of Tennant's Wellpark Brewery.

13th Corps: Formed on 5 December 1859.

Upon amalgamation the above corps were designated as 'A' to 'F' Companies in their order of seniority. In July 1861 three new companies were added when the following corps were absorbed—

60th Corps: Formed on 18 February 1860 and also known as the '1st Highland' Corps.

61st Corps: Formed on 18 February 1860 and also known as the '2nd Highland' Corps.

93rd Corps: Formed on 8 August 1860. This was the '3rd Highland' Corps and was also known as the 'Glasgow Highland Rifle Rangers'.

The above corps became 'G', 'H' and 'I' Companies of the 4th and as the sub-titles suggest were formed by Highlanders resident in Glasgow.

Under General Order 181 of December 1887 the 4th Lanarks became the 4th Volunteer Battalion of the Cameronians (Scottish Rifles). The corps provided the regiment's 8th Battalion upon transfer to the Territorial Force in April 1908.

The Kelvinside Academy Cadet Corps was formed in September 1893 and was associated with the 4th Volunteer Battalion from that date. In 1908 the Academy became part of the Junior Division, Officers Training Corps.

5TH CORPS

In the *Army List* for February 1860 the following Glasgow corps are shown as being amalgamated under the title of 19th Lanarkshire (Glasgow, 2nd Northern) Rifle Volunteer Corps—

19th Corps: Formed on 5 December 1859 with the sub-title 'Glasgow, 2nd Northern'. This company was formed by members of the Western and Clyde Engineering Works.

23rd Corps: Formed on 5 December 1859 and known as the 'Warehousemen' Company. Members were all workers in drapery firms.

24th Corps: Formed in the Cowcaddens district on 6 December 1859. Also known as the 'North Western' Corps.

28th Corps: Formed on 22 December 1859 from employees of the Edinburgh and Glasgow Railway.

36th Corps: Formed on 28 December 1859 by workers of Messrs Edington & Co's Phoenix Ironworks at Port Dundas.

41st Corps: Also known as the 'North Western Artisans' and consisted chiefly of masons. Formation of the company was on 31 December 1859.

By September 1860 the corps that until then had constituted the 5th Admin. Battalion of Lanarkshire Rifle Volunteers were also included in the 19th. These were—

51st Corps: Formed on 11 January 1860 by newspaper workers and known as the '2nd Press' Corps.

67th Corps: Formed on 17 February 1860 by employees of Messrs D. Laidlaw & Sons.

74th Corps: This company was known as the 'Grenadiers' and would not accept recruits under 5 feet 9 inches in height. Formation date was 29 February 1860.

80th Corps: Formed on 29 March 1860 by employees of Messrs M'Gavin & Co a firm of ironworkers at Windmill Croft.

81st Corps: Formed on 2 April 1860 mainly from employees of Law & Co's Iron Works at Port Dundas. Also known as the 'Northern Artisans'.

83rd Corps: Formed on 24 April 1860 mainly by joiners.

Before the end of 1860 three other Glasgow companies were to be absorbed, these were—

85th Corps: Formed on 7 May 1860 from ironworkers and also known as the '2nd North Eastern' Corps.

89th Corps: Formed on 9 May 1860 by workers in textile firms. Known as the 'Manufacturers' Corps.

91st Corps: Formed on 24 May 1860 and known as the '3rd Abstainers'. This company was formed chiefly by total abstainers from the Whitevale district.

The 19th Corps now consisted of fifteen companies which were divided into two battalions. In 1864, however, a reduction in the establishment to twelve companies took place. At this time the two battalions became one.

The 19th were redesignated as 5th Corps in 1880 and as the 1st Volunteer Battalion of the Highland Light Infantry in 1887 (General Order 181 of December). They remained with the regiment and in 1908 provided their 5th Battalion.

The Glasgow Academy Cadet Corps was formed in August 1902 and was from that date affiliated to the 1st Volunteer Battalion. The Academy became part of the Junior Division of the Officers Training Corps in 1908.

6TH CORPS

The corps included in the 6th Battalion of Lanarkshire Rifle Volunteers were all formed by employees of Clyde shipbuilding and engineering yards. The battalion was first seen in the *Army List* for July 1860.

25th Corps: Formed on 14 December 1859 at Messrs Barclay, Curle & Co.

26th Corps: Formed on 14 December 1859 at Messrs R. Napier & Sons, Govan.

27th Corps: Formed on 14 December 1859 by Messrs R. Napier & Sons Engineering Department.

40th Corps: Formed on 29 December 1859 from various smaller yards.

68th Corps: Formed on 17 February 1860 by Messrs Neilson & Co's Locomotive Works.

69th Corps: Formed on 17 February 1860 at Messrs J. & G. Thompson's.

70th Corps: Formed on 17 February 1860 at A. & J. Inglis and Todd and MacGregor's.

71st Corps: Formed on 17 February 1860 at Lancefield Forge and the Anderston Foundry.

In April 1861 the battalion was consolidated as the 25th Lanarkshire Rifle Volunteer Corps. The eight companies were organised as follows—

'A' Company late 26th Corps	'E' Company late 70th Corps
'B' Company late 68th Corps	'F' Company late 27th Corps
'C' Company late 71st Corps	'G' Company late 69th Corps
'D' Company late 40th Corps	'H' Company late 25th Corps

Two new companies were formed in 1882.

The 25th was redesignated as the 6th Corps in 1880 and as the 2nd Volunteer Battalion, The Highland Light Infantry in 1887 (General Order 181 of December). In 1901 the Govan High School at Hillhead formed a cadet corps which was affiliated to the battalion.

The 2nd VB became the 6th Battalion of the Highland Light Infantry in 1908. Govan High School remained unattached until transfer to the Junior Division, Officers Training Corps in 1911.

7TH CORPS

The 4th Admin. Battalion of Lanarkshire Rifle Volunteers was formed with headquarters at Airdrie on 14 May 1862. The corps included then or upon formation were as follows—

29th Corps: Formed at Coatbridge on 13 February 1860.

32nd Corps: Formed at Summerlee by employees of Messrs Neilson's Iron Works on 10 January 1860.

43rd Corps: Formed at Gartsherrie on 10 January 1860. This company was formed by workers of W. Baird & Co's Iron Works and transferred its headquarters to Shotts in 1872.

48th Corps: Formed on 11 February 1860 at Airdrie.

95th Corps: Formed at Bailliestown on 16 October 1860.

97th Corps: Formed at Woodhead on 11 January 1865. This company, which was the 2nd to hold this number, later moved to Coatbridge.

98th Corps: Formed at Gartness on 12 May 1865 and was raised by workers of the Calderbank and Chapelhall Iron and Steel Works. Headquarters were moved to Wattstown in 1869.

99th Corps: Formed at Clarkston on 27 July 1865. Heaaquarters were moved to Caldercruix, Airdrie in 1866.

100th Corps: Headquarters of this company were moved to Caldercruix in 1866 having been formed at Calderbank on 8 July 1865.

101st Corps: Formed at Newarthill on 7 June 1866.

104th Corps: Formed at Holytown, Bellshill on 18 April 1868, its members being recruited from Messrs Neilson's Mossend Works.

On 19 September 1873 the 4th Admin. Battalion was consolidated as the 29th Lanarkshire Corps. Headquarters remained at Airdrie and the twelve companies were organised as follows—

'A' Company at Coatbridge	Late 29th Corps
'B' Company at Airdrie	Late 32nd Corps and No 1 Company of the 48th
'C' Company at Shotts	Late 43rd Corps
'D' Company at Airdrie	Late No 2 Company of 48th Corps
'E' Company at Bailliestown	Late 95th Corps
'F' Company at Coatbridge	Late 97th Corps
'G' Company at Greengairs	Late 98th Corps
'H' Company at Clarkston	Late 99th Corps
'I' Company at Calderbank	Late 100th Corps
'K' Company at Newarthill	Late 101st Corps
'L' Company at Bellshill	Late 104th Corps
'M' Company at Harthill & Benhar	Late 100th Corps

In 1875 'E' and 'F' Companies were amalgamated as 'E' at Coatbridge and a new 'F' Company formed at Cheyston. Two years later, due to a fall off in numbers, the establishment of the corps was reduced to eight companies. This required the following reorganisations—

'A' Company at Coatbridge	Late 'A' Company
'B' Company at Airdrie	Late 'B' Company
'C' Company at Shotts	Late 'C' and 'M' Companies
'D' Companies at Airdrie	Late 'D' and 'L' Companies
'E' Company at Coatbridge	Late 'E' Company
'F' Company at Cheyston	Late 'F' Company
'G' Company at Caldecruix	Late 'G' and 'H' Companies
'H' Company at Newarthill	Late 'I' and 'K' Companies

The corps was renumbered as 7th in 1880 and in 1887 under General Order 181 of December redesignation as the 5th Volunteer Battalion of the Cameronians (Scottish Rifles) was conferred.

On 1 April 1897 the 5th Volunteer Battalion was disbanded as a result of severe criticism by the officer commanding 26th Regimental District on its discipline.

8TH CORPS

On 4 July 1860 the following Glasgow Rifle Corps were grouped together as the 4th Battalion of Lanarkshire Rifle Volunteers—

30th Corps: Formed on 28 December 1859 and known as the '1st Central' Corps. Disbanded in 1865.

31st Corps: The 31st was formed on 21 December 1859 by workers in the leather trade.

38th Corps: Formed on 29 December 1859 from mechanics. Also known as 'Rifle Rangers'.

45th Corps: Formed by Glasgow grocers on 10 January 1860.

46th Corps: Formed by Glasgow grocers on 10 January 1860.

47th Corps: Formed by Glasgow grocers on 10 January 1860.

75th Corps: Formed by workers in the leather trade on 29 February 1860.

84th Corps: Formed on 24 April 1860 from members of the grain and provision trades.

In March 1861 the 4th Battalion was redesignated as the 2nd Admin. Battalion and at the same time the following corps added—

86th Corps: Formed by tailors on 7 May 1860.

96th Corps: Formed on 29 November 1860.

88th Corps: This corps did not join the battalion until October 1861 having been raised on 9 May by members of the fleshers' trade. Disbanded in 1864.

The 2nd Admin. Battalion was consolidated as the 31st Corps on 10 May 1865 and in June 1869 received the additional title of 'The Blythswood Rifles' in honour of its commanding officer, Lt-Col Campbell of Blythswood.

The 7th Battalion of Lanarkshire Rifle Volunteer appeared for the first time in the *Army List* for September 1860. It included the following Glasgow companies—

5th Corps: Formed on 24 September 1859 and also known as the '1st Eastern'.

21st Corps: This corps was also known as the 'Parkhead Artisans' and was formed on 5 December 1859.

34th Corps: Formed on 27 December 1859 and also known as the '1st Rifle Rangers'.

35th Corps: The 35th or '2nd Rifle Rangers' was formed on 27 December 1859.

58th Corps: Formed on 10 February 1860 and known as the 'Eastern Artisans'.

59th Corps: The 59th were also known as the 'Eastern Artisans' and was formed from the overspill of the 58th on 21 February 1860.

64th Corps: The 64th (1st Rutherglen) Corps was the first of two companies to be formed in the Royal Burgh on 18 February 1860.

65th Corps: The '2nd Rutherglen' Corps formed on 18 February 1860.

66th Corps: Formed and also known as the 'Eastern Rifle Rangers' on 17 February 1860.

90th Corps: Formed in the Whitevale district on 24 May 1860.

In November 1860 the 7th Battalion was consolidated as the 5th Lanarkshire Rifle Volunteer Corps with an establishment of twelve companies. The corps was reduced to ten companies in 1864 and from then on suffered a steady decline in its numbers.

By 1873 the 5th Corps had all but vanished and in September what remained of it was absorbed into the 31st. At this time no increase in establishment was gained by the Blythswood Corps but in 1877 the fomation of an additional two companies was sanctioned.

In 1880 the 31st became the 8th and in 1887, General Order 181 of December, the 3rd (The Blythswood) Volunteer Battalion of the Highland Light Infantry. The next change in designation occurred in April 1908 upon transfer to the Territorial Force as the regiment's 7th Battalion.

9TH CORPS

The 9th Corps of 1880 was originally the 8th Battalion of Lanarkshire Rifle Volunteer which was formed from the following corps in December 1860—

37th Corps: Formed at Lesmahagow on 3 February 1860.

55th Corps: Formed at Lanark on 23 February 1860.

73rd Corps: Formed at Carluke on 12 March 1860.

94th Corps: Formed at Douglas on 21 September 1860.

In March 1861 the 8th was redesignated as the 3rd Admin. Battalion of Lanarkshire Rifle Volunteers with headquarters at Lanark. The battalion was later joined by—

62nd Corps: The original 62nd Corps was formed at Biggar on 22 February 1860 but was disbanded in September of the same year. A new company was raised at Biggar on 17 March 1863 and once again numbered as 62nd.

107th Corps: As previously mentioned this was the last corps to be raised in Lanarkshire and held the highest number allotted to any volunteer unit. Formation was in May 1875 at Leadhills.

In 1880 the battalion was consolidated as the 37th Lanarkshire Rifle Volunteer Corps being renumbered as 9th before the end of the year. Headquarters of the new corps remained at Lanark and the six companies were lettered 'A' to 'F' in the order of seniority formally held by the six corps.

The 9th Lanarks joined the Highland Light Infantry as one of its allotted volunteer battalions in 1881 but although serving as 4th did not give up its rifle volunteer corps title. Before transfer to the Territorial Force as the regiment's 8th Battalion in 1908 'E' Company was to move to Forth in 1894 and 'F' to Law in 1901.

10TH CORPS

On 21 July 1868 twelve companies were formed from Highlanders resident in the City of Glasgow. Designated as the 105th Lanarkshire (Glasgow Highland) Rifle Volunteer Corps the new battalion attracted many men from the Highland

Companies of the 4th Corps. Although the twelve companies recruited in general from all over the city 'C' was made up by residents of Partick 'E' from Crosshill; 'F' by natives of Islay and 'G' by exiles from Argyllshire.

Redesignation as the 10th Corps occurred in 1880 and as the 5th (Glasgow Highland) Volunteer Battalion of the Highland Light Infantry in 1887 (General Order 181 of December). A new company consisting of cyclists was formed in 1900 and in 1908 the 5th VB became the 9th Battalion, HLI.

On 25 July 1891 a cadet corps was formed and affiliated to the battalion at Blairlodge School. The company was disbanded in 1904 and was to be found at Polmont Station in Stirlingshire.

LANCASHIRE

The last rifle corps to be raised and numbered in Lancashire was that formed at Flixton in 1872. This company received the title of 91st Corps and as such held the second highest number allotted to any volunteer unit in the country. Not all the positions in the county list were used as several numbers, 16, 18, 20, 34, 35, 50, 58, 85 and 89, were reserved for corps but never used.

The county was to provide the usual administrative battalions for its smaller corps. Of the nine created three were to be consolidated before the reorganisations of 1880. The remaining six together with the larger corps were in 1880 to form twenty-one corps with a 22nd following in 1882.

1ST CORPS

The 1st Admin. Battalion of Lancashire Rifle Volunteers was formed in May 1860 from corps within the Liverpool area.

1st Corps: Formed on 11 June 1859.

22nd Corps: Formed on 30 January 1860.

38th Corps: Formed in the Fairfield area of Liverpool as the 1st Sub-division on 20 January 1860. Appeared for the first time as 38th Corps in the *Army List* for March 1860.

45th Corps: Formed on 27 February 1860.

66th Corps: Formed on 25 April 1860.

69th Corps: Formed on 31 May 1860.

In December 1861 the 1st Admin. was consolidated to form the 1st Corps with an establishment of eight companies. Not included in the merger was the 22nd Corps which remained independent until 1863 when it disappeared from the *Army List*. To replace the 22nd the 14th Corps at Edge Hill was brought in. The 14th had been formed as the 2nd Sub-division on 10 November 1859. It first appeared as 14th in the *Army List* for December 1859 and was until the merger with the 1st Corps included in the 2nd Admin. Battalion.

The 74th Corps, which was formed on 2 July 1860, was absorbed into the 1st in 1862 and in 1863 the 13th, 48th, 54th and 83rd were attached for administrative purposes. A cadet corps was also formed by the battalion in April 1865. The 82nd

Corps was disbanded in 1872 and in 1873 the 13th was transferred to the 15th Corps. In 1880 the 48th was merged with the 47th to form the 21st and the 54th became part of the 13th Corps.

The cadet corps was removed from the *Army List* during 1884 and in 1888, under Army Order 81 of March, the 1st Corps was redesignated as the 1st Volunteer Battalion, The King's (Liverpool Regiment). Became the 5th Battalion in 1908.

2ND CORPS

The following corps were all included in the 8th Admin. Battalion, formed with headquarters at Blackburn in March 1864—

2nd Corps: Formed at Blackburn on 4 October 1859 and in February of the following year absorbed the 3rd Corps which was also formed at Blackburn on the 4th. The 81st Corps was attached in 1861 until 1876.

62nd Corps: Formed at Clitheroe on 27 March 1860.

81st Corps: Formed at Withnell on 20 February 1861. This corps was included in the 2nd Admin. Battalion for a short time but before the end of 1861 was attached to the 2nd Corps. The 81st disappeared from the *Army List* during 1876 having moved its headquarters from Withnell to Wheelton in July 1864.

The 8th Admin. Battalion was consolidated as the 2nd Corps in 1880. Headquarters remained at Blackburn and the corps' ten companies were organised as follows—

'A' to 'F' at Blackburn	Late 2nd Corps
'G' 'H' at Over Darwen	Late 2nd Corps
'J' 'K' at Clitheroe	Late 62nd Corps

Redesignation as the 1st Volunteer Battalion, The East Lancashire Regiment occurred in June 1889 and in 1908 the 4th Battalion of the regiment was formed upon transfer to the Territorial Force.

Affiliated to the 1st VB was the Stonyhurst College Cadet Corps which was formed in January 1901. This unit became part of the Junior Division of the Officers Training Corps in 1908.

3RD CORPS

Burnley was the first headquarters of the 3rd Admin. Battalion which was formed in September 1860. These were moved to Rossendale in 1862, to Accrington in 1865 and back to Burnley in 1874. The corps included in the battalion were as follows—

4th Corps: Formed at Rossendale on 4 July 1859.

7th Corps: Formed at Accrington on 20 September 1859 and absorbed the 36th Corps in 1861.

17th Corps: Formed at Burnley on 16 January 1860.

29th Corps: Formed at Lytham on 28 January 1860 and remained independent until joining the 3rd Admin. in 1864.

36th Corps: Formed at Accrington on 7 January 1860 and was absorbed into the 7th Corps in 1861.

57th Corps: Formed at Ramsbottom on 26 March 1860. Did not join battalion until late 1861.

84th Corps: Formed at Padiham on 18 February 1861.

87th Corps: Formed at Nelson on 7 February 1862 and disappeared from the *Army List* in June 1865.

88th Corps: Formed at Haslingden on 27 February 1863.

90th Corps: Formed at Fleetwood on 3 June 1868. Disappeared from the *Army List* during 1870.

Upon consolidation in 1880 the battalion was at first numbered as 4th Corps. This was changed by September, however, to 3rd. Headquarters remained at Burnley and the corps' twelve companies were organised as follows—

'A' to 'D' Companies at Burnley	Late 17th Corps
'E' Company at Padiham	Late 84th Corps
'F' to 'H' Companies at Accrington	Late 7th Corps
'J' Company at Haslington	Late 88th Corps
'K' Company at Ramsbottom	Late 57th Corps
'L' Company at Stackshead	Late 4th Corps
'M' Company at Lytham	Late 29th Corps

The 3rd Corps became the 2nd Volunteer Battalion, The East Lancashire Regiment under Army Order 263 of June 1889 and the regiment's 5th Battalion in 1908.

4TH CORPS

The 4th Admin. Battalion was formed with headquarters at Eccles in October 1860 and contained the following corps—

21st Corps: Formed at Wigan on 20 January 1860. The 21st was attached to the 8th Corps in 1862 and transferred to the 4th Admin. in 1869.

46th Corps: Formed at Swinton on 24 February 1860 and in October absorbed the No 12 Company of the 6th Corps.

55th Corps: Formed at Leigh on 3 March 1860. Joined the battalion in October 1861.

60th Corps: Formed at Atherton on 6 March 1860. Joined the battalion in October 1861.

67th Corps: Formed at Worsley on 7 May 1860.

76th Corps: Formed at Farnworth on 3 July 1860.

91st Corps: Formed at Flixton on 14 August 1872.

Headquarters of the battalion moved to Manchester in 1862, to Wigan by the beginning of 1877 and back to Manchester in 1879.

The 4th Admin. was consolidated in 1880 and was at first numbered as 21st Corps. This was changed to 4th, however, by September. Headquarters of the 4th were at Manchester and its thirteen companies organised as follows—

'A' to 'E' Companies at Wigan	Late 21st Corps
'F' Company at Swinton	Late 46th Corps
'G' Company at Eccles	Late 46th Corps
'H' Company at Leigh	Late 55th Corps
'J' Company at Atherton	Late 60th Corps
'K' Company at Worsley	Late 67th Corps
'L' 'M' Companies at Farnworth	Late 76th Corps
'N' Company at Flixton	Late 91st Corps

The 4th Corps became the 1st Volunteer Battalion of the Manchester Regiment in 1888 (Army Order 409) and that regiment's 5th Battalion in 1908.

5TH CORPS

Formed in May 1860 the 2nd Admin. Battalion of Lancashire Rifle Volunteers contained the following Liverpool corps—

5th Corps: Formed on 19 August 1859.

14th Corps: Formed as the 2nd Sub-division at Edge Hill on 10 November 1859. Shown for the first time as 14th Corps in the *Army List* for December 1859.

19th Corps: Formed as the 19th Liverpool Scottish Corps on 18 January 1860. The word 'Scottish' was dropped from the title from March 1860.

39th Corps: Formed on 2 February 1860.

63rd Corps: Formed in the Toxteth Park area on 9 April 1860.

64th Corps: Formed on 25 April 1860.

68th Corps: Formed on 31 May 1860.

71st Corps: Formed on 24 May 1860.

86th Corps: Formed on 18 May 1861.

The 81st Corps was shown in the *Army List* as being included in the battalion for a few months during 1861. It subsequently joined the 8th Admin.

In March 1862 the 2nd Admin. Battalion was consolidated as the 5th Lancashire (The Liverpool Rifle Volunteer Brigade) Rifle Volunteer Corps. Not included in the merger were the 14th Corps which was absorbed into the 1st Corps, the 64th which remained independent and later became the Liverpool Irish Corps and the 71st which remained independent until disbandment in 1863. To make up for the loss of these corps both the 32nd, formed 28 January 1860, and the 79th, formed 16 February 1861 were absorbed.

Attached to the 5th Corps was the 2nd Lancashire Light Horse from 1864 until its disbandment in 1874, the 42nd Corps from 1864 until 1870 and the 15th Corps for a few months during 1866.

The 5th became the 2nd Volunteer Battalion of the King's (Liverpool Regiment) in 1888 (AO81) and in 1908 that regiment's 6th Battalion.

6TH CORPS

The 6th Lancashire Rifle Volunteer Corps was formed in Manchester on 25 August 1859 and by March 1860 was shown in the *Army List* with the additional title, (1st Manchester). The No 12 Company of the 6th was transferred to the 46th Corps in October 1860 but the following year its strength was increased when the 43rd Corps was absorbed. The 43rd had been formed at Fallowfield on 11 February 1860.

Under Army Order 409 of September 1888 the 6th was redesignated as the 2nd Volunteer Battalion of the Manchester Regiment. In 1908 that regiment's 6th Battalion was provided by the 2nd VB except for one company, 'N', which became part of the Manchester University Officers Training Corps.

7TH CORPS

The 7th Admin. Battalion of Lancashire Rifle Volunteers was formed with headquarters at Ashton-Under-Lyne in November 1863. The corps included were as follows—

23rd Corps: Formed at Ashton-Under-Lyne on 7 February 1860.

31st Corps: Formed at Oldham on 1 February 1860.

Upon consolidation in 1880 the 7th Admin. was designated as the 23rd Corps. This was changed to 7th, however, after a few months. Headquarters of the 7th were placed at Ashton-Under-Lyne and the corps' twelve companies were organised as follows—

'A' to 'F' Companies at Ashton-Under-Lyne   Late 23rd Corps
'G' 'H' 'J' and 'K' to 'M' Companies at Oldham   Late 31st Corps

In 1882 the establishment of the corps was reduced to six companies when the Oldham personnel were removed to form a new corps designated as 22nd.

The 7th was redesignated as the 3rd Volunteer Battalion of the Manchester Regiment in 1888 (Army Order 409) and in 1908 provided that regiment's 9th Battalion.

8TH CORPS

The 8th Lancashire Rifle Volunteer Corps was formed at Bùry on 22 August 1859. Attached to the 8th between 1862 and 1869 was the 21st Corps but this was transferred to the 4th Admin. Battalion.

The 8th became the 1st Volunteer Battalion of the Lancashire Fusiliers in February 1883 (General Order 14) and in 1908 that regiment's 5th Battalion. The Bury Grammar School Cadet Corps was formed and affiliated to the battalion in 1892 and in 1908 became part of the Officers Training Corps.

9TH CORPS

The 9th Lancashire Rifle Volunteer Corps was formed at Warrington on 16 September 1859. In 1862 the 49th Corps which was formed at Newton-le-Willows on 3 March 1860 was attached to the 9th for drill and administration.

In September 1865 the 9th Admin. Battalion was created with headquarters at Warrington and included in it was the above corps. The 9th Admin. was consolidated as the 9th Corps in 1880. Headquarters remained at Warrington and the corps' seven companies were organised as follows—

'A' to 'F' Companies at Warrington   Late 9th Corps
'G' Company at Newton-le-Willows   Late 49th Corps

The 9th became the 1st Volunteer Battalion of the South Lancashire Regiment in 1886 (General Order 78 of July) and in 1908 provided that regiment's 4th Battalion.

10TH CORPS

The 37th Lancashire Rifle Volunteer Corps was formed at Ulverston on 29 February 1860 and by May appeared in the *Army List* with the additional title (North Lonsdale). In the *London Gazette* dated 9 April 1861 it is recorded that the 37th is to be divided to form the following corps; 37A at Ulverston, 37B at Barrow, 37C at Hawkshead, 52nd at Dalton, and the 53rd at Cartmel. All corps were to be included in the 5th Admin. Battalion whose headquarters were to be at Ulverston.

Other corps to join the 5th Admin. were—

10th Corps: Formed at Lancaster on 20 September 1859 and joined the battalion in 1862.

65th Corps: Formed at Rossall on 27 April 1860. An entry in *The Times* dated 16 June 1860 records the swearing in of the first members of the 65th. The corps was formed by masters and senior boys of Rossall School and the paper notes that this was the first instance of a large public school enrolling under the provisions of the Volunteer Act. The 65th joined the 5th Admin. in 1863 and in 1873 a cadet corps was formed by the school's junior boys.

75th Corps: The 75th was formed at Broughton-in-Furness on 28 August 1860 but was removed from the *Army List* in February of the following year. The corps returns to the *List* in April 1861 and is now shown as being part of the 5th Admin. The 75th was disbanded in 1863.

The 52nd Corps was absorbed into 37B in 1870 but in 1875 the Dalton personnel were transferred to 37A. The 53rd disappeared from the *Army List* in 1875.

The 5th Admin. Battalion was consolidated as the 10th Corps in 1876. Headquarters were placed at Ulverston and the Corps' nine companies were organised as follows—

'A' 'B' Companies at Lancaster	Late 10th Corps
'C' 'D' Companies at Ulverston	Late 37A Corps
'E' 'F' Companies at Barrow	Late 37B Corps
'G' Company at Hawkshead	Late 37C Corps
'H' Company at Rossall	Late 65th Corps
'J' Company at Grange	Newly-formed

The newly-raised 'J' Company also included a detachment at Cartmel which was formed by members of the old 53rd Corps.

In 1877 two new companies, 'K' and 'L' were formed at Dalton but in 1889 the headquarters of 'L' were transferred to Millom and in 1890 the Rossall Company was disbanded and the cadet corps transferred to the 1st Lancashire Engineer Volunteers.

Under General Order 14 of February 1883 the 10th was redesignated as the 1st Volunteer Battalion of the King's Own (Royal Lancaster Regiment). In 1900 it was decided to split the battalion and form a 2nd VB for the regiment. This was done and the following reorganisation took place—

1st Volunteer Battalion: Headquarters Ulverston
              'A' 'B' Companies at Ulverston
              'C' 'D' Companies at Barrow
              'E' Company at Hawkshead
              'F' Company at Barrow
              'G' Company at Dalton
              'H' Company at Millom

2nd Volunteer Battalion: Headquarters Lancaster
              'A' to 'D' Companies at Lancaster
              'E' Company at Morecambe
              'F' Company at Grange

In 1908 both the 1st and 2nd Volunteer Battalions transferred to the Territorial Force forming the 4th and 5th Battalions of the King's.

11TH CORPS

The 6th Admin. Battalion of Lancashire Rifle Volunteers was formed with headquarters at Preston in September 1861 and included the following corps—

11th Corps: Formed at Preston on 4 October 1859 and in February 1860 absorbed two other Preston corps, the 12th, formed 7 October 1859 and the 30th, formed in the Fishwick area on 16 January 1860. In 1865 (Preston) was also included in the title of the corps. The 44th Corps at Longton was absorbed in 1866 followed by the 61st in November 1868.

44th Corps: Formed at Longton on 2 March 1860 and absorbed into the 11th Corps in 1866.

59th Corps: Formed at Leyland on 29 February 1860.

61st Corps: Formed at Chorley on 6 March 1860 and absorbed into the 11th Corps in 1868.

The battalion was consolidated as the 11th Corps in 1880. Headquarters remained at Preston and the corps' nine companies were organised as follows—

'A' to 'E' Companies at Preston   Late 11th Corps
'F' Company at Leyland   Late 59th Corps
'G' 'H' 'J' Companies at Chorley   Late 11th Corps

The 11th Corps was designated as the 1st Volunteer Battalion of the North Lancashire Regiment in 1883 (General Order 14 of February) and in 1908 provided that regiment's 4th Battalion.

12TH CORPS

The 24th Lancashire Rifle Volunteer Corps was formed at Rochdale on 24 February 1860. The 24th was redesignated as 12th Corps in 1880 and as the 2nd Volunteer Battalion of the Lancashire Fusiliers in 1883 (General Order 14 of February). In 1908 the 2nd VB provided the 6th Battalion of the Lancashire Fusiliers.

13TH CORPS

The 13th Corps of 1880 was formed by the amalgamation of the 13th and 54th Corps. The 13th first appeared in the *Army List* for October 1859 and was listed as the 1st Sub-division at Southport. In the list for December the corps is shown as 13th and with officers' commissions dated 6 December 1859. The 13th was attached to the 1st Corps for drill and administration in 1863 and in 1873 was transferred to the 15th Corps.

Formed at Ormskirk on 15 March 1860 the 54th Corps was attached to the 1st Corps in 1863

The new 13th remained attached to the 15th Corps and in 1888 (Army Order 81 of March) became the 3rd Volunteer Battalion of The King's (Liverpool Regiment). The 3rd VB was disbanded in March 1908.

14TH CORPS

The 3rd Sub-division of Lancashire Rifle Volunteers was formed at Bolton on 2 December 1859. In February 1860 the 3rd SD was increased to a full company and thereafter designated as the 27th Corps. In 1863 the 82nd Corps, formed at Hindley on 14 June 1861 was attached to the 27th, and in 1876 an amalgamation between the two corps took place.

The 27th was renumbered as the 14th Corps in 1880 and in 1883 the title of 2nd Volunteer Battalion, The North Lancashire Regiment was assumed under General Order 14 of February. The 2nd VB provided the regiment's 5th Battalion upon transfer to the Territorial Force in 1908.

15TH CORPS

Formed on 10 January 1860 the 15th Corps had its headquarters in Liverpool. In 1865 the 15th was temporarily attached to the 5th Corps for drill and administration until 1866.

In 1873 both the 13th Lancashire and the 2nd Isle of Man Corps were attached to the 15th. The 13th remained until 1880 and in the same year the Isle of Man Corps was renumbered as 1st and once again attached to the 15th having been removed in 1877. The 1st Isle of Man was transferred to the 19th Corps in 1884.

Under Army Order 81 of March 1888 the 15th became the 4th Volunteer Battalion, The King's (Liverpool Regiment). In 1908 the 4th VB became the 7th Battalion of the King's.

16TH CORPS

The 40th or (3rd Manchester) Corps was formed on 29 February 1860. It was renumbered as 16th in 1880 and in 1888, (Army Order 409 of September) redesignation as the 4th Volunteer Battalion of the Manchester Regiment was assumed. The 7th Battalion of the same regiment was provided in 1908.

17TH CORPS

The 56th Corps was formed at Salford on 5 March 1860 and in 1881 joined the Manchester Regiment as one of its allotted volunteer battalions. No change in designation was assumed and in March 1886 the corps was transferred to the Lancashire Fusiliers and designated as its 3rd Volunteer Battalion. Both the 7th and 8th Battalions of the regiment were provided in 1908.

Attached to the battalion was the Salford Cadet Corps which was formed in July 1888 and disbanded in 1891.

18TH CORPS

The 64th Lancashire Rifle Volunteer Corps was formed in Liverpool on 25 April 1860 and in May was included in the 2nd Admin. Battalion. Upon consolidation of that battalion in 1862 the 64th was made independent and in November 1864 was allowed to include (Liverpool Irish) in its title. The 2nd Isle of Man Corps was attached between 1877 and 1880.

The 64th became the 18th in 1880 and in March 1888 the 5th (Irish) Volunteer Battalion of the King's (Liverpool Regiment). That regiment's 8th Battalion was provided upon transfer to the Territorial Force in 1908.

19TH CORPS

Formed by members of the newspaper and printing trades the 80th Lancashire Rifle Volunteer Corps was formed in Liverpool on 8 January 1861. The additional title, (Liverpool Press Guard) was included in 1862 and in 1863 the 73rd Corps at Newton was absorbed. The 73rd was formed on 8 June 1860.

The 80th became the 19th in 1880 and the 6th Volunteer Battalion of the King's (Liverpool Regiment) in 1888. The 6th VB provided the regiment's 9th Battalion in 1908.

20TH CORPS

Formed at Ardwick on 28 January 1860 the 33rd Corps absorbed the 78th in 1862. The 78th which was also known as the (4th Manchester) Corps was formed on 2 November 1860.

The corps known as the (2nd Manchester) was formed as the 28th Lancashire Rifle Volunteers on 21 February 1860. The 28th absorbed the 70th Corps, formed at Droylesden on 5 May 1860, in 1862 and in 1864 was itself absorbed into the 33rd at Ardwick. From 1864 the 33rd also included (2nd Manchester) in its title.

The 33rd became the 20th in 1880 and in 1888 (Army Order 409 of September) the 5th (Ardwick) Volunteer Battalion of the Manchester Regiment. A cadet corps was formed in 1888 and in 1908 the 5th VB transferred to the Territorial Force as the 8th Manchesters.

21ST CORPS

The 21st Corps was formed in 1880 by the amalgamation of the 47th and 48th Lancashire Corps. The 47th was formed at St Helens on 29 February 1860 while the 48th originated in Preston on 15 March 1860 and was from 1863 attached to the 1st Corps for drill and administration.

The 21st became the 2nd Volunteer Battalion, The South Lancashire Regiment in July 1886 and in 1908 that regiment's 5th Battalion.

22ND CORPS

The 22nd Lancashire Rifle Volunteer Corps was formed on 29 July 1882 by the withdrawal of the Oldham Companies of the 7th Corps. These companies had originated in February 1860 and until 1880 were known as the 31st Corps.

The 22nd became the 6th Volunteer Battalion of the Manchester Regiment under Army Order 409 of September 1888 and in 1908 provided that regiment's 10th Battalion.

Other Lancashire Corps that existed before 1880 and were not involved in the reorganisations of that year were as follows—

25th Corps: Formed at Liverpool on 9 January 1860. The 25th was absorbed into the 8th Lancashire Artillery Volunteers in April 1864.

26th Corps: Formed at Haigh on 9 February 1860 and was disbanded in April 1864.

41st Corps: Formed at Liverpool on 16 February 1860 and disappeared from the *Army List* in February 1864.

42nd Corps: Formed at Childwall on 3 March 1860 and was attached to the 5th Corps in 1864. The 42nd disappeared from the *Army List* in 1870.

51st Corps: Formed in Liverpool on 3 March 1860 and in March 1862 absorbed the 72nd Corps. The 51st disappeared from the *Army List* in August 1866.

72nd Corps: Formed at Old Swan on 8 June 1860 and was absorbed into the 51st Corps in 1862.

77th Corps: Formed at Widnes on 1 October 1860. This corps disappeared from the *Army List* in August 1863.

83rd Corps: Formed at Knowsley on 11 February 1861 and in 1863 was attached to the 1st Corps for drill and administration. The 83rd disappeared from the *Army List* in December 1872.

The 8th (Scottish) Volunteer Battalion of the King's (Liverpool Regiment) was raised by Scotsmen resident in the City of Liverpool during the South African War. Formation date is 4 October 1900 and the establishment of the battalion was set at eight companies. The 8th transferred to the Territorial Force in 1908 as the 10th Battalion of the King's.

Lancashire also formed three cadet battalions. The 1st CB Manchester Regiment was formed in February 1889 followed by the 1st CB King's Liverpools in October 1890. A 2nd CB was formed for the King's in January 1902 which in 1904 was merged with the 1st.

LEICESTERSHIRE

Formed with headquarters at Leicester on 10 July 1860 the 1st Admin. Battalion of Leicestershire Rifle Volunteers contained the following corps—

1st Corps: Formed at Leicester on 31 August 1859.

2nd Corps: Formed at Belvoir on 13 February 1860.

3rd Corps: Formed at Melton Mowbray on 2 March 1860.

4th Corps: Formed at Leicester on 4 March 1860.

5th Corps: Formed at Leicester on 3 March 1860.

6th Corps: Formed at Loughborough on 7 July 1860.

7th Corps: Formed at Lutterworth on 6 October 1860. Disbanded in 1873.

8th Corps: Formed at Ashby-de-la-Zouch on 16 September 1860.

9th Corps: Formed at Leicester on 24 December 1860.

10th Corps: Formed at Hinckley on 27 November 1860.

The battalion was consolidated in 1880 as the 1st Leicestershire Rifle Volunteers. Headquarters remained at Leicester and its eleven companies were organised as follows—

'A' Company at Leicester	Late 1st Corps
'B' Company at Belvoir	Late 2nd Corps
'C' Company at Melton Mowbray	Late 3rd Corps
'D' 'E' Company at Leicester	Late 4th Corps
'F' 'G' Company at Leicester	Late 5th Corps
'H' Company at Loughborough	Late 6th Corps
'J' Company at Ashby-de-la-Zouch	Late 8th Corps
'K' Company at Leicester	Late 9th Corps
'L' Company at Hinckley	Late 10th Corps

In 1882 the establishment of the corps was increased when a new company was raised at Market Harborough. The following year and under General Order 14 of February the corps was redesignated as the 1st Volunteer Battalion, The Leicestershire Regiment.

Yet another increase in the strength of the battalion occurred in 1900 when on this occasion four new companies were formed, two at Leicester; one at Wigston and one at Mountsorrel. With sixteen companies the 1st VB now constituted a 'double battalion'.

When the Territorial Force was created in 1908 the Leicestershire Regiment was allotted two battalions; 4th and 5th. These were provided by the 1st VB as follows; 4th Bn by the Leicester and Wigston personnel; 5th Bn by the remainder less the Belvoir Company which was disbanded.

LINCOLNSHIRE

There were three administrative battalions formed in Lincolnshire to control the various rifle corps formed within the county. Of these the 3rd which was formed on 6 July 1860 with headquarters in Boston contained the 4th, 13th, 14th, 16th and 17th Corps. In 1862 this battalion was broken up and its corps transferred to the 2nd Admin. The 14th, however, which was formed at Swineshead on 6 March 1860, was not included as this company was disbanded in 1861.

The 1st Admin. Battalion was formed on 15 May 1860 with headquarters at Lincoln. The corps included then or upon formation were—

1st Corps: Formed at Lincoln on 26 October 1859.

2nd Corps: The 2nd Corps was formed as the 1st Sub-division on 21 November 1859. Redesignated as 2nd in January of the following year. Headquarters were at Louth.

6th Corps: Formed at Great Grimsby on 20 March 1860.

7th Corps: Formed at Spilsby on 17 March 1860.

9th Corps: Formed at Horncastle on 22 March 1860.

11th Corps: Formed at Alford on 23 February 1860.

12th Corps: Formed at Barton upon Humber as the 1st Sub-division on 12 January 1860. Appeared for the first time as 12th Corps in the *Army List* for March 1860.

19th Corps: Formed at Gainsborough on 10 July 1860.

20th Corps: Formed at Market Rasen on 16 July 1860.

Consolidation as the 1st Lincolnshire Rifle Volunteer Corps came in 1880. Headquarters of the new corps remained at Lincoln and its eleven companies were organised as follows—

'A' 'B' 'C' Companies at Lincoln	Late 1st Corps
'D' Company at Louth	Late 2nd Corps
'E' Company at Great Grimsby	Late 6th Corps
'F' Company at Spilsby	Late 7th Corps
'G' Company at Horncastle	Late 9th Corps
'H' Company at Alford	Late 11th Corps
'I' Company at Barton	Late 12th Corps
'J' Company at Gainsborough	Late 19th Corps
'K' Company at Market Rasen	Late 20th Corps

The headquarters of 'K' Company were moved to Frodingham by 1881 and in 1883 under General Order 63 of May the corps became the 1st Volunteer Battalion of the Lincolnshire Regiment. In 1887 the 1st Lincoln Light Horse Volunteer Corps was disbanded having been attached to the battalion since its formation in 1867.

In 1900 the establishment of the battalion was reduced to seven companies; 'A' 'B' 'C' and 'D' at Lincoln, 'E' and 'F' at Gainsborough and 'G' at Horncastle. The remainder of the battalion was detached to form the 3rd Volunteer Battalion.

Grantham was the headquarters of the 2nd Admin. Battalion which was formed on 21 May 1860. The corps included were—

3rd Corps: Formed at Grantham on 28 February 1860.

5th Corps: Formed at Stamford on 14 February 1860.

8th Corps: Formed at Sleaford on 23 February 1860.

15th Corps: Formed at Bourne on 23 April 1860. This Corps was disbanded in 1873.

18th Corps: Formed at Folkingham on 13 March 1860. Headquarters were moved to Billingborough in 1872.

As previously mentioned the 3rd Admin. Battalion was broken up in 1862 and its corps added to the 2nd. These were—

4th Corps: Formed at Boston on 9 February 1860.

13th Corps: Formed at Spalding on 28 February 1860.

16th Corps: Formed at Holbeach on 20 March 1860. This corps was later disbanded and was last seen in the *Army List* for November 1871.

17th Corps: Formed at Donington on 17 March 1860. Moved to Gosberton in 1876.

Upon consolidation in 1880 the battalion was originally designated as 3rd Corps. This was changed, however, to 2nd after a few months. Headquarters remained at Grantham and the eight companies of the corps were organised as follows—

'A' 'B' Companies at Grantham	Late 3rd Corps
'C' Company at Boston	Late 4th Corps
'D' Company at Stamford	Late 5th Corps
'E' Company at Sleaford	Late 8th Corps
'F' Company at Spalding	Late 13th Corps
'G' Company at Gosberton	Late 17th Corps
'H' Company at Billingborough	Late 18th Corps

The 2nd Corps was designated as the 2nd Volunteer Battalion, The Lincolnshire Regiment in 1883, the change being notified in General Order 63 of that year.

The 3rd Volunteer Battalion of the Lincolnshire Regiment was formed on 20 June 1900 by withdrawing the Louth, Grimsby, Spilsby, Alford, Barton and Frodingham Companies from the 1st VB. Headquarters of the battalion were placed at Grimsby.

Several cadet units have been associated with the Lincolnshire Rifle Volunteers. The first of these was formed at Lincoln Grammar School in 1903 and affiliated to the 1st VB. This was followed in 1904 by a company raised by the King's School in Grantham which became affiliated to the 2nd VB. Two units were connected with the 3rd VB. The King Edward VI Grammar School, Louth provided a company in 1905 which was followed in 1906 by Grimsby Municipal College.

Upon transfer to the Territorial Force in 1908 the 1st, 2nd and 3rd VBs were amalgamated to form the 4th and 5th Battalions of the Lincolnshire Regiment. The reorganisation went as follows—

> 4th Battalion: Formed by the 2nd VB plus the Lincoln and Horncastle companies of the 1st.
>
> 5th Battalion: Formed by the 3rd VB plus the Gainsborough Companies of the 1st.

With the exception of the Lincoln Grammar School, which was not recognised by the TF, all cadet units became part of the Junior Division of the Officers Training Corps.

LINLITHGOWSHIRE

On 8 October 1862 the rifle corps then in existence within the county were grouped together as the 1st Admin. Battalion of Linlithgowshire Rifle Volunteers. Two additional corps were later formed and also included.

1st Corps: Formed at Linlithgow on 19 March 1860.

2nd Corps: Formed at Bo'ness on 19 March 1860.

3rd Corps: Formed at Bathgate on 25 April 1860. Headquarters were transferred to Torphichen in 1864.

4th Corps: Formed at Bathgate on 9 August 1862 its members being recruited in the main from Young's Chemical Works.

5th Corps: Formed at Uphall on 18 March 1872.

6th Corps: Formed at West Calder on 17 April 1878, as one and a half companies.

The battalion, whose headquarters were at Linlithgow, was consolidated as the 1st Linlithgowshire Rifle Volunteers in March 1880. The establishment was set at seven companies which were formed, 'A' to 'E' by the 1st to 5th Corps respectively, 'F', whose headquarters were at Addiewell, by the half company of the 6th Corps and 'G' by the 6th Corps.

In 1881 headquarters of 'C' Company were moved to Armadale and in April 1888 and by Army Order 144, the corps was redesignated as the 8th Volunteer Battalion, The Royal Scots. Before transfer to the Territorial Force in 1908 as the 10th (Cyclist) Battalion of the regiment two new companies were raised. This occurred in 1900 and the additions were, 'H' Company at South Queenferry and 'I' Company at Kirkliston. Also that year 'F' Company moved to Fauldhouse and in 1906 'I' was re-lettered as 'H' after the disbandment of the South Queensbury Company.

LONDON

1ST CORPS

On 14 December 1859 the first officer was commissioned into the City of London Rifle Volunteer Brigade. Ranked as 1st in London the corps soon consisted of fifteen companies which were divided into two battalions.

The first mention of a cadet corps having been formed by the brigade was in the *Army List* for May 1877. There was in fact a unit formed as early as 1860 which according to one source had a strength of some 400 boys.

In 1870 the strength of the brigade was increased when the 12th Tower Hamlets Corps was absorbed. The brigade became a volunteer battalion of the King's Royal Rifle Corps in 1881 but no change in title was assumed.

Included in the *c*1860 cadet unit mentioned above were boys from the Merchant Taylors, City of London, University College and King's College Schools. In 1900 these schools together with the corps mentioned in 1877 are shown in the *Army List* as forming five companies affiliated to the brigade. By 1902 the five appear under the heading of '1st City of London Cadet Corps'. The five companies were later reduced to three when in 1904 University College School transferred to the 20th Middlesex and in 1905 the City of London School Company went to the 2nd London Corps.

In 1908 the brigade became the 5th (City of London) Battalion, The London Regiment. Both Merchant Taylors and King's College Schools became part of the Junior Division, Officers Training Corps.

2ND CORPS

The 2nd London Rifle Volunteer Corps was formed on 16 May 1860. Like the 1st the 2nd was also a strong corps. It consisted of many employees from the newspaper and printing industry, two complete companies were provided by the *Daily Mail*, and was known as the 'Printers Battalion'. The 48th Middlesex Corps was absorbed in 1872. The corps joined the King's Royal Rifle Corps as one of its allotted volunteer battalions in 1881. No change in designation, however, was assumed. In 1908 the battalion became the 6th (City of London) Battalion, The London Regiment. Also in 1908 the City of London School Cadet Corps, which had been transferred to the 2nd Londons in 1905 from the 1st, became part of the Officers Training Corps.

3RD CORPS

The 3rd Corps was formed on 8 March 1861 and in 1881 became a volunteer battalion of the King's Royal Corps. By 1904 the *Army List* shows the corps with the additional (City of) included in its title. In 1908 the 3rd Corps became the 7th (City of London) Battalion, The London Regiment.

4TH CORPS

The first London corps to bear this number was formed on 2 October 1861. It later disappeared from the *Army List* and was not seen again after March 1865.

In 1900 a new 4th Corps appears as having been formed by the Grocer's Company's Schools. The first officers commission was 18 May. With headquarters at Clapton the 4th was attached to the 1st Corps and constituted a volunteer battalion of the King's Royal Rifle Corps. The 4th was disbanded in 1905.

5TH CORPS

The 5th London appeared for the first time in the *Army List* for February 1862. No officers were appointed to it and it was last seen in the *List* for April 1863.

MERIONETHSHIRE

The first unit to bear the title of 1st Merionethshire Rifle Volunteer Corps was formed at Bala on 11 November 1859. This company was disbanded in March 1864. At this time the county's 2nd Corps which was formed at Dolgelly on 15 May 1860, became 1st and was united to the 1st Admin. Battalion of Montgomery Rifle Volunteers. The Dolgelly Corps was also disbanded and was last seen in the *Army List* for February 1872.

A 3rd Corps was raised by the county on 15 September 1860 and is first shown as being formed at Corwen. This was changed to Festiniog in 1861 and in February 1864 the unit disappeared from the *Army List*.

MIDDLESEX

Like the counties of Kent and Essex, Middlesex also recruited its volunteer corps throughout the County of London. Previous to 1880 fifty numbered corps were raised and to administer those of insufficient strength seven administrative battalions were formed. Of the seven only two, the 2nd and 7th, survived up to 1880 and the reorganisations of that year. The 6th was absorbed into the 2nd and the remaining four were broken up and their corps made independent. The 1st Admin. Battalion was formed in August 1860 and had its headquarters at Tyndale Place, Islington. The corps included were the 4th and 7th and the battalion was removed from the *Army List* in March 1861 upon their amalgamation. The 3rd Battalion, whose headquarters were never recorded in the *Army List*, was formed in August 1860. Its corps were the 39th and 40th and the battalion was broken up in April 1861. Also broken up in April 1861 was the 4th Admin. Battalion. The 4th had its headquarters at Cardington Street, Euston and was formed in August 1860 containing the 20th, 29th and 37th Corps. The 5th Admin. which was also formed in August 1860, had its headquarters at Custom House. The corps included were the 26th and 42nd who in 1864 were amalgamated.

In 1880 the remaining two admin. battalions and the surviving independent corps were organised into twenty-five corps. A 26th and 27th were later raised.

1ST CORPS

Upon the general disbandment of volunteers in 1814 the Duke of Cumberland's Sharpshooters, after the most strenuous of efforts, were permitted to continue service. Although not formally recognised as a military organisation the Duke's were allowed to establish themselves as a rifle club. In 1835 permission was granted to style the club as The Royal Victoria Rifle Club and in 1853 sanction to form a volunteer corps was given. As the Victoria Volunteer Rifle Corps, whose first officers' commissions were dated 4 January 1853, the club subsequently, in 1859, became the 1st Middlesex Corps. The additional title of (Victoria) was added by March 1860.

Headquarters of the corps were at Kilburn but these were moved to St John's Wood in 1867. Attached to the 1st in 1863 were the 18th and 47th Corps. The 47th was disbanded in 1865 and in 1870 the 18th was transferred to the 9th Corps. At the same time the 1st became attached to the 11th Corps.

In 1881 the 1st joined the King's Royal Rifle Corps as one of its allotted volunteer battalions although no change in designation was assumed.

Headquarters of the corps were moved to Davies Street, Westminster in 1892 and in that same year, on 1 June, an amalgamation took place with the 6th Corps. From then on the corps became known as the 1st Middlesex (Victoria and St George's) and in 1908 was once again involved in a merger, this time with the 19th Corps, to form the 9th (County of London) Battalion of the London Regiment.

A cadet corps was formed for the 1st corps towards the end of 1866 but this was later disbanded and was last seen in the *Army List* for January 1898.

2ND CORPS

Formed on 14 October 1859 the 2nd Corps first appeared in the *Army List* as the 2nd The South Middlesex Rifle Volunteer Corps. By March 1860 the corps, whose headquarters were at Waltham Green, was styled as the 2nd Middlesex (South Middlesex) Corps.

The 2nd joined the King's Royal Rifle Corps in 1881 as one of its allotted volunteer battalions although no change in designation was assumed. Headquarters were moved to Fulham House, Putney Bridge in 1902 and in that same year the 26th Corps was attached for drill and administration.

A cadet corps was formed for the 2nd in February 1865 but this company was removed from the *Army List* in 1880. In November 1890 a new unit, The St Paul's School, West Kensington Cadet Corps was formed and affiliated to the corps.

In 1908 much of the 2nd, some 300, provided a nucleus for the 10th Battalion of the Middlesex Regiment. Some were also to join the 13th (County of London) Battalion of the London Regiment. The St Paul's School Cadets joined the Officers Training Corps as part of its Junior Division.

3RD CORPS

The 3rd Corps of 1880 was derived from two of the county's admin. battalions the first of which, the 2nd, was formed with headquarters at Highgate on 28 November 1860. The corps included were—

3rd Corps: Formed at Hampstead on 6 December 1859. Permission to include '(Hampstead)' in the title was granted in 1862.

13th Corps: Formed at Hornsey on 2 November 1859.

14th Corps: Formed at Highgate on 2 November 1859. In 1864 a cadet corps was formed for the 14th by Christ College Finchley but this was disbanded in 1867. Corps headquarters were moved to Hornsey in 1870 and then back to Highgate in 1879.

Included in the 6th Admin. Battalion of Middlesex Rifle Volunteers, formed during 1860 with headquarters at Barnet, were the following corps—

12th Corps: Formed at Barnet on 20 October 1859. A cadet corps was formed at the Brunswick House School but this existed for two years only.

33rd Corps: The services of the 33rd (Tottenham and Edmonton) Corps were accepted on 16 February 1860. A cadet corps was formed for the company at Bruce Castle School.

35th Corps: Formed at Enfield on 20 April 1860. Absorbed into the 40th Corps in April 1861.

41st Corps: The services of this corps, which was mainly recruited from employees of the Royal Small Arms Factory at Enfield Lock, were accepted on 11 June 1860.

The two battalions were amalgamated as 2nd on 17 January 1862. Headquarters were moved to Hornsey in October 1870 and in March 1880 the battalion was consolidated as the 3rd Middlesex Rifle Volunteer Corps. Headquarters remained at Hornsey and the nine companies were organised as follows—

'A' Company at Hampstead	Late 3rd Corps
'B' Company at Hampstead	Late 3rd Corps
'C' Company at Barnet	Late 12th Corps
'D' Company at Hornsey	Late 13th Corps
'E' Company at Highgate	Late 14th Corps
'F' Company at Highgate	Late 14th Corps
'G' Company at Tottenham	Late 33rd Corps
'H' Company at Enfield Lock	Late 41st Corps
'I' Company at Enfield Lock	Late 41st Corps

In 1881 the corps became the 1st Volunteer Battalion of the Middlesex Regiment but it was not until 1898 (Army Order 46 of March) that this title was assumed.

During 1881 formation began at Enfield Town of a new company and in 1883 a cadet corps appears in the *Army List* as having been formed at Highgate School.

No officers were appointed to the corps which was removed from the *Army List* by the end of 1884. In 1892, however, the school appears again and this time an officer is listed with a commission dated 5 March.

On 1 April 1908 the 1st VB became the 7th Battalion of the Middlesex Regiment. The Highgate School Cadet Corps transferred to the Officers Training Corps as part of the Junior Division.

4TH CORPS

Formed in Islington during 1859 were the following corps—

4th Corps: Formed on 15 October.

5th Corps: Formed on 27 December.

6th Corps: Formed in November.

7th Corps: Formed on 26 November.

8th Corps: Formed in November.

In June 1860 both the 5th and 6th Corps were absorbed into the 4th and in August the 8th was also included. For a few months in 1860 the *Army List* indicated that the 4th and 7th Corps were part of the 4th Admin. Battalion. They were in fact included in the 1st and are shown as such from December 1860. The 1st Admin. ceased to exist in 1861 when upon the amalgamation of the 4th and 7th the 4th was made independent.

The 1st Middlesex Light Horse Volunteers were attached to the 4th from 1863 until their disbandment in 1866.

The additional title (West London) was given to the corps in July 1864 and in 1881 the 4th joined the King's Royal Rifle Corps as one of its allotted volunteer battalions. Headquarters of the corps were moved to Kensington in 1885 having been situated in the West End of London since 1864.

The 14th Corps was attached to the 4th between 1893 and 1899 and in September 1905 the full title of the corps became 4th Middlesex (Kensington). The next change was in 1908 when the 4th provided the 13th (County of London) Battalion of the London Regiment.

5TH CORPS

The 9th Middlesex Rifle Volunteer Corps was formed on 14 October 1859 and chose for its headquarters the Lord's Cricket Ground at St John's Wood. From February 1860 the corps appeared in the *Army List* as The West Middlesex Rifle Volunteers but in the following month 9th Middlesex (West Middlesex) is the title given. The 18th Corps was attached for drill and administration in 1870.

The 9th was renumbered as 5th in 1880 and the following year became a volunteer battalion of the Royal Fusiliers. Under General Order 99 of July 1883 the 5th was transferred to the King's Royal Rifle Corps.

In 1899 the 18th Corps at Harrow, which had been renumbered as 9th in 1880, was absorbed into the 5th and at the same time its cadet corps at Harrow School affiliated. On 1 April 1902 the Harrow School Cadets were withdrawn from the 5th Corps and constituted as the 27th Middlesex Volunteer Rifle Corps. They remained as such until January 1906 when the 27th was disbanded and its personnel returned to the 5th Corps as a cadet company.

The 5th became the 9th Battalion of the Middlesex Regiment in 1908 and the school part of the Officers Training Corps.

6TH CORPS

The 11th (St George's) Corps was renumbered as 6th Corps in 1880 having been formed on 14 January 1860 in the Parish of St George's, Westminster. The 32nd Corps was attached in 1863 and remained with the 11th until disbandment in 1868. In 1870 the 1st Corps, which had just been reduced in strength, was also attached.

The 6th joined the King's Royal Rifle Corps in 1881 and was to serve as one of its volunteer battalions until 1892 when it was amalgamated with the 1st Corps to form the 1st (Victoria and St George's) Volunteer Rifles.

7TH CORPS

The services of a rifle corps composed of Scotsmen living in the London area were accepted by the War Office on 2 November 1859. The corps consisted of six companies and was designated as the 15th Middlesex (London Scottish) Rifle Volunteers. Corps headquarters were placed at 8 Adelphi Terrace and the six companies were located as follows—

No 1 (Highland)	10 Pall Mall, East.
No 2 (City)	The Oriental Bank.
No 3 (Northern)	Rosemary Hall, Islington.
No 4 (Central)	Scottish Corporation House.
No 5 (Southern)	68 Jermyn Street.
No 6 (Western)	Chesterfield House.

In 1861 No 2 Company became No 7 and a new No 2 together with a No 8 were raised. No 3 Company was absorbed into the rest in 1865 and the following year company numbers were replaced by letters. This required the following reorganisation—

'A' Company	Formed from No 1
'B' Company	Newly-raised
'C' Company	Formed from No 4
'D' Company	Formed from No 5
'E' Company	Formed from No 2 and No 6
'F' Company	Formed from No 7
'G' Company	Left vacant
'H' Company	Formed from No 8

The 15th was renumbered as 7th in September 1880 and the following year a new 'G' Company was formed. At the same time the corps became a volunteer battalion of the Rifle Brigade but no change in designation was assumed. 'I' and 'K' Companies were formed in 1884.

The 7th became the 14th (County of London) Battalion, The London Regiment upon transfer to the Territorial Force in 1908 having moved its headquarters to Adam Street in 1873 and to Buckingham Gate in 1886.

8TH CORPS

The 7th Admin. Battalion of Middlesex Rifle Volunteers was formed with headquarters at Whitton Park, Hounslow in April 1861. It was also permitted the additional title (South West Middlesex) and the corps included were as follows—

16th Corps: Formed at Hounslow on 6 January 1860.

24th Corps: Formed at Uxbridge on 22 February 1860.

30th Corps: Formed at Ealing on 29 February 1860.

43rd Corps: Formed at Hampton on 25 September 1860. The 43rd absorbed the 45th Corps in 1863 and in 1870 moved its headquarters to Sunbury.

44th Corps: Formed at Staines on 7 December 1860.

45th Corps: Formed at Sunbury on 20 December 1860 and was absorbed into the 43rd Corps in 1863.

The battalion was consolidated as the 16th (South West Middlesex) Corps in 1880 but this was changed to 8th after a few months. Headquarters remained at Hounslow and the corps' eight companies were organised as follows—

'A' to 'D' Companies at Hounslow	Late 16th Corps
'E' Company at Uxbridge	Late 24th Corps
'F' Company at Ealing	Late 30th Corps
'G' Company at Sunbury	Late 43rd Corps
'H' Company at Staines	Late 44th Corps

The 8th was redesignated as the 2nd Volunteer Battalion, The Middlesex Regiment in 1887 and in 1908 became that regiment's 8th Battalion.

A cadet corps is shown as having been formed by the battalion in 1901 and from May 1904 is listed as being provided by Ealing Schools. This unit was affiliated to the 8th Battalion after 1908.

9TH CORPS

The 18th Middlesex Rifle Volunteer Corps was formed with headquarters at Harrow on 30 December 1859. Much of the corps was recruited from the staff and senior members of Harrow School which in 1870 also provided a cadet corps. The 18th was attached to the 1st Corps in 1863 but in 1870 was transferred to the 9th.

The 18th was renumbered as 9th in 1880 and the following year joined the Royal Fusiliers as one of its allotted volunteer battalions. It was transferred to the King's Royal Rifle Corps in 1883 (General Order 99 of July) and in 1899 was amalgamated with the 5th Corps.

10TH CORPS

The 19th Middlesex Corps was formed on 13 December 1859 by members of the Working Men's College in Bloomsbury. By 1862 the corps consisted of nine companies of which three were supplied by the college and the remainder by the St John's and Literate Institutes and the Price Belmont Works at Battersea.

The 19th became the 10th Corps in 1880 and in 1881 was allotted to the King's Royal Rifle Corps as one of its volunteer battalions. No change in designation was assumed but in 1883, under General Order 99 of July, the 10th transferred to the Royal Fusiliers as its 1st Volunteer Battalion. In 1908 the 1st VB transferred to the Territorial Force as the 1st (City of London) Battalion of the London Regiment.

11TH CORPS

On 13 December 1859 the 20th Corps was formed with headquarters at Euston Square. The corps was raised in the main by employees of the London and North Western Railway Company. The 20th was placed in the 4th Admin. Battalion upon its formation in August 1860 but in May of the following year was made independent.

In 1880 the 20th was redesignated as the 11th (Railway) Corps and in 1881 was allotted to the King's Royal Rifle Corps as one of its volunteer battalions. Under General Order 237 of 1882 the 11th was transferred to the Middlesex Regiment and in 1890 (General Order 74 of March) was again transferred this time to the Royal Fusiliers and as its 3rd Volunteer Battalion.

The corps occupied several headquarters in the Euston area and in 1908 became the 3rd (City of London) Battalion of the London Regiment.

12TH CORPS

During 1860 the following Middlesex corps were formed by Government departments—

21st Corps: Formed on 2 January by the Audit Office and Post Office. Headquarters Somerset House.

27th Corps: Formed on 10 February by the Inland Revenue. Headquarters Somerset House.

31st Corps: Formed on 25 February by various offices in Whitehall.

34th Corps: Formed on 22 February at the Admiralty.

From the very beginning of the Volunteer Movement it had been intended to merge all units raised by government departments into one corps. This was later achieved and in June 1860 the above corps were amalgamated under the title of 21st Middlesex (Civil Service) Rifle Volunteers. Headquarters were placed at Somerset House and the eight companies were organised as follows—

'A' (Audit Office) Company
'B' (Post Office) Company
'C' (Post Office) Company
'D' (Inland Revenue) Company
'E' (Inland Revenue) Company
'F' (Whitehall) Company
'G' (Whitehall) Company
'H' (Admiralty) Company

In July 1866 an additional company, 'K', was raised by clerks and senior members of the Bank of England and at the same time the two 'Whitehall' Companies, 'F' and 'G', were amalgamated as 'G'.

On 1 December 1875 the first officer was commissioned to the 50th Middlesex (Bank of England) Rifle Volunteer Corps. This new unit was attached to the 21st and consisted of porters and messengers from the bank.

The 21st was renumbered as the 12th Corps in September 1880 and in the following year joined the King's Royal Rifle Corps as one of its allotted volunteer battalions. No change in designation, however, was assumed. The next change in title was in May 1898 when the corps became known as The Prince of Wales's Own 12th Middlesex (Civil Service) Rifle Volunteers. His Royal Highness had been Hon Colonel of the corps since its formation.

Two new companies were raised in 1900 and designated as 'F' and 'I'. The former was recruited from employees of the London County Council and the latter consisted of all cyclists.

In 1902 the 26th Corps, which had been attached to the 12th since 1893, was transferred to the 2nd and in 1907 the Bank of England Corps, now 25th, was disbanded.

Upon transfer to the Territorial Force in April 1908 the 12th Corps became the 15th (County of London) Battalion, The London Regiment. The Civil Service Cadet Corps, which had been formed in 1903, continued its association and was eventually recognised by the TF in 1911.

13TH CORPS

The 13th Corps was originally formed as the 22nd (Queen's) Rifle Volunteers at Pimlico on 25 February 1860. Headquarters are given as Westminster from March 1860.

The 22nd was renumbered as 13th in 1880 and in 1881 joined the King's Royal Rifle Corps as one of its allotted volunteer battalions.

By 1900 the establishment of the corps had reached sixteen companies distributed as follows—

'A' to 'D' Pimlico Division	'E' 'F', St John's Division
'G' St Margaret's Division	'H' St James' Division
'I' 'K' St Martin's Division	'L' Shoolbread Company
'M' St Clement Dane's Division	'O' Royal Welsh
'R' Greater Westminster	'S' Mounted Infantry
'T' Cyclists	

A cadet corps was also formed in November 1900.

The 13th became the 16th (County of London) Battalion, The London Regiment in 1908.

14TH CORPS

Formed at Lincoln's Inn on 15 February 1860 the 23rd (Inns of Court) Corps was renumbered as 14th in 1880. Without any change in designation the corps joined the Rifle Brigade in 1881 as one of its allotted volunteer battalions. The 26th Corps was attached in 1889 and in 1893 the 14th was itself attached to the 4th Corps until 1899. The St Peter's College, Westminster Cadet Corps was formed and affiliated to the 14th in May 1902 and was from May 1904 shown in the *Army List* simply as Westminster School.

It was the intention in 1908 to transfer the 14th to the Territorial Force as the 27th Battalion of the London Regiment. The regiment was not happy with this designation and chose to continue service as the Inns of Court Officers Training Corps.

15TH CORPS

The 5th Admin. Battalion of Middlesex Rifle Volunteers was formed in October 1860 and contained the 26th and 42nd Corps.

26th Corps: Formed on 9 February 1860 by Customs Officers in the London Docks. Headquarters were at Custom House.

42nd Corps: Formed on 19 June 1860 from employees of St Catherine's Docks.

In 1864 the 26th Corps was amalgamated with the 9th Tower Hamlets Rifle Volunteers which was formed by members of the London Docks. From 1864 the title of the corps became 15th Middlesex (The Customs and the Docks) Rifle Volunteers. By 1866 the other member of the 5th Admin., which had now ceased to exist, was absorbed into the 26th and at the same time the 2nd Middlesex Artillery Volunteer Corps was attached for administration.

The 26th absorbed the 8th Tower Hamlets, another dockland corps, in 1868 and in 1880 was renumbered as 15th. The corps joined the Rifle Brigade in 1881 as one of its allotted volunteer battalion.

In 1908 the 15th Middlesex and the 2nd Tower Hamlets were amalgamated to form the 17th (County of London) Battalion of the London Regiment.

16TH CORPS

The 28th Corps was formed on 28 February 1860 and by July was shown in the *Army List* as the 28th (London Irish) Corps. The first headquarters occupied by the 28th were at Burlington House. These were moved to York Buildings, Adelphi in 1866, to Leicester Square in 1869 and to King William Street in 1873.

The 28th became the 16th Corps in 1880 and the following year became a volunteer battalion of the Rifle Brigade. Yet another move, this time to Duke Street, Charing Cross, occurred in 1897 and in 1908 the corps became the 18th (County of London) Battalion of the London Regiment.

17TH CORPS

The 29th Corps was formed at St Pancras on 1 March 1860 and in August of the same year was included in the 4th Admin. Battalion of Middlesex Rifle Volunteers.

The 29th was removed from the 4th Admin. in December 1860 and in 1861 moved its headquarters to the Regent's Park area. In 1864 the corps was given permission to include (North Middlesex) as part of its title and in the same year headquarters were moved yet again this time to Camden Town.

The 29th became the 17th Corps in 1880 and in 1881 joined the Middlesex Regiment as one of its allotted volunteer battalions. In 1908 the corps transferred to the Territorial Force as the 19th (County of London) Battalion, The London Regiment.

18TH CORPS

Formed in Paddington on 29 February 1860 the 36th Corps became the 18th in 1880. It joined the Rifle Brigade in 1881 and in 1908 became the 10th (County of London) Battalion, The London Regiment.

19TH CORPS

The 37th Corps was formed on 31 March 1860 with headquarters at the Local Board of Works, Holborn. The corps joined the 4th Admin. in August 1860 but was made independent in May of the following year.

In 1861 headquarters were moved to the Foundling Hospital and in 1869 the corps was given permission to include (St Giles and St George's, Bloomsbury) in its title.

The 37th became the 19th in 1880 and in 1881 joined the Rifle Brigade as one of its volunteer battalions. Headquarters were moved to Chenies Street, Bedford Square in 1887 and in 1908 after amalgamation with the 1st Corps the 19th became the 9th (County of London) Battalion of The London Regiment.

20TH CORPS

On 25 May 1860 a corps of rifle volunteers was formed and numbered as the 38th Middlesex. Headquarters were placed at Burlington House and the corps included painters, sculptors, musicians, architects, actors and other members of artistic occupations.

In 1869 headquarters were moved to The Arts Club, Hanover Square and in 1877 the corps were given permission to include (Artists) in its title.

Renumbered as the 20th in 1880 the corps joined the Rifle Brigade in 1881 and in 1908 became the 28th (County of London) Battalion, The London Regiment.

Attached to the 20th in 1904 was the University College School Cadet Corps. This unit had previously been affiliated to the 1st London Corps and in 1908 became part of the Junior Division of the Officer Training Corps.

21ST CORPS

Included in the 3rd Admin. Battalion upon its formation in August 1860 was the 39th Corps. The 39th had been formed at Clerkenwell on 6 March 1860.

The corps was removed from the 3rd Admin. in 1861 and in September 1862 the 39th was allowed to include (The Finsbury Rifle Volunteer Corps) in its title.

The 39th became the 21st in 1880 and in 1881 joined the Rifle Brigade as one of its volunteer battalions. The corps was transferred to the King's Royal Rifle Corps in 1883 and in 1908 became the 11th (County of London) Battalion, The London Regiment.

22ND CORPS

The 40th Middlesex Rifle Volunteer Corps was formed at Gray's Inn on 30 April 1860 and in August was placed into the 3rd Admin. Battalion. In 1861 the corps appeared in the *Army List* with the additional title (Gray's Inn Rifle Rangers) but before the end of that year (Central London Rifle Rangers) was substituted.

In April 1861 the 40th absorbed the 35th which had been formed at Enfield on 26 March 1860 and hitherto been part of the 6th Admin. Battalion. At the same time the 40th was removed from the 3rd Admin. and made independent.

The 40th became the 22nd Corps in 1880 and in 1881 joined the Royal Fusiliers as one of its volunteer battalions. The corps was transferred to the King's Royal Rifle Corps in 1882 (General Order 237) and in 1908 became the 12th (County of London) Battalion of the London Regiment.

In 1891 the Mayall College Cadet Corps at Herne Hill was transferred to the 22nd from the 8th Surrey Corps. This company was removed from the *Army List* during 1899.

23RD CORPS

The 46th Corps was formed on 16 April 1861 with headquarters at Victoria Street, Westminster and in 1880 was renumbered as the 23rd Corps. Under General Order 99 of July 1883 the 23rd was redesignated as the 2nd Volunteer Battalion, The Royal Fusiliers and in 1908 provided the 2nd (City of London) Battalion of the London Regiment.

Affiliated to the battalion in 1900 was the St John's, Westminster Cadet Corps which had been formed in October. This company was not recognised by the Territorial Force in 1908.

24TH CORPS

The formation of a rifle corps at the General Post Office in London was sanctioned by the War Office on 13 February 1868. Designated as the 49th Middlesex the new corps consisted of seven companies and was recruited from the minor staff of the Post Office. Senior members were already serving as part of the 21st (Civil Service) Corps.

'A' Company Formed by staff of the E.C. District.

'B' Company Formed by staff of the Inland Office.

'C' Company Formed by staff of the Newspaper and Money-Order offices.

'D' Company Formed by staff of the W.C. District.

'E' Company Formed by staff of the W., S.W. and S. Districts.

'F' Company Formed by staff of the N. and N.W. Districts.

'G' Company Formed by staff of the E. and S.E. Districts.

In June 1869 a new company, 'H', was formed by the S.W. District. This was followed in July 1870 by 'I' Company which was raised by the Telegraph Branch. By the end of 1876 sufficient numbers had been attained by the E. and S.E. Districts to increase the establishment by one company. From January 1877 'G' Company was recruited from E. District only while the S.E. men provided the new 'K'.

The 49th was renumbered as 24th in September 1880 and in the following year the corps became one of the volunteer battalions allotted to the Rifle Brigade. No change in designation, however, was assumed.

On 18 July 1882 the War Office approved a scheme for the formation by the 24th of an Army Postal Corps. The idea of the new unit was for it to undertake all the postal duties connected with an army on active service overseas.

The Army Post Office Corps was to consist of two officers and 100 men all recruited from the 24th. Of these two officers and fifty men were to serve overseas while the remainder remained at home as part of the Army Reserve. Within a short time nearly all the officers and 350 of the men had volunteered their services and on 8 August the APOC detachment embarked to joined the expeditionary force then in Egypt.

In 1883 the telegraph company, 'I', was recruited up to 200. It was subsequently divided into two divisions, 'A' and 'B', and shown in the *Army List* as 'Field Telegraph Companies'.

Formation of a Field Telegraph Corps was authorised in 1884 and was to be run along the same lines as the APOC. The FTC was to consist of fifty rank and file and when formed was duly enrolled upon the reserve strength of the Royal Engineers.

In 1889 both the APOC and the FTC were constituted as companies of the 24th. The former provided 'M' Company while the telegraph personnel formed 'L'.

Additional companies were raised during the Boer War period and in 1908 the 24th became the 8th (City of London) Battalion, The London Regiment (Post Office Rifle).

25TH CORPS

In July 1866 the clerks and senior staff of the Bank of England raised a company of rifle volunteers which was to become part of the 21st (Civil Service) Corps. On 1 December 1875 a new company was formed this time by the porters and messengers of the bank. The new unit on this occasion did not join the 21st and instead constituted a separate corps designated as the 50th Middlesex (Bank of England) Rifle Volunteers. It was, however, attached to the 21st for drill and administration.

The Bank of England Corps was disbanded with effect from 1 April 1907 having been renumbered as 25th in 1880.

26TH CORPS

The 26th Corps was raised in 1888 and bears the distinction of being the first volunteer corps completely dedicated to a cyclist roll. Notification of the acceptance of the corps services was received on 11 February. It was organised into three troops which were lettered 'A', 'B' and 'C' and received the title 26th Middlesex (Cyclist) Rifle Volunteer Corps, although according to the *London Gazette* of 24 February 1888 the word 'Rifle' was not included.

Upon formation the 26th was allotted to the King's Royal Rifle Corps as one of its volunteer battalions. In 1889, however, it was transferred to the Rifle Brigade and at the same time attached to the 14th Corps for drill. This association was to last until 1893 when the Cyclists became attached to the 12th Civil Service Corps. Yet another change was made in 1902, this time to the 2nd Corps.

The first headquarters to be recorded in the *Army List* were at Ashley Place S.W. but by the end of 1888 a move had been made to Hare Court E.C. This was to be the first of a series of moves by the corps. In 1890 No 2 Queen's Road, West Chelsea was taken over as HQ. This was followed in 1899 by No 69 Lillie Road, West Brompton and in 1904 by Horseferry Road, Wetminster.

In 1908 the 26th became the 25th (County of London) (Cyclist) Battalion of the London Regiment.

27TH CORPS

On 1 April 1902 the cadet corps formed by Harrow School and hitherto attached to the 5th Middlesex became a corps in its own right. The new corps was designated as the 27th Middlesex (Harrow School) Volunteer Rifles and allotted to the King's Royal Rifle Corps as one of its volunteer battalions.

The 27th appeared as such for the last time in the *Army List* for April 1906 being officially disbanded on 31 January. It reappeared as the Harrow School Cadet Corps, affiliated to the 5th Middlesex, and subsequently, in 1908, became part of the Junior Division, Officers Training Corps.

CADET BATTALIONS

Formation of the 2nd Cadet Battalion of the Queen's (Royal West Surrey Regiment) has already been recorded in this work under the Surrey section. As mentioned the 2nd CB Queen's became the 1st CB King's Royal Rifle Corps in 1894. At this time a new headquarters was found at Finsbury Square E.C. and the boys then recruited from the London area.

The next cadet battalion to be formed and associated with Middlesex Rifle Volunteers was on 8 May 1901. This was designated as the 1st CB Royal Fusiliers and had its headquarters in St Pancras. A move to Pond Street in Hampstead was, however, made in 1904.

In 1900 over half the strength of the 1st CB KRRC, which at that time stood at 700, volunteered for service in South Africa. Subsequently some ninety-six members went overseas and in doing so earned for their battalion the battle honour 'South Africa 1900–02'. This also granted the battalion the distinction of being the only cadet unit to hold a battle honour.

Both the 1st CB KRRC and the 1st CB Royal Fusiliers continued their associations with their regiments after 1908.

Other Middlesex Corps were—

10th Corps: It was intended to raise a 10th Corps with headquarters at Marylebone and its existence is recorded in the *Army List* for the first time in November 1859. No officers were gazetted and the corps was removed in February 1860.

25th Corps: The February 1860 *Army List* indicates that a 25th Corps was to be formed at St Martin's in The Fields. No officers were gazetted and the corps was removed in March 1860.

32nd Corps: Formed with headquarters in Seymore Place, Marylebone on 14 February 1860. The 32nd was attached to the 11th Corps in 1863 until its disbandment in 1868.

47th Corps: Formed at Stanmore on 13 January 1862 and attached to the 1st Corps in 1863. The 47th was disbanded in 1865.

48th Corps: Formed on 27 February 1862 with headquarters at Lincoln's Inn Fields. The corps was raised by the cartoonist George Cruikshank who had previously been involved with the 24th Surrey Corps. The 48th was, like the 24th Surrey, formed from members of the Temperance League and consisted entirely of total abstainers. Included in the title of the corps was '(or Havelock's)', General Sir Henry Havelock being one of the noted leaders of the Temperance Movement. The 48th was absorbed into the 2nd London Corps in January 1872.

MIDLOTHIAN

The 1st Midlothian Rifle Volunteer Corps originated in 1859 when four companies were raised on 6 December at Leith. By 1861 eight companies were in existence which in 1863 were increased to nine upon the absorption of the 4th Midlothian Corps at Corstorphine. The 4th had been raised on 26 November 1860 and had since then been attached to the 1st.

Redesignation as the 5th Volunteer Battalion, The Royal Scots was notified in Army Order 144 of 1888. A cyclist company was raised in 1900 and in 1908 the battalion transferred to the Territorial Force as the 7th Bn Royal Scots.

The remaining Midlothian corps were all placed into the 1st Admin. Battalion of Midlothian Rifle Volunteers which was formed on 22 January 1862 with headquarters at Dalkeith.

2nd Corps: Formed at Dalkeith on 22 May 1860.

3rd Corps: The 3rd Corps was formed on 22 May 1860 with a strength of three companies. Headquarters and No 1 Company were at Penicuik, No 2 at Valleyfield and No 3 which was disbanded in 1864, at Roslin.

5th Corps: Formed at Musselburgh on 19 April 1861.

6th Corps: Formed at Loanhead on 29 April 1876.

In 1863 the 1st, 2nd and 3rd Peebleshire Corps were added to the battalion. The 2nd Peebles was disbanded ten years later and in 1880 the battalion was consolidated as the 2nd Midlothian Rifle Volunteer Corps. Headquarters were placed at Penicuik and the eleven companies were organised as follows—

'A' Company at Dalkeith	Late 2nd Midlothian Corps
'B' Company at Dalkeith	Late 2nd Midlothian Corps
'C' Company at Dalkeith	Late 2nd Midlothian Corps
'D' Company at Dalkeith	Late 2nd Midlothian Corps
'E' Company at Penicuik	Late 3rd Midlothian Corps
'F' Company at Valleyfield	Late 3rd Midlothian Corps
'G' Company at Musselburgh	Late 5th Midlothian Corps
'H' Company at Loanhead	Late 6th Midlothian Corps
'I' Company at Peebles	Late 1st Peebles Corps
'K' Company at Peebles	Late 1st Peebles Corps
'L' Company at Inverleithen	Late 3rd Peebles Corps

The sub-title (Midlothian and Peebleshire) was also held by the 2nd Corps which in 1888 (Army Order 144 of April) was redesignated as the 6th Volunteer Battalion of the Royal Scots.

In 1895 the headquarters of 'D' Company was moved to Bonnyrigg and in 1907 that for the battalion to Peebles. The following year the 6th and 7th Volunteer Battalions of the regiment were merged as the 8th Battalion, The Royal Scots, the 6th VB providing four companies.

MONMOUTHSHIRE

The 1st Admin. Battalion of Monmouthshire Rifle Volunteers was formed in August 1860. Headquarters were placed at Newport and the corps included then or upon formation were as follows—

1st Corps: Formed at Chepstow on 9 September 1859.

3rd Corps: Formed at Newport on 11 February 1860. Appeared for the first time in the *Army List* for March 1860 as 2nd Corps but in the following month was listed as 3rd.

4th Corps: Formed at Tredegar on 17 February 1860. This corps was later disbanded and last seen in the *Army List* for March 1864. A new 4th Corps was later formed but this was included in the 2nd Admin. Battalion.

10th Corps: Formed at Risca on 19 November 1860. Disappeared in 1875.

11th Corps: Formed at Tredegar on 12 October 1878.

The battalion was consolidated as the 1st Monmouthshire Rifle Volunteer Corps in 1880. Headquarters remained at Newport and the companies were organised as follows—

'A' Company at Chepstow	Late 1st Corps
'B' 'C' Companies at Newport	Late 3rd Corps
'D' 'E' Companies at Pantegmister	Late 3rd Corps
'F' Company at Tredegar	Late 11th Corps
'G' Company at Bassaleg	Newly-formed

Under General Order 70 of July 1885 the 1st Corps became the 2nd Volunteer Battalion, The South Wales Borderers. The strength of the battalion grew steadily until in 1900 the establishment stood at eleven companies. In 1908 the 2nd VB became the 1st Battalion of the Monmouthshire Regiment.

The 2nd Monmouthshire Corps was formed at Pontypool on 31 December 1859. It first appeared in the *Army List* as 3rd Corps but from April 1860 was listed as 2nd. The 11th Corps was absorbed into the 2nd in May 1861, having been formed on 21 November 1860.

The 2nd Corps became the 3rd Volunteer Battalion of the South Wales Borderers in 1885, the change being notified in General Order 70 of that year. The establishment reached ten companies in 1900 and in 1908 the 3rd VB became the 2nd Battalion of the Monmouthshire Regiment.

The 3rd Corps of 1880 was formed as a result of the consolidation that year of the 2nd Admin. Battalion. The 2nd had been formed in September 1860 and had its headquarters at Pontypool. Included in the battalion were the following corps—

4th Corps: The original 4th Corps had been disbanded in 1864 and until then was included in the 1st Admin. Battalion. A new 4th was formed at Blaenavon in 1866 from part of the 5th Corps.

5th Corps: Formed at Pontypool on 11 February 1860. One company of the 5th was recruited at Blaenavon. In 1866 this portion of the unit was withdrawn to form the 4th Corps.

6th Corps: Formed at Monmouth on 29 February 1860.

7th Corps: Formed at Newport on 1 March 1860.

8th Corps: Formed at Usk on 14 June 1860.

9th Corps: Formed at Abergavenny on 11 August 1860.

Upon consolidation the battalion took on the number of its senior corps and was for a few months known as the 4th. Headquarters remained at Pontypool and the corps' eight companies were organised as follows—

'A' Company at Blaenavon	Late 4th Corps
'B' Company at Pontypool	Late 5th Corps
'C' Company at Monmouth	Late 6th Corps
'D' 'E' 'F' Companies at Newport	Late 7th Corps
'G' Company at Usk	Late 8th Corps
'H' Company at Abergavenny	Late 9th Corps

The 3rd Corps became the 4th Volunteer Battalion of the South Wales Borderers under General Order 70 of July 1885. The strength of the battalion reached ten companies in 1900 and in 1904 a cadet corps was provided by the Monmouth Grammar School. Headquarters of the battalion were moved to Newport in 1901.

In 1908 the 4th VB became the 3rd Battalion, The Monmouthshire Regiment. The cadet corps was eventually recognised by the TF in 1911 and affiliated to the 2nd Monmouths.

MONTGOMERYSHIRE

The 1st Admin. Battalion of Montgomeryshire Rifle Volunteers was formed with headquarters at Welshpool on 28 March 1861. In addition to Montgomeryshire corps the battalion also included the 2nd (later 1st) Cardiganshire and the 1st Merionethshire. Both joined in 1864 and were disbanded in 1866 and 1872 respectively. The Montgomeryshire Corps were—

1st Corps: Formed at Newtown on 19 February 1860. Disbanded in 1872.

2nd Corps: Formed at Welshpool on 26 March 1860. Disbanded in 1876.

3rd Corps: Formed at Welshpool on 14 August 1860. Disbanded in 1872.

4th Corps: Formed at Machynlleth on 10 January 1861. Disbanded in March 1864.

5th Corps: Formed at Lanidloes on 2 March 1861. Became 4th Corps upon the disbandment of the above unit in 1864. Disbanded in 1876.

Battalion headquarters were moved to Newtown in 1864 and then back to Welshpool in 1870. Due to a steady fall off in numbers the 1st Admin. was broken up and its corps added to the 1st Shropshire Admin. in 1873. This was not popular with the 2nd and 4th and led to many resignations. Both corps were disbanded in 1876.

The county once again provided rifle volunteers in 1897 when on 1 April the 5th Volunteer Battalion of the South Wales Borderers was formed at Newtown. Establishment was four companies.

Two new companies were later added and according to the *Territorial Yearbook* of 1909 one of them, 'E', was formed by Aberystwyth University College on 17 March 1900.

In 1908 the 5th VB formed Headquarters and four companies of the 7th Battalion, Royal Welsh Fusiliers. The University College personnel became part of the Senior Division of the Officers Training Corps.

NAIRN

Formed as one company on 14 April 1860, the 1st Corps was the only rifle volunteer unit to be raised within the county. Headquarters were at Nairn and in 1862, due to a fall off in numbers, the corps was disbanded.

NEWCASTLE-UPON-TYNE

Formation of the 1st Newcastle-upon-Tyne Rifle Volunteers began in 1859 when the Newcastle Rifle Club decided to form a corps. By the end of the year sufficient names had been enrolled to form a battalion of nine companies. This was done and on 22 February 1860 the first officers were gazetted.

The nine companies were made up from all sections of the Newcastle community. Each was given names such as the 'Quaysiders' or 'Oddfellows' and there was even a kilted company which was recruited from Scotsmen resident in the city. One company, which required its members to be six feet or more in height, was sub-titled 'Guards'.

An increase in establishment to thirteen companies was achieved by 1861 but this was later reduced to eight. Redesignation as the 3rd Volunteer Battalion of the Northumberland Fusiliers was notified in General Order 14 of February 1883. Two new companies were formed in 1900 and in 1908 the 3rd VB became the 6th Battalion, The Northumberland Fusiliers. One of the companies raised in 1900 was by members of Durham University. They were designated as 'K' and in 1908 provided part of the newly-raised Officers Training Corps.

NORFOLK

In the *Army List* for February 1860 the 1st, 2nd and 3rd Norfolk Corps are shown as having been amalgamated under the title of 1st City of Norwich Rifle Volunteers. All three companies were situated in Norwich and were formed in 1859 on 31 August, 15th and 2nd September respectively. By the following month the corps appeared as the 1st Norfolk (City of Norwich) RVC. The 1st Norfolk Mounted Rifles, later Light Horse, was attached to the corps from March 1861 until its disbandment in 1867.

In 1883 the 1st Corps, which consisted of six companies, was redesignated as the 1st Volunteer Battalion of the Norfolk Regiment. A cadet corps was formed by the battalion in 1893 but in January 1895 this was absorbed into the 1st Cadet Battalion.

In 1908 and after amalgamation with the 4th VB the 1st VB became the 4th Battalion, The Norfolk Regiment.

The 4th Norfolk Rifle Volunteer Corps was formed on 3 September 1859 and by July 1860 was permitted to include the name of its headquarters, (Great Yarmouth), in its title. In the *Army List* for September 1860 the corps is shown as 2nd and filling the gap left by the Norwich Company at the beginning of the year.

With an establishment of five companies the 2nd Corps managed to remain independent of any administrative battalion. In 1876, however, it appears as being 'temporarily' attached to the 1st Corps. By the beginning of 1877 we find the 2nd, together with the 4th, 14th and 17th Corps from the neighbouring county of Suffolk, forming the 1st Admin. Battalion of Norfolk Rifle Volunteers. This battalion was consolidated in March 1880 as the 2nd Norfolk (Norfolk and Suffolk) Corps. It contained nine companies with headquarters at Great Yarmouth and was organised as follows—

'A' 'B' 'C' 'D' Companies at Gt Yarmouth	Late 2nd Norfolk.
'E' Company at Gorleston	New company formed upon consolidation in Norfolk.
'F' Company at Bungay	Late 4th Suffolk.
'G' Company at Beccles	Late 14th Suffolk.
'H' 'I' Companies at Lowestoft	Late 17th Suffolk.

Redesignation as the 2nd Volunteer Battalion, The Norfolk Regiment was notified in General Order 79 of June 1883. In 1908 the battalion was amalgamated with the regiment's 3rd VB to form its 5th Battalion of the new Territorial Force. Some personnel provided a nucleus for the Norfolk and Suffolk Brigade Company of the Army Service Corps.

On 4 April 1861 the original 1st Admin. Battalion of the county was formed with headquarters at Fakenham. The corps included then or upon formation were—

5th Corps: Formed at King's Lynn on 5 September 1859. The 5th was not included in the battalion until 1863.

6th Corps: Formed as the 1st Sub-division at Aylsham on 23 September 1859. Appeared for the first time as 6th Corps in the *Army List* for March 1860.

10th Corps: Formed as the 5th Sub-division at Fakenham on 20 October 1859. Appeared as 10th for the first time in the *Army List* for March 1860 and was disbanded in 1866.

11th Corps: Formed at Holkham as the 6th Sub-division on 21 October 1859. Shown as 11th From March 1860.

12th Corps: Formed at Eynesford on 26 April 1860. Headquarters moved to Reepham by the end of the year.

13th Corps: Formed at Cromer on 16 April 1860. Disbanded during 1866.

15th Corps: Formed at East Dereham on 27 April 1860.

16th Corps: Formed at Swaffham on 12 June 1860. Joined the 2nd Admin. Battalion in 1863 until transfer to the 1st the following year.

17th Corps: Formed at Snettisham on 4 September 1860. Was not included in the battalion until 1863 and in 1867 moved headquarters to Heacham.

19th Corps: Formed at Holt on 1 March 1861.

23rd Corps: Formed at Downham Market on 23 February 1861. Served with the 2nd Admin. from 1863 until transfer to the 1st in 1864.

24th Corps: Formed at North Walsham on 13 November 1862.

Headquarters of the battalion moved to Norwich in 1862 and then to East Dereham in 1866. On 3 July 1872 the battalion was consolidated as the 3rd Norfolk Rifle Volunteer Corps. Headquarters remained at East Dereham.

Redesignation as the 3rd Volunteer Battalion, The Norfolk Regiment occurred in 1883 and was notified in General Order 79 of June. In 1908 the battalion amalgamated with the 2nd VB to form the 5th Battalion, Norfolk Regiment.

Several cadet units have been associated with the battalion. The first appeared in 1867 and was shown in the *Army List* as being attached to the 5th Corps at King's Lynn. From 1883 this unit was listed as being at East Dereham but in 1885 it once again appears at King's Lynn. The company finally disappeared from the *Army List* in February 1888. Another cadet corps, this time raised by the Norfolk County School at North Elmham, was affiliated to the battalion in 1888. This too was disbanded and is last seen in 1893. Next came the Gresham's School Cadet Corps in 1902. This school was situated at Holt and in 1908 became part of the Junior Division of the Officers Training Corps.

The county's 2nd Admin. Battalion was formed with headquarters at Norwich on 25 March 1861. It contained the following corps—

7th Corps: Formed at Harleston as the 2nd Sub-division on 30 September 1859. Shown as 7th Corps for the first time in the *Army List* for March 1860.

8th Corps Formed at Diss as the 3rd Sub-division on 7 October 1859. Shown as 8th Corps from March 1860.

9th Corps: Formed as the 4th Sub-division on 8 October 1859 at Loddon. Shown as 9th Corps from March 1860.

14th Corps: Formed at Stalham on 18 April 1860.

18th Corps: Formed at Blofield on 16 August 1860.

20th Corps: Formed at Attleborough on 6 October 1860.

21st Corps: Formed at Wymondham on 11 October 1860.

22nd Corps: Formed at Thetford on 13 December 1860.

The 2nd Admin. Battalion was also to include the 16th and 23rd Corps. These joined in 1863 but by April 1864 had been transferred to the 1st Admin.

The battalion was consolidated as the 4th Norfolk Rifle Volunteer Corps in July 1872. This title was changed to the 4th Volunteer Battalion, The Norfolk Regiment in General Order 79 of June 1883. In 1908 the 1st and 4th VBs were amalgamated to form the 4th Battalion, The Norfolk Regiment.

The 1st Cadet Battalion, The Norfolk Regiment was formed with headquarters at the Drill Hall, Theatre Street, Norwich on 23 January 1895. It contained four companies one of which had been absorbed from the 1st Volunteer Battalion. By 1898 the battalion had moved into Britannia Barracks and was last seen in the *Army List* for March 1900.

NORTHAMPTONSHIRE

The 1st Admin. Battalion of Northamptonshire Rifle Volunteers was formed on 8 August 1860 and in addition to the several rifle corps that were formed also contained the 1st Northamptonshire Mounted Rifles. This unit was attached to the battalion from 1862 until disbandment in 1869. Another volunteer corps to be associated with the 1st Admin. was the 1st Northants Engineers who were raised in 1867 at Peterborough. They later, in 1872, transferred to the 2nd Tower Hamlets Engineer Corps. Headquarters of the battalion were at Northampton and the rifle corps included were—

1st Corps: Formed at Althorpe on 29 August 1859.

2nd Corps: Formed at Towcester on 19 October 1859.

3rd Corps: A 3rd Corps appeared in the *Army List* for March 1860 but this disappeared in the April issue having had no officers or location allotted to it. This position in the county list was to remain vacant until 1872 when upon the amalgamation of the two Northampton Corps, 4th and 5th, the space was filled.

4th Corps: Formed at Northampton on 15 February 1860. Amalgamated with the 5th Corps in 1872 and renumbered as 3rd.

5th Corps: Formed at Northampton on 3 March 1860. Amalgamated with the 4th Corps in 1872.

6th Corps: Formed at Peterborough on 3 March 1860.

7th Corps: Formed at Wellingborough on 20 September 1860.

8th Corps: Formed at Daventry on 23 November 1860.

9th Corps: Formed at Kettering on 22 April 1867.

One other corps to be recorded in the *Army List* was the 1st Sub-division. This appeared in the issue for March 1860 only and had its headquarters at Overstone. No officers were gazetted.

The 1st Admin. Battalion was consolidated as the 1st Northamptonshire Rifle Volunteer Corps in 1880. Headquarters remained at Northampton and the thirteen companies were organised as follows—

'A' Company at Althorpe	Late 1st Corps
'B' Company at Towcester	Late 2nd Corps
'C' to 'G' Companies at Northampton	Late 3rd Corps
'H' 'I' Companies at Peterborough	Late 6th Corps
'K' 'L' Companies at Wellingborough	Late 7th Corps
'M' Company at Daventry	Late 8th Corps
'N' Company at Kettering	Late 9th Corps

It would appear from the list of consolidated units issued in November 1880 by HMSO that the above companies were originally numbered.

Redesignation as the 1st Volunteer Battalion of the Northamptonshire Regiment occurred in 1887 and was notified in General Order 181 of that year. Three new companies were raised in 1900 in addition to a cadet corps at Wellingborough Grammar School. In 1902 Oundle School also provided a company.

In 1908 the main portion of the battalion transferred to the Territorial Force as the 4th Bn Northamptons. Two of the Peterborough Companies, however, together with personnel from the Northampton RE (Vols) formed the Northamptonshire Battery, RFA and the East Midland Brigade Company ASC. Both cadet units became part of the Junior Division of the Officers Training Corps.

NORTHUMBERLAND

The following corps were formed in Northumberland between 1859 and 1878—

1st Corps: Formed at Tynemouth on 16 August 1859. Absorbed the 2nd Corps in February 1860 and in August 1861 was divided to form the 1st, 8th and 9th. The 1st Corps disappeared from the *Army List* in November 1862 having been disbanded the previous month.

2nd Corps: Formed at Tynemouth on 4 January 1860. Absorbed into the 1st Corps the following month. A new 2nd Corps, this time with headquarters at Hexham was formed on 10 March 1860.

3rd Corps: Formed at Morpeth on 12 March 1860.

4th Corps: Formed at Wooler-in-Glendale on 23 April 1860. Headquarters moved to Belford in 1861.

5th Corps: Formed at Alnwick on 27 March 1860.

6th Corps: Formed at Tynedale on 23 April 1860.

7th Corps: Formed at Allendale on 11 September 1860.

8th Corps: Formed at Walker from three companies of the 1st Corps in August 1861.

9th Corps: Formed at Crumlington from one company of the 1st Corps in August 1861. This corps was disbanded in December 1864.

10th Corps: Formed at Lowick on 20 December 1861.

11th Corps: Formed at St John-Lee on 25 April 1868. Headquarters moved to Corbridge in 1876.

12th Corps: Formed at Haltwhistle on 3 July 1878.

The 1st Admin. Battalion of Northumberland Rifle Volunteers was formed in November 1860 and contained, with the exception of the 1st Corps, those then in existence. Headquarters of the battalion, which also included the 1st Berwick-upon-Tweed Corps, were at Alnwick.

When the 1st Corps was divided in August 1861 into the 1st, 8th and 9th these three corps were grouped into the 2nd Admin. Battalion. Headquarters were at Tynemouth until 1863 when they moved to Walker.

By 1865 only the 8th Corps was still in existence. In February of that year the 2nd Admin. was removed from the *Army List* and the 8th corps made independent.

In 1880 the corps then constituting the 1st Admin. Battalion were consolidated as the 1st Northumberland (Northumberland and Berwick-upon-Tweed) Rifle Volunteer Corps. The new corps consisted of ten companies organised as follows—

'A' Company at Hexham	Late 2nd Northumberland
'B' Company at Morpeth	Late 3rd Nortumberland
'C' Company at Belford	Late 4th Northumberland
'D' Company at Alnwick	Late 5th Northumberland
'E' Company at Bellingham	Late 6th Northumberland
'F' Company at Allendale	Late 7th Northumberland
'G' Company at Berwick-upon-Tweed	Late 1st Berwick-upon-Tweed
'H' Company at Lowick	Late 10th Northumberland
'I' Company at Corbridge	Late 11th Northumberland
'K' Company at Haltwhistle	Late 12th Northumberland

Under General Order 14 of February 1883 the 1st Corps became the 1st Volunteer Battalion, The Northumberland Fusiliers. Headquarters were moved from Alnwick to Hexham in 1891.

Two new companies were raised in 1900 and in 1908 the battalion transferred to the Territorial Force as the 4th Bn Northumberland Fusiliers. The Alnwick portion of the battalion provided a nucleus for the regiment's 7th Battalion.

The 8th Corps, in 1880, was renumbered as 2nd and in February, 1883 provided the Northumberland Fusiliers with their 2nd Volunteer Battalion.

The battalion consisted of six companies lettered 'A' to 'F'. In 1900, additional personnel were raised which became 'G' (Cyclist) Company at Walker, 'H' Company at Newburn, and 'I' and 'K' which were both at Gosforth. In 1908 the 2nd VB became the 5th Battalion, The Northumberland Fusiliers.

NOTTINGHAMSHIRE

In the *Army List* for October 1859 five companies of rifle volunteers are shown as having been formed in Nottingham. In that for December the five appear as having been amalgamated under the title of The Robin Hood Rifle Volunteer Corps. Officers' commissions were dated 15 November 1859. By March 1860 the corps had been designated as the 1st Nottinghamshire (Robin Hood) Rifle Volunteers.

The corps joined the Sherwood Foresters (Derbyshire) Regiment in 1881. Although serving as the regiment's 3rd Volunteer Battalion no change in designation was conferred.

In 1900 the corps reached a strength of eighteen companies. It was then divided into two battalions of nine companies each. On 20 June 1900 a cadet corps was formed by Nottingham High School.

Upon transfer to the Territorial Force in 1908 the Robin Hoods provided the 7th Battalion of the Sherwood Foresters. The cadet corps became part of the Junior Division, Officers Training Corps.

The remaining Nottinghamshire corps were numbered 2nd to 8th and were in May 1861 grouped into the county's 1st Admin. Battalion.

2nd Corps: Formed at East Retford on 3 March 1860.

3rd Corps: Formed at Newark on 3 March 1860.

4th Corps: Formed at Mansfield on 9 March 1860.

5th Corps: This corps was formed at Thorney Wood Chase on 9 March 1860. It appeared as 4th Corps in the March 1860 *Army List* but in that for April was shown as 5th. The 5th was not included in the battalion until mid-1862.

6th Corps: Formed at Collingham on 9 March 1860.

7th Corps: Formed at Worksop on 28 April 1860.

8th Corps: Formed at Southwell on 7 July 1860.

Although the battalion was first shown in the *Army List* in May 1861 it was not until 1863 that its Newark headquarters were recorded. This, however, changed in 1865 to East Retford.

The battalion was consolidated in 1880 as the 2nd Nottinghamshire Rifle Volunteer Corps. Headquarters remained at East Retford and the corps' eight companies were organised as follows—

'A' Company at East Retford	Late 2nd Corps
'B' 'C' Companies at Newark	Late 3rd Corps
'D' Company at Mansfield	Late 4th Corps
'E' Company at Thorney Wood Chase	Late 5th Corps
'F' Company at Collingham	Late 6th Corps
'G' Company at Worksop	Late 7th Corps
'H' Company at Southwell	Late 8th Corps

In 1887 and under General Order 39 of April the 2nd Corps became the 4th (Nottingham) Volunteer Battalion of the Sherwood Foresters. Headquarters were moved to Newark in 1890.

Two cadet corps have been associated with the battalion. The first was formed by Worksop College in September 1900 and in 1906 a company was formed by the Queen Elizabeth School in Mansfield.

In 1908 the 4th VB became the 8th Battalion, Sherwood Foresters. Both cadet units transferred to the Junior Division, Officers Training Corps.

ORKNEY

Formed at Lerwick in the Shetland Isles on 24 April 1860, the 1st Orkney Rifle Volunteers consisted of one sub-division. In 1864 the Lerwick Volunteers were included in the 1st Admin. Battalion of Sutherland Rifles upon its formation in January. Shortly after achieving full company strength in August 1866 the title of the corps was changed to the 1st Orkney and Shetland. This was retained until 1880 when the 1st Sutherland Rifle Volunteer Corps was formed by the consolidation of the 1st Admin. Battalion, the Shetlanders forming 'F' Company.

OXFORDSHIRE

On 8 August 1859 three companies of rifle volunteers were formed within Oxford University. A 4th followed on 16 December. In the *Army List* for February 1860 all four companies are shown as having amalgamated under the title of 1st University of Oxford Rifle Volunteer Corps. A 5th and 6th Company were later formed.

In 1887 and under General Order 181 of December the corps became the 1st (Oxford University) Volunteer Battalion, The Oxfordshire Light Infantry. The battalion subsequently, in 1908, became part of the Senior Division, Officers Training Corps.

On 3 May 1873 a cadet corps was formed and affiliated to the battalion. This unit consisted of one company and in 1883 was shown in the *Army List* as having its headquarters at Magdalen College School. The corps was later disbanded and removed from the *Army List* in December 1884. Another unit known as the Oxford Military College Cadet Corps was raised in July 1885. This also was disbanded and was last seen in January 1898.

The remaining Oxfordshire Corps were placed into an administration battalion. This was formed in May 1860 and was at first numbered as 2nd. In 1861 the battalion was renumbered as 1st and its headquarters listed as being at Oxford.

2nd Corps: Formed at Oxford on 4 February 1860.

3rd Corps: Formed at Banbury on 13 February 1860.

4th Corps: Formed at Henley-on-Thames on 13 March 1860.

5th Corps: Formed at Woodstock on 26 May 1860. In 1861 the corps was divided to form the 5th and 9th. The new 9th Corps retained the Woodstock headquarters while the 5th was located at Witney. The 5th Corps was disbanded in December 1864.

6th Corps: Formed at Deddington on 25 April 1860.

7th Corps: Formed at Bicester on 12 May 1860. This corps was disbanded in 1870.

8th Corps: Formed at Thame on 27 November 1860.

9th Corps: As mentioned above the 5th Corps was divided in 1861 to form the 5th and 9th Corps. With headquarters at Woodstock the 9th is first seen in the *Army List* for October.

The 1st Oxfordshire Light Horse Volunteers were attached to the battalion from 1864 until their disbandment in 1870.

In 1875 the battalion appears in the *Army List* as having been consolidated and that for August 1875 indicates that the title of 2nd Corps has been assumed. Headquarters remained at Oxford and the establishment of the new corps was set at six companies.

The title of 2nd Volunteer Battalion of the Oxfordshire Light Infantry was assumed under General Order 181 of December 1887. Three new companies had been formed by 1900 and in 1908 the battalion provided the regiment's 4th Battalion.

PEEBLESHIRE

The following companies of rifle volunteers were formed in Peebleshire and in 1863 included in the 1st Admin. Battalion of Midlothian Rifle Volunteers—

1st Corps: Formed at Peebles on 31 August 1860.

2nd Corps: Formed at Broughton on 31 August 1860. Disbanded during the later part of 1873.

3rd Corps: Formed at Inverleithen on 31 August 1860.

4th Corps: Formed at Linton on 16 October 1860. Disbanded in 1862.

The 1st Midlothian Admin. Battalion was consolidated in 1880 to form the 1st Midlothian (Midlothian and Peebleshire) Rifle Volunteer Corps. The 1st Peebles Corps provided 'I' and 'K' Companies while the 3rd formed 'L'.

PEMBROKESHIRE

The 1st Admin. Battalion of Pembrokeshire Rifle Volunteers was formed in June 1861. Headquarters are given in the *Army List* as Haverfordwest by 1863 and the corps included were as follows—

1st Corps: Formed at Milford on 23 June 1859.

2nd Corps: Formed with headquarters at Pembroke Dock on 26 September 1860. This corps was later converted to artillery and became the 2nd Pembrokeshire Artillery Volunteers in April 1864.

3rd Corps: Formed at Pembroke on 26 September 1860.

4th Corps: Formed at New Milford on 2 July 1861. Disbanded in 1863.

In 1862 the 1st Haverfordwest Corps was also included in the battalion as was the 2nd Cardigan in 1864. Further additions were made in 1875 when the 1st, 2nd, 3rd and 5th Carmarthen joined but the 3rd was lost due to disbandment before the end of the year.

The battalion was consolidated in 1880 as the 1st Pembrokeshire (Pembroke, Carmarthen, Cardigan and Haverfordwest) Rifle Volunteer Corps. Headquarters remained at Haverfordwest and the corps' ten companies were organised as follows—

'A' Company at Milford	Late 1st Pembroke Corps
'B' 'C' 'D' Companies at Haverfordwest	Late 1st Haverfordwest Corps
'E' Company at Pembroke	Late 3rd Pembroke Corps
'F' Company at Cardigan	Late 1st Cardigan Corps
'G' Company at Llandilo	Late 1st Carmarthen Corps
'H' 'I' Companies at Carmarthen	Late 2nd Carmarthen Corps
'K' Company at Llanelly	Late 5th Carmarthen Corps

Under General Order 181 of December 1887 the corps became the 1st (Pembroke-shire) Volunteer Battalion of the Welsh Regiment and in 1908 provided that regiment's 4th Battalion.

PERTHSHIRE

The following corps were all raised within the County of Perthshire and on 20 November 1860 included in the 1st Admin. Battalion.

1st Corps: Formed at Perth on 13 December 1859. A 2nd Corps was also formed at Perth on the same date and in June 1860 was absorbed as No 2 Company of the 1st Corps.

5th Corps: Formed at Blairgowrie on 16 March 1860.

6th Corps: Formed at Dunblane on 13 December 1859.

7th Corps: Formed at Coupar Angus on 5 May 1860.

8th Corps: Formed at Crieff on 5 May 1860. Absorbed the 19th Corps in 1878.

9th Corps: Formed at Alyth on 26 May 1860.

11th Corps: Formed at Doune on 26 May 1860.

12th Corps: Formed at Callander on 26 May 1860. Disbanded in 1861.

13th Corps: Formed at St Martin's on 22 August 1860.

14th Corps: Formed at Birnam on 10 November 1860.

Subsequent companies to be formed and included were—

15th Corps: Formed at Auchterarder on 4 December 1860.

16th Corps: Formed at Stanley on 22 January 1861. Disbanded in 1863.

17th Corps: A 17th Corps was first shown in the *Army List* for February 1861 but had disappeared by May having had no officers appointed. Head-quarters were given as being at Comrie. A new 17th Corps was later formed at Bridge of Earn in April 1863. Once again no officers were gazetted and the corps was disbanded in June.

18th Corps: Formed at Perth on 8 May 1863.

19th Corps: Formed at Crieff on 7 December 1868 and absorbed into the 8th Corps in 1878.

21st Corps: Formed at Comrie in July 1875. Disbanded in March of the follow-ing year.

In 1869 the 5th, 7th, 9th, 13th and 14th Corps were all transferred to the 2nd Admin. Battalion and in 1880 the 1st Admin. was consolidated as the 1st Perth-shire Rifle Volunteer Corps. The new corps consisted of seven companies and retained the Perth headquarters of the former 1st Admin. Battalion. The compan-ies were organised as follows—

'A' Company at Perth	Late 1st Corps
'B' Company at Perth	Late 1st Corps
'C' Company at Dunblane	Late 6th Corps
'D' Company at Crieff	Late 8th Corps

'E' Company at Doune	Late 11th Corps
'F' Company at Auchterarder	Late 15th Corps
'G' Company at Perth	Late 18th Corps

A new company 'H' was formed at Bridge of Allan in 1885 and in 1887 redesignation as the 4th (Perthshire) Volunteer Battalion of the Black Watch was conferred in General Order 181 of December.

Three additional companies were formed in Perth during 1900. 'I', however, was disbanded in 1902 as were 'K' and 'L' in 1905.

A cadet corps was formed and affiliated to the battalion in February 1875 by Glenalmond College.

In April 1908 the 4th VB transferred to the Territorial Force as the 6th Battalion, Black Watch. The cadet corps became part of the Junior Division of the Officers Training Corps.

On 29 February 1860 four companies of Rifle Volunteers were raised by the Marquess of Breadalbane and designated as the 3rd Perthshire (Breadalbane) Rifle Volunteer Corps. Corps headquarters were placed at Taymouth Castle and the four companies were located; No 1 Kenmore, No 2 Aberfeldy, No 3 Killin and No 4 Strathfillan. The 10th Perthshire Corps was formed on 19 May 1860 and from then recorded in the *Army List* as being 'united for drill and administrative purposes' with the 3rd Corps.

In November 1861 a 2nd Admin. Battalion for the Perthshire area was formed with headquarters at Taymouth. The corps included were the 3rd and 10th Perthshire which were joined by the 9th Corps from the neighbouring county of Argyllshire. The latter, who had previously been attached to the 3rd Corps, was transferred to the 1st Argyllshire Admin. Battalion in 1865.

During 1869 the 1st and 4th Companies of the 3rd Corps were disbanded and the 3rd Company was constituted as a separate corps and designated 4th, the Killin headquarters being retained. The 3rd (Breadalbane) Corps now consisted of just one company, the former No 2 at Aberfeldy. Also that year the strength of the battalion was increased when, as previously mentioned, the 5th, 7th, 9th, 13th and 14th Corps were removed from the 1st Admin. and included, and the 20th Corps formed at Pitlochry on 27 May. Yet another change occurred in 1869 when battalion headquarters were moved from Taymouth to Birnam.

In 1873 the 10th Corps was disbanded and the following year the sub-title 'Perthshire Highland' was granted to the battalion.

When the battalion was consolidated in 1880 the title originally assumed was 3rd Perthshire (Perthshire Highland) Rifle Volunteer Corps but this was changed to 2nd after a few months. Headquarters of the new corps remained at Birnam and the eight companies were organised as follows—

'A' Company at Aberfeldy	Late 3rd Corps
'B' Company at Killin	Late 4th Corps
'C' Company at Blairgowrie	Late 5th Corps
'D' Company at Coupar Angus	Late 7th Corps
'E' Company at Alyth	Late 9th Corps

'F' Company at St Martin's	Late 13th Corps
'G' Company at Birnam	Late 14th Corps
'H' Company at Pitlochry	Late 20th Corps

Redesignation as the 5th (Perthshire Highland) Volunteer Battalion of the Black Watch was assumed in 1887 and notified in General Order 181 of December. In 1899 the headquarters of 'F' Company were moved to New Stone and two new companies, 'I' and 'K' were formed at Blairgowrie and Birnam respectively. The new additions were, however, later disbanded, 'I' going in 1904 and 'K' in 1905.

When the battalion transferred to the Territorial Force in 1908 it was originally designated as the 8th (Cyclist) Battalion, The Black Watch. In 1909, however, the new title of the Highland Cyclist Battalion was conferred.

RADNORSHIRE

Three rifle corps were formed in Radnorshire which in 1864 appeared in the *Army List* as being part of the 1st Admin. Battalion of Herefordshire Rifle Volunteers.

1st Corps: Formed at Presteigne on 8 March 1860.

2nd Corps: Formed at Knighton on 25 April 1860. This corps was later disbanded and disappeared from the *Army List* in 1878. A new 2nd Corps was raised at Rhayader on 11 September 1878.

3rd Corps: Formed at New Radnor on 6 August 1860. Was later disbanded, disappearing from the *Army List* in September 1872.

In 1880 the 1st Herefordshire Admin. Battalion was consolidated as the 1st Herefordshire (Hereford and Radnor) Rifle Volunteer Corps. The two Radnorshire Corps providing 'I' and 'K' Companies.

RENFREWSHIRE

In February 1860 an amalgamation took place between four of the seven companies of rifle volunteers then in existence in the Burgh of Greenock. The corps concerned were—

1st Corps: Formed on 10 September 1859.

2nd Corps: Formed on 10 September 1859.

13th Corps: Formed on 24 January 1860.

18th Corps: Formed on 6 February 1860.

The four were merged under the title of 1st Renfrewshire Rifle Volunteer Corps and in August 1860 became part of the newly-formed 1st Admin. Battalion of Renfrewshire Rifle Volunteers. Headquarters of the battalion were at Greenock and in addition to the 1st the following corps were included—

5th Corps: Formed at Port Glasgow on 15 November 1859.

10th Corps: Formed at Greenock on 3 February 1860. From 1863 this corps was also listed as 'The Greenock Highlanders'.

11th Corps: Formed at Greenock on 3 February 1860. Absorbed into the 10th Corps as its No 2 Company in 1863.

22nd Corps: Formed at Gourock on 6 April 1860.

In 1863 the 1st Bute Rifle Volunteer Corps was also included in the battalion which in 1880 was consolidated as the 1st Renfrewshire Corps. The new battalion retained its headquarters at Greenock and the nine companies were organised as follows—

'A' to 'D' Companies at Greenock	Late 1st Renfrew Corps
'E' Company at Port Glasgow	Late 5th Renfrew Corps
'F' 'G' Companies at Greenock	Late 10th Renfrew Corps
'H' Company at Gourock	Late 22nd Renfrew Corps
'I' Company at Rothesay	Late 1st Bute Corps

Under General Order 181 of December 1887 the 1st Renfrewshires became the 1st (Renfrewshire) Volunteer Battalion, The Argyll and Sutherland Highlanders. In 1900 a new company dedicated to a cyclist role was formed and in 1906 'I' Company the old 1st Buteshires was disbanded due to a fall off in numbers. The 5th Battalion, the Argyll and Sutherland Highlanders was formed upon transfer to the Territorial Force in April 1908.

The 2nd Admin. Battalion of Renfrewshire Rifle Volunteers was formed with headquarters at Paisley on 2 June 1860. The corps included were—

3rd Corps: Formed at Paisley on 22 September 1859.

6th Corps: Formed at Paisley on 23 November 1859.

9th Corps: Formed at Johnstone on 6 February 1860.

14th Corps: Formed at Paisley on 8 February 1860.

15th Corps: Formed at Kilbarchan on 20 January 1860.

17th Corps: Formed at Lochminnoch on 20 January 1860.

20th Corps: Formed at Renfrew on 1 March 1860.

24th Corps: Formed at Paisley on 10 April 1860.

Upon consolidation in 1880 the battalion was at first numbered as 3rd Corps but after a few months this was changed to 2nd. Headquarters remained at Paisley and the eight companies were organised as follows—

'A' Company at Paisley	Late 3rd Corps
'B' Company at Paisley	Late 6th Corps
'C' Company at Johnstone	Late 9th Corps
'D' Company at Paisley	Late 14th Corps
'E' Company at Kilbarchan	Late 15th Corps
'F' Company at Lochwinnoch	Late 17th Corps
'G' Company at Renfrew	Late 20th Corps
'H' Company at Paisley	Late 24th Corps

A new company, 'I', was formed at Paisley in 1884 and in 1887 the title of 2nd (Renfrewshire) Volunteer Battalion, the Argyll and Sutherland Highlanders was conferred in General Order 181 of December. 'K' (Cyclist) Company was formed at Paisley in 1900 and in 1903 'E' was disbanded and 'F' moved to Elderslie.

The 2nd VB was amalgamated with the 3rd VB of the regiment in April 1908 to form the 6th Battalion, the Argyll and Sutherland Highlanders. The 2nd VB providing headquarters and five companies.

Included in the 3rd Admin. Battalion, formed on 4 August 1860 with headquarters at Barrhead, were the following corps, the 25th being added upon formation in 1862.

4th Corps: Formed at Pollockshaws on 22 September 1859.

7th Corps: Formed at Barrhead on 15 February 1860.

8th Corps: Formed at Neilston on 6 March 1860.

16th Corps: Formed at Thornliebank on 15 February 1860.

19th Corps: Formed at Hurlet on 6 March 1860.

21st Corps: Formed at Barrhead on 12 March 1860.

23rd Corps: Formed at Cathcart on 6 April 1860.

25th Corps: Formed at Thornliebank on 15 May 1862.

The battalion was consolidated in 1880 as the 4th Renfrewshire Rifle Volunteer Corps, changing to 3rd after a few months. Headquarters remained at Barrhead and the eight companies were organised as follows—

'A' Company at Pollockshaws	Late 4th Corps
'B' Company at Barrhead	Late 7th Corps
'C' Company at Neilston	Late 8th Corps
'D' Company at Thornliebank	Late 16th Corps
'E' Company at Hurlet	Late 19th Corps
'F' Company at Barrhead	Late 21st Corps
'G' Company at Cathcart	Late 23rd Corps
'H' Company at Thornliebank	Late 25th Corps

In 1881 headquarters of 'E' Company were moved from Hurlet to Newton-Mearns and those for the battalion from Barrhead to Pollockshaws. Redesignation as the 3rd (Renfrewshire) Volunteer Battalion of the Argyll and Sutherland Highlanders was notified in General Order 181 of December 1887. Two new companies, 'I' and 'K' (Cyclist) were formed at Barrhead in 1900 but the former was disbanded in 1903.

Upon transfer to the Territorial Force in 1908 the battalion provided three companies of the 6th Bn The Argyll and Sutherland Highlanders.

One other corps was formed in Renfrewshire which was not included in either of the three Admin. Battalions that were formed. The 12th Corps was raised at Greenock on 3 February 1860 but disbanded before the end of the year.

ROSS-SHIRE

The 1st Admin. Battalion of Ross-shire Rifle Volunteers was formed with headquarters at Dingwall on 30 September 1861. At that time six corps were then in existence, the 3rd, however, was not shown as being included in the battalion until

1863. Three additional companies were raised and added in the period 1866–1867.

1st Corps: Formed at Invergordon on 15 February 1860. Headquarters m ꞈd to Tain in 1869.

2nd Corps: Formed at Dingwall on 15 February 1860.

3rd Corps: Formed at Avoch on 17 February 1860. Headquarters moved to Fortrose in 1876.

4th Corps: Formed at Knockbain on 22 March 1860. Headquarters moved to Munlochy in 1876.

5th Corps: Formed at Alness on 20 May 1861 and disbanded in September 1864. Reformed at Ullapool on 24 May 1865.

6th Corps: Formed at Alness on 21 May 1861. Headquarters moved to Invergordon in 1871.

7th Corps: Formed at Evanton on 12 May 1866.

8th Corps: Formed at Moy near Dingwall on 11 August 1866.

9th Corps: Formed at Gairloch on 23 February 1867.

The battalion was consolidated as the 1st Ross-shire (Ross Highland) Rifle Volunteer Corps in 1880. Headquarters remained at Dingwall and the nine companies, 'A' to 'I', were formed in order of seniority by the former corps of the battalion.

In December 1887 and under General Order 181 the title of 1st (Ross Highland) Volunteer Battalion, the Seaforth Highlanders was conferred. Also that year the headquarters of 'G' and 'H' Companies were moved to Dingwall and Fairburn and in April 1908 the Ross-shires became the 4th Battalion, Seaforth Highlanders.

ROXBURGHSHIRE

Included in the 1st Admin. Battalion of Roxburghshire Rifle Volunteers, formed in November 1861 with headquarters at Melrose, were the 1st to 5th Roxburghshire Corps.

1st Corps: Formed at Jedburgh with a detachment at Denholm on 15 September 1859. In 1863 the Denholm personnel were absorbed into the 4th Corps as its No 2 Company.

2nd Corps: Formed at Kelso on 29 March 1860.

3rd Corps: Formed at Melrose on 15 June 1860.

4th Corps: Formed at Hawick on 11 June 1860. Increased to two companies in 1863 after absorbing the Denholm Detachment of the 1st Corps.

5th Corps: Formed at Hawick on 15 January 1861. Disbanded in 1867.

In 1862 the 1st and 2nd Selkirkshire Corps were also included in the battalion which in 1868 added the additional title of '(The Border)' to its full designation.

Headquarters were moved to Newtown St Boswells in 1873 and in 1880 the battalion was consolidated as the 1st Roxburgh and Selkirk (The Border) Rifle

Volunteer Corps. The nine companies of the new corps were organised as follows—

'A' Company at Jedburgh	Late 1st Roxburgh Corps
'B' Company at Kelso	Late 2nd Roxburgh Corps
'C' Company at Melrose	Late 3rd Roxburgh Corps
'D' Company at Hawick	Late 4th Roxburgh Corps
'E' Company at Hawick	Late 4th Roxburgh Corps
'F' Company at Galashiels	Late 1st Selkirk Corps
'G' Company at Galashiels	Late 1st Selkirk Corps
'H' Company at Selkirk	Late 2nd Selkirk Corps
'I' Company at Selkirk	Late 2nd Selkirk Corps

In 1881 the corps became one of the volunteer battalions allotted to the Royal Scots Fusiliers. They remained with the regiment until 1887 when under General Order 61 of May they joined the King's Own Scottish Borderers. Although ranked as 1st Volunteer Battalion no change in designation was assumed and the corps retained its rifle volunteer title until 1908.

At the same time as the transfer from the Royal Scots Fusiliers to the King's Own Scottish Borderers, 'H' Company of the battalion moved from Selkirk to Galashiels. In 1892 a new company, 'K', was raised at Hawick followed by two more lettered 'L' and 'M' in 1901. Two years later both 'L' and 'M' were disbanded; battalion headquarters were moved to Melrose and a new 'L' (Cyclist) Company was formed at Newcastleton.

Upon transfer to the Territorial Force in April 1908 the 1st Roxburgh and Selkirk were merged with the 2nd VB of the regiment to form the 4th Battalion, the King's Own Scottish Borderers. The 1st providing headquarters and six companies.

A cadet corps was formed by the Kelso High School in 1901 and affiliated to the battalion. Recognition was not gained from the Territorial Force in 1908 and the company was eventually disbanded on 19 January 1911.

SELKIRKSHIRE

Known unofficially as the 'Gala Forest Rifles' the 1st Selkirkshire Rifle Volunteer Corps was formed on 27 March 1860. The original establishment of the corps, whose headquarters were at Galashiels, was one company but this was increased to two in 1870. In 1880 the 1st Admin. Battalion of Roxburghshire Rifle Volunteers, with whom the 1st Selkirks had been united since 1862, was consolidated as the 1st Roxburgh and Selkirk RVC. The Galashiels Volunteers forming 'F' and 'G' Companies of the new battalion.

Selkirk means 'the church in the forest' and it was in this Royal Burgh that the 2nd Selkirkshire Corps was formed on 15 June 1860. The forest referred to is the Royal Forest of Ettrick giving rise to the corps' unofficial title of 'the Ettrick Forest Rifles'. Like the 1st Corps the 2nd also joined the Roxburghshire Admin. Battalion in 1862 and in 1880 became part of the 1st Roxburgh and Selkirk Corps. In this case providing 'H' and 'I' Companies.

SHETLAND

A sub-division of rifle volunteers was raised at Lerwick in the Shetland Isles on 24 April 1860 and designated as the 1st Orkney Corps. As such details of the corps have been dealt with under the 'Orkney' section of this work.

In 1884 and as 'F' Company of the 1st Sutherland Rifle Volunteer Corps the corps mentioned above was disbanded. This left the islands without volunteers until 1900 when on 19 December three companies were formed and designated as the 7th Volunteer Battalion of the Gordon Highlanders. Headquarters were placed at Lerwick and the three companies were situated, 'A' and 'B' at Lerwick and 'C' at Scalloway.

The battalion, who in view of its strength were attached to the 1st VB Gordons, transferred to the Territorial Force in 1908 and is shown in the *Army List* as, The Shetland Companies, The Gordon Highlanders.

SHROPSHIRE

The following companies of rifle volunteers were all raised within the County of Shropshire and with the exception of the 9th Corps included in one or other of the two administrative battalions to be formed in July 1860.

1st Corps: Formed at Shrewsbury on 14 December 1859.

2nd Corps: Formed at Market Drayton on 15 February 1860.

3rd Corps: Formed at Whitchurch on 13 February 1860.

4th Corps: Formed at Bridgnorth on 13 February 1860.

5th Corps: Formed at Condover on 5 March 1860.

6th Corps: Formed at Much Wenlock on 13 February 1860. Headquarters moved to Ironbridge in 1863.

7th Corps: Formed at Wellington as the 1st Sub-division on 17 September 1859. Redesignated as 7th Corps in February 1860.

8th Corps: Formed at Hodnet on 2 March 1860.

9th Corps: Formed at Shrewsbury on 2 March 1860. Converted to artillery and redesignated as the 1st Shropshire Artillery Volunteers in July 1860.

10th Corps: Formed at Ludlow on 2 March 1860.

11th Corps: Formed at Cleobury Mortimer on 4 May 1860.

12th Corps: Formed at Wem on 3 May 1860.

13th Corps: Formed at Ellesmere on 2 June 1860. Disbanded in 1879.

14th Corps: Formed at Shifnal on 21 April 1860.

15th Corps: Formed at Oswestry on 28 April 1860.

16th Corps: Formed at Munslow on 24 May 1860. Disbanded in 1863.

17th Corps: Formed at Shrewsbury on 8 January 1861.

18th Corps: Formed at Newport on 17 January 1862.

Headquarters of both battalions were placed at Shrewsbury and the corps included in each were—

1st Battalion: 1st, 4th, 5th, 6th, 10th, 11th, 14th, 16th, 17th.
2nd Battalion: 2nd, 3rd, 7th, 8th, 12th, 13th, 15th, 18th.

In 1873 the 2nd and 4th Montgomeryshire Corps are shown in the *Army List* as being 'United' with the 2nd Shropshire Admin. Battalion. This attachment was not a popular one in Montgomeryshire and brought about many resignations. Both corps were disbanded by 1876.

In 1880 the 1st and 2nd Admin. Battalions were consolidated as the 1st and 2nd Shropshire Rifle Volunteer Corps. Headquarters of the 1st Corps remained at Shrewsbury and its eight companies were organised as follows—

'A' Company at Shrewsbury	Late 1st Corps
'B' Company at Shrewsbury	Late 17th Corps
'C' Company at Condover	Late 5th Corps
'D' Company at Ironbridge	Late 6th Corps
'E' Company at Shifnal	Late 14th Corps
'F' Company at Bridgnorth	Late 4th Corps
'G' Company at Ludlow	Late 10th Corps
'H' Company at Cleobury Mortimer	Late 11th Corps

The 2nd Corps, who moved its headquarters from Shrewsbury to Newport shortly after consolidation, only had seven companies and these were formed in order of seniority by the seven corps that previously constituted the 2nd Admin. Battalion.

In 1885 the old 13th Ellesmere Corps, which was disbanded in 1879, was re-raised as 'H' Company of the 2nd Corps. Two years later and under General Order 181 of December, the titles of 1st and 2nd Volunteer Battalions, the King's (Shropshire Light Infantry) were conferred upon the 1st and 2nd Corps. These were retained until April 1908 when after amalgamation the two battalions formed the 4th Battalion of the regiment.

Three cadet units have been associated with the 1st Corps. Shrewsbury School had a drill company of some seventy boys between 1860 and 1863 and in 1900 formed a cadet corps. In 1908 the school transferred to the Junior Division of the Officers Training Corps.

The Bridgnorth Cadet Company was also formed in 1900 followed in 1906 by the Shrewsbury Town Cadet Corps. Recognition eventually came for the former but the Shrewsbury Town Company were not included in the new Territorial Cadet Force.

The Ellesmere College Cadet Corps is shown in the *Army List* as being affiliated to the 2nd Volunteer Battalion, the King's (Shropshire LI). Formation of the company began in 1900 and its first officers' commissions were dated 27 February 1901. The college transferred to the Officers Training Corps in 1908.

SOMERSETSHIRE

There were twenty-eight independent rifle corps formed within the county all of which were placed into one or other of the three administrative battalions that were formed. In 1880 these battalions were consolidated into three corps.

The 1st Admin. Battalion was formed in August 1860 with headquarters at Bath. The corps included were—

1st Corps: Formed at Bath on 20 October 1859.

2nd Corps: Formed at Bathwick on 21 October 1859.

7th Corps: Formed at Keynsham as the 1st Sub-division on 25 February 1860. Appeared for the first time as 7th Corps in the *Army List* for April 1860.

14th Corps : Formed at Warleigh Manor on 5 March 1860.

17th Corps: Formed at Lyncombe on 2 March 1860.

18th Corps: Formed at Walcot on 3 March 1860.

22nd Corps: Formed at Temple Cloud on 10 September 1860. Headquarters were moved to Kilmersdon in 1869.

The battalion was consolidated in 1880 as the 1st Somersetshire Rifle Volunteers Corps. Headquarters remained at Bath and the corps' seven companies were organised as follows—

'A' Company at Bath	Late 1st Corps
'B' Company at Bathwick	Late 2nd Corps
'C' Company at Keynsham	Late 7th Corps
'D' Company at Warleigh Manor	Late 14th Corps
'E' Company at Lyncombe	Late 17th Corps
'F' Company at Walcot	Late 18th Corps
'G' Company at Kilmersdon	Late 22nd Corps

Under General Order 261 of October 1882 the 1st Corps became the 1st Volunteer Battalion, The Prince Albert's (Somersetshire Light Infantry). The establishment of the battalion was increased to eight companies in 1885 and then to ten in 1900.

Three school cadet companies have been associated with the 1st VB. The first was formed at Bath College in March 1900. This was followed in May of that year by one at King Edward's School in Bath and in 1904 by a company at Monkton Combe School near Bath.

Also formed in August 1860 was the 2nd Admin. Battalion. This had its headquarters at Taunton and included the following corps—

3rd Corps: Formed at Taunton on 22 October 1859.

5th Corps: Formed at Bridgwater on 14 January 1860.

8th Corps: Formed at Wellington on 28 February 1860.

9th Corps: Formed at Williton on 22 February 1860.

11th Corps: Formed at Stogursey on 21 February 1860. This corps moved its headquarters to Nether Stowey in 1868 and was disbanded in 1873.

12th Corps: Formed at Wiveliscombe on 29 February 1860.

16th Corps: Formed at Yeovil on 4 April 1860.

20th Corps: Formed at Crewkerne on 25 April 1860.

21st Corps: Formed at Langport on 12 April 1860.

26th Corps: Formed at Bridgwater on 5 February 1861.

28th Corps: Formed at South Petherton on 4 November 1876.

The 2nd Admin. Battalion was consolidated in 1880 as the 3rd Somersetshire Rifle Volunteer Corps. This was changed, however, to 2nd Corps after a few months. Headquarters remained at Taunton and the corps' twelve companies were organised as follows—

'A' 'B' Companies at Taunton	Late 3rd Corps
'C' Company at Wellington	Late 8th Corps
'D' Company at Williton	Late 9th Corps
'E' Company at Wiveliscombe	Late 12th Corps
'F' Company at Yeovil	Late 16th Corps
'G' Company at Crewkerne	Late 20th Corps
'H' Company at Langport	Late 21st Corps
'I' Company at Bridgwater	Late 5th Corps
'K' 'L' Companies at Bridgwater	Late 26th Corps
'M' Company at South Petherton	Late 28th Corps

The 2nd Corps became the 2nd Volunteer Battalion, The Prince Albert's (Somersetshire Light Infantry) under General Order 261 of October 1882. A new company was formed in 1900 and in 1901 and 1903 respectively both the County School, Wellington and the King's College, Taunton provided cadet companies.

Headquarters of the 3rd Admin. Battalion, which was formed in August 1860, were at Wells. Its corps were—

4th Corps: Formed at Burnham on 12 January 1860.

6th Corps: Formed at Weston-super-Mare on 11 February 1860.

10th Corps: Formed at Wells on 14 February 1860.

13th Corps: Formed at Frome on 9 March 1860.

15th Corps: Formed at Shepton Mallet on 24 March 1860.

19th Corps: Formed at Glastonbury on 17 March 1860.

23rd Corps: Formed at Wincanton on 30 June 1860. Headquarters were moved to Castle Cary in 1863.

24th Corps: Formed at Somerton on 20 July 1860. This corps was disbanded in 1871.

25th Corps: Formed at Baltonsborough on 14 January 1861. Headquarters were moved to Keinton in 1870.

27th Corps: Formed at Wrington on 23 July 1861. Moved to Langford in 1866.

The 3rd Admin. Battalion was consosidated in 1880 as the 4th Somersetshire Rifle Volunteer Corps. This was changed after a few months, however, to 3rd. Headquarters remained at Wells and the corps' nine companies were organised as follows—

'A' Company at Burnham	Late 4th Corps
'B' Company at Weston-super-Mare	Late 6th Corps
'C' Company at Wells	Late 10th Corps
'D' Company at Frome	Late 13th Corps
'E' Company at Shepton Mallet	Late 15th Corps
'F' Company at Glastonbury	Late 19th Corps
'G' Company at Castle Cary	Late 23rd Corps
'H' Company at Keinton	Late 25th Corps
'I' Company at Langford	Late 27th Corps

In 1882 headquarters were moved to Weston-super-Mare and under General Order 261 of October the corps became the 3rd Volunteer Battalion, The Prince Albert's (Somersetshire Light Infantry).

Upon transfer to the Territorial Force in 1908 the 1st, 2nd and 3rd Volunteer Battalions were amalgamated to form the 4th and 5th Battalions of the Somersetshire LI. All cadet units became part of the Junior Division, Officers Training Corps.

STAFFORDSHIRE

During 1860 the Staffordshire rifle volunteers were organised into five administrative battalions. In the *Army List* for August 1861 a 6th Admin. Battalion is shown with headquarters at Stafford. Included in the battalion were the 21st and 25th, who had previously been with the 2nd Admin., and the 38th and 40th formerly of the 1st. The *list* for September omits the 6th and shows its corps as having returned to their original battalions.

In 1880 the five admin. battalions were consolidated into the 1st to 5th Staffordshire Corps. Under General Order 142 of June 1882 the 1st, 3rd and 4th Corps became part of the South Staffordshire Regiment and the 2nd and 5th part of the North. Previous to this and since 1881 the 1st, 3rd and 4th had been with the North Staffords while the 2nd and 5th were with the South. The following headings are based on the 1880 numbering.

1ST CORPS

The 3rd Admin. Battalion was formed in July 1860 and had its headquarters at Handsworth. The corps included were—

1st Corps: Formed at Handsworth on 15 August 1859.

15th Corps: Formed at Brierley on 1 August 1860.

17th Corps: Formed at Seisdon on 21 February 1860. In 1873 the 17th was absorbed into the 27th as its No 2 Company.

18th Corps: Formed at Kingswinford on 21 February 1860.

20th Corps: Formed at West Bromwich on 25 February 1860.

27th Corps: Formed at Patshull on 7 March 1860. In 1873 the strength of the corps was increased to two companies when the 17th Corps at Seisdon was absorbed.

31st Corps: Formed at Smethwick on 19 April 1860.

35th Corps: Formed at Kinver on 3 July 1860. Disbanded in 1864.

Upon consolidation as 1st Corps in 1880 headquarters remained at Handsworth and the companies organised as follows—

'A' 'B' Companies at Handsworth	Late 1st Corps
'C' Company at Brierley	Late 15th Corps
'D' Company at Kingswinford	Late 18th Corps
'E' Company at West Bromwich	Late 20th Corps
'F' Company at Seisdon	Late 27th Corps
'G' Company at Patshull	Late 27th Corps
'H' Company at Smethwick	Late 31st Corps

Under General Order 63 of May 1883 the 1st Corps was redesignated as the 1st Volunteer Battalion of the South Staffordshire Regiment. The headquarters of 'D' Company were later moved from Kingswinford to Wordsley. In 1900 two new companies were formed, 'I' at Smethwick and 'K' at West Bromwich, followed in 1901 by a cyclist company, 'L', at Handsworth. 'G' was later disbanded.

In 1908 the bulk of the battalion was converted to engineers and formed the 1st North Midland Field Company RE. Some of the Handsworth personnel, however, remained as infantry and merged with the 2nd VB S Staffs as the regiment's 5th Battalion. Also in 1908 the Handsworth Grammar School Cadet Corps, which had been formed and affiliated to the 1st VB in 1907, became part of the Junior Division, Officers Training Corps.

2ND CORPS

The 2nd Corps of 1880 was formed by the consolidation of the 1st Admin. Battalion. This was created in May 1860 and with headquarters at Stoke-upon-Trent contained the following corps—

2nd Corps: Formed at Longton on 30 September 1859.

3rd Corps: Formed at Hanley on 27 September 1859.

6th Corps: Formed at Burslem on 28 December 1859.

9th Corps: Formed at Tunstall on 4 January 1860.

10th Corps: Formed at Stoke-upon-Trent on 19 January 1860.

13th Corps: Formed at Kidsgrove on 26 February 1860.

16th Corps: Formed at Newcastle-under-Lyne on 24 February 1860.

28th Corps: Formed at Leek on 26 April 1860. Not included in the battalion until May 1861.

36th Corps: Formed at Hanley on 18 June 1860.

37th Corps: Formed at Cheadle on 30 August 1860. This corps was later disbanded and was last seen in the *Army List* for November 1872.

38th Corps: Formed at Eccleshall on 17 September 1860. Disbanded in 1869.

40th Corps: Formed at Stone on 1 December 1860.

Upon consolidation the above corps were organised as follows—

'A' Company at Longton	Late 2nd Corps
'B' Company at Hanley	Late 3rd Corps
'C' Company at Burslem	Late 6th Corps
'D' Company at Tunstall	Late 9th Corps
'E' Company at Stoke-upon-Trent	Late 10th Corps
'F' Company at Kidsgrove	Late 13th Corps
'G' 'H' Companies at Newcastle-under-Lyne	Late 16th Corps
'J' Company at Leek	Late 28th Corps
'K' Company at Hanley	Late 36th Corps
'L' Company at Stone	Late 40th Corps

Shortly after the formation the 2nd Corps was permitted to include 'The Staffordshire Rangers' as part of its title. In 1883 a new title, that of 1st Volunteer Battalion, The Prince of Wales's (North Staffordshire Regiment), was assumed under General Order 14 of February.

On 13 November 1875 a cadet corps was formed by the 10th (Stoke-upon-Trent). This remained with the corps until 1884 when it was removed from the *Army List*.

The establishment of the battalion reached fourteen companies in 1900 but this was later reduced to thirteen. In 1908 the 1st VB became the North Stafford's 5th Battalion.

3RD CORPS

The 5th Admin. Battalion was formed in November 1860 with headquarters at Walsall. Its corps were as follows—

4th Corps: Formed at Walsall on 4 November 1859.

14th Corps: Formed as the 1st Sub-division at Bloxwich on 10 December 1859. Appeared as 14th Corps for the first time in the *Army List* for March 1860.

22nd Corps: Formed at Brownhills on 24 February 1860.

33rd Corps: Formed at Cank on 14 July 1860. Headquarters were moved to Cannock in 1873.

34th Corps: Formed at Wednesbury on 11 May 1860.

With the exception of the 33rd, who were hitherto unattached, the above corps previous to formation of the 5th Admin. were included in the 2nd Battalion.

Upon consolidation the battalion originally took on the number of its senior corps, 4th. This was changed by September 1880 to 3rd Corps. Headquarters remained at Walsall and the corps' six companies were organised as follows—

'A' 'B' Companies at Walsall	Late 4th Corps
'C' Company at Bloxwich	Late 14th Corps
'D' Company at Brownhills	Late 22nd Corps
'E' Company at Cannock	Late 33rd Corps
'F' Company at Wednesbury	Late 34th Corps

In May 1883 and under General Order 63 the 3rd Corps became the 2nd Volunteer Battalion, The South Staffordshire Regiment. A new company was later raised at Walsall but was soon disbanded. In 1884 yet another company was formed at Walsall together with one at Wednesbury. Also that year the headquarters of 'E' moved from Cannock to Brownhills. Before 1901 the Brownhills Company, 'D', was disbanded but this was later reformed at Walsall. The last company to be formed by the battalion, 'I', was raised at Walsall in 1901.

In 1908 the battalion together with one of the Handsworth Companies of the 1st VB formed the 5th Battalion of the South Staffordshire Regiment. Queen Mary's School at Walsall, who had provided a cadet corps in 1901, became part of the Junior Division of the Officers Training Corps.

4TH CORPS

Headquarters of the 4th Admin. Battalion were at Wolverhampton. It was formed in May 1860 and the corps included were as follows—

5th Corps: Formed at Wolverhampton on 26 December 1859. Absorbed 26th Corps at Willenhall in 1874.

11th Corps: Formed at Tipton on 11 January 1860.

12th Corps: Formed at Bilston on 26 January 1860.

23rd Corps: Formed at Wolverhampton on 1 March 1860.

26th Corps: Formed at Willenhall on 27 February 1860. Absorbed into 5th Corps as No 4 Company in 1874.

29th Corps: Formed at Sedgley on 9 April 1860.

30th Corps: Formed at Tettenhall on 30 March 1860.

32nd Corps: Formed at Wolverhampton on 19 April 1860.

The battalion was consolidated in March 1880 and at first took on the number of its senior corps, 5th. This was changed to 4th in September. Headquarters remained at Wolverhampton and the twelve companies were organised as follows—

'A' 'B' 'C' Companies at Wolverhampton	Late 5th Corps
'D' Company at Willenhall	Late 5th Corps
'E' Company at Tipton	Late 11th Corps
'F' Company at Sedgley	Late 29th Corps
'G' 'H' Companies at Bilston	Late 12th Corps
'I' Company at Wolverhampton	Late 23rd Corps
'K' 'L' Companies at Wolverhampton	Late 32nd Corps
'M' Company at Tettenhall	Late 30th Corps

Redesignation as the 3rd Volunteer Battalion, South Staffordshire Regiment took place in 1883 and was notified in General Order 63 of May. In 1900 'N' (Cyclist) Company was formed at Wolverhampton. Also that year the headquarters of 'H' Company moved from Bilston to Darlaston. The 3rd VB became the 6th Battalion of the South Staffordshire Regiment in 1908.

5TH CORPS

Formed on 10 July 1860 with headquarters at Lichfield the 2nd Admin. Battalion contained the following corps—

7th Corps: Formed at Burton-on-Trent on 10 February 1860.

8th Corps: Formed at Burton-on-Trent on 10 February 1860.

19th Corps: Formed at Tamworth on 21 February 1860.

21st Corps: Formed at Rugeley on 24 February 1860.

24th Corps: Formed at Lichfield on 6 March 1860.

25th Corps: Formed at Stafford on 6 March 1860.

39th Corps: Formed at Burton-on-Trent on 27 September 1860.

The 4th, 14th, 22nd and 34th Corps also formed part of the 2nd Admin. but these were transferred to the 5th Admin. in November 1860.

In 1880 the battalion became the 7th Staffordshire Rifle Volunteer Corps but this was changed to 5th Corps after a few months. There were eight companies organised as follows—

'A' Company at Burton-on-Trent	Late 7th Corps
'B' Company at Burton-on-Trent	Late 8th Corps
'C' Company at Tamworth	Late 19th Corps
'D' Company at Rugeley	Late 21st Corps
'E' Company at Lichfield	Late 24th Corps
'F' 'G' Company at Stafford	Late 25th Corps
'H' Company at Burton-on-Trent	Late 39th Corps

Redesignation as the 2nd Volunteer Battalion, The Prince of Wales's (North Staffordshire Regiment) took place in 1883 and was notified in General Order 14 of February. Headquarters were moved to Burton-on-Trent in 1884 and in 1900 the establishment of the battalion was increased when a new company was formed at Uttoxeter.

In 1908 the 2nd VB became the North Staffs 6th Battalion. Denstone College, who had provided a cadet corps in 1900, became part of the Junior Division, Officers Training Corps.

STIRLINGSHIRE

The following corps were all formed within the County of Stirlingshire and included, with the exception of the 10th and 14th, in the 1st Admin. Battalion—

1st Corps: Formed at Stirling on 14 October 1859.

2nd Corps: Formed at Stirling on 3 February 1860.

3rd Corps: Formed at Falkirk on 27 March 1860.

4th Corps: Formed at Lennoxtown on 6 March 1860.

5th Corps: Formed at Balfron on 1 May 1860. Was later disbanded and was not seen in the *Army List* after September 1877.

6th Corps: Formed at Denny on 11 April 1860.

7th Corps: Formed at Lennox Mill on 1 May 1860.

8th Corps: Formed at Strathblane on 25 May 1860. Disbanded in 1863.

9th Corps: Formed at Bannockburn on 21 May 1860.

10th Corps: Formed at Stirling on 10 November 1860. Did not join any admin. battalion and was disbanded in February 1864.

11th Corps: Formed at Stirling on 6 December 1860.

12th Corps: Formed at Carron on 10 February 1862.

13th Corps: Formed at Kilsyth on 19 July 1866.

14th Corps: Formed at Alva on 17 October 1868 and included in the 1st Clackmannan and Kinross Admin. Battalion. This battalion was consolidated as the 1st Clackmannan and Kinross Rifle Volunteer Corps in 1880, the 14th Stirlingshire providing 'F' Company.

The 1st Stirlingshire Admin. Battalion was formed on 9 June 1860 with headquarters at Stirling. The 1st and 2nd Clackmannan Corps were also included in 1862 but in 1867 these were transferred to the 1st Clackmannan Admin.

The battalion was consolidated in 1880 as the 1st Stirlingshire Rifle Volunteer Corps. Headquarters remained at Stirling and the ten companies were organised as follows—

'A' Company at Stirling	Late 1st Corps
'B' Company at Stirling	Late 2nd Corps
'C' Company at Falkirk	Late 3rd Corps
'D' Company at Lennox Mill	Late 7th Corps
'E' Company at Lennoxtown	Late 4th Corps
'F' Company at Stirling	Late 11th Corps
'G' Company at Denny	Late 6th Corps
'H' Company at Bannockburn	Late 9th Corps
'I' Company at Carron	Late 12th Corps
'K' Company at Kilsyth	Late 13th Corps

Shortly after consolidation the headquarters of 'D' Company were moved to Falkirk and in 1887 the title of 4th (Stirlingshire) Volunteer Battalion, The Argyll and Sutherland Highlanders was conferred under General Order 181 of December.

In 1904 the headquarters of 'H' and 'I' Companies were moved to Stenhousemuir and two year later those for 'F' went to Falkirk.

The battalion transferred to the Territorial Force in April 1908 and together with the 7th VB of the regiment formed the 7th Battalion, The Argyll and Sutherland Highlanders. The 4th VB providing headquarters and four companies.

SUFFOLK

The 1st Admin. Battalion of Suffolk Rifle Volunteers was formed with headquarters at Stowmarket on 30 July 1860. From August 1861 the *Army List* gives the battalion's HQ as being at Bury St Edmunds and from April 1864 as Sudbury. Included in the battalion were the following corps—

6th Corps: Formed at Stowmarket on 13 February 1860.

10th Corps: Formed at Eye on 6 March 1860.

11th Corps: Formed at Sudbury on 14 April 1860.

13th Corps: Formed at Bury St Edmunds on 11 May 1860.

16th Corps: Formed at Hadleigh on 2 July 1860.

18th Corps: Formed at Wickhambrook on 22 October 1860. Disbanded in 1870.

19th Corps: Formed at Brandon on 23 April 1861. Disbanded in 1863.

20th Corps: Formed at Mildenhall on 23 May 1861. Absorbed the 9th Cambridgeshire Corps in 1863 and in 1871 moved to Newmarket.

Also included were the 12th Corps from December 1860 until May 1861 when they transferred to the 2nd Admin. and the 9th Cambridgeshire Corps who are shown as being 'united' with the battalion from July 1862. The 9th, however, were in 1863 absorbed into the 20th Suffolk.

Headquarters of the 2nd Admin. Battalion of Suffolk Rifle Volunteers was at Woodbridge. The battalion was formed on 24 October 1860 and contained the following corps—

1st Corps: Formed as the 1st Sub-division at Ipswich on 11 October 1859. Became 1st Corps in January 1860.

2nd Corps: Formed at Framlingham on 1 March 1860.

3rd Corps: Formed at Woodbridge on 26 January 1860.

5th Corps: Formed at Wickham Market on 16 February 1861. Disbanded in 1875.

8th Corps: Formed at Saxmundham on 29 February 1860.

12th Corps: Formed at Bosmere on 1 June 1860. This corps was at first placed into the 1st Admin. but from June 1861 is shown as being with the 2nd. Headquarters were moved to Needham Market in 1861 and the corps was disbanded in 1866.

21st Corps: The 21st Corps, with headquarters at Aldborough, was first seen in the *Army List* for June 1861 and had been formed from part of the 9th Corps. In 1864 it was decided to convert the 21st to an artillery unit. This was done and in April the corps were enrolled as the 3rd Suffolk Artillery Volunteers.

The 9th Corps was also included in the battalion from December 1860 until May 1861 when it was transferred to the 3rd Admin. Also attached were the 2nd Suffolk Artillery Volunteers from May 1861 until late 1863.

Halesworth was the first headquarters of the 3rd Admin. Battalion which was formed on 12 November 1860.

4th Corps: Formed at Bungay on 20 July 1860.

7th Corps: Formed at Halesworth on 28 February 1860.

9th Corps: Formed at Aldborough on 9 March 1860 and in December placed into the 2nd Admin. Battalion. Much of the 9th was recruited in the Leiston area and in the early part of 1861 the corps was divided. The Aldborough portion became the 21st Corps and remained with the 2nd Admin. Leiston now became the headquarters of the 9th Corps but was transferred to the 3rd Admin. Battalion.

14th Corps: Formed at Beccles on 1 May 1860.

15th Corps: Formed at Wrentham on 9 June 1860. This corps was disbanded in 1865.

17th Corps: Formed at Lowestoft on 11 September 1860.

Also attached to the battalion were the 1st Suffolk Artillery Volunteers from 1861–1863.

Battalion headquarters were moved to Lowestoft in 1865 and in January 1877 the battalion was broken up. The 7th and 9th Corps were transferred to the 2nd Admin. Battalion while the 4th, 14th and 17th joined the 1st Admin. Battalion of the neighbouring county of Norfolk.

In 1880 both the Suffolk Admin. Battalions were consolidated taking on the numbers of their senior corps. The 2nd Admin. became the 1st Corps with eight companies organised as follows—

'A' 'B' 'C' Companies at Ipswich	Late 1st Corps
'D' Company at Framlingham	Late 2nd Corps
'E' Company at Woodbridge	Late 3rd Corps
'F' Company at Halesworth	Late 7th Corps
'G' Company at Saxmundham	Late 8th Corps
'H' Company at Leiston	Late 9th Corps

Headquarters of the new 1st Corps were at first given as being at Ispwich but by 1881 Woodbridge is shown in the *Army List*.

Under General Order 181 of December 1887 the 1st Corps became the 1st Volunteer Battalion of the Suffolk Regiment. A 9th Company was formed in 1900 and in 1908 the battalion became the 4th Bn Suffolk Regiment.

In 1889 a cadet corps was formed and affiliated to the 1st VB by the Queen Elizabeth's School at Ipswich. The corps was to disappear from the *Army List* by the end of 1891 but was again included in 1900. Framlingham College also provided a company of cadets during 1901. In 1908 both schools became part of the Junior Division of the Officers Training Corps.

In 1880 the 1st Admin. Battalion became the 6th Corps and was after a few months given the opportunity to renumber as 2nd. This was the general practice in 1880 as the system of taking on the senior corps' number in a battalion upon consolidation left many gaps in the county's sequence of numbers. The 6th chose to remain as such making Suffolk the only county without a clear run of numbers after 1880.

Headquarters of the 6th were at Sudbury and its eight companies were organised as follows—

'A' Company at Stowmarket	Late 6th Corps
'B' 'C' Companies at Eye	Late 10th Corps
'D' Company at Sudbury	Late 11th Corps
'E' 'F' Companies at Bury St Edmunds	Late 13th Corps
'G' Company at Hadleigh	Late 16th Corps
'H' Company at Newmarket	Late 20th Corps

The 6th were redesignated as the 2nd Volunteer Battalion of the Suffolk Regiment under General Order 181 of December 1887 and in 1889 moved its headquarters to Bury St Edmunds.

A reduction in establishemnt to seven companies occurred in 1889 but this was brought back up to eight in 1900. A cadet company was also provided in 1900 by the King Edward's School at Bury St Edmunds.

The 2nd VB provided the 5th Battalion of the Suffolk Regiment in 1908. At the same time King Edward's School cadets joined the Officers Training Corps as part of its Junior Contingent.

SURREY

Of the twenty-six numbered corps that were raised in Surrey between 1859 and 1862 only three were of sufficient strength not to be included in one or other of the four administrative battalions that were formed. Other corps omitted were the 3rd, who were absorbed into the 1st a few months after formation, and the 24th which was disbanded in 1862 having been formed at Southwark on 9 March 1861. The 24th consisted entirely of members of the Temperance League.

In 1880 eight corps of battalion strength were created from those then in existence. It is this series of numbers that has been used in the following as headings.

1ST CORPS

The 1st Surrey Corps was formed in Camberwell on 14 June 1859. This was followed by the 3rd Corps, also at Camberwell, on 26 August. In the *Army List* for February 1860 the 3rd Corps is shown as forming the No 2 Company of the 1st. The 1st at this time was listed as The South London Rifle Volunteer Corps but in the *List* for March, 1st Surrey (South London), is the title allotted.

By 1861 the establishment of the 1st Corps had reached eight companies. A cadet corps was formed by Dulwich College in 1878 and in 1881 the corps joined the East Surrey Regiment as one of its allotted volunteer battalions. Although ranked as 1st VB in the regiment's volunteer line-up the 1st Surreys retained their rifle volunteer title until transferred to the Territorial Force in 1908 as the 21st (County of London) Battalion, The London Regiment. The cadet corps also became part of the TF in 1908 providing the Dulwich College Contingent of the Junior Division Officers Training Corps.

2ND CORPS

This corps was formed at Croydon on 16 June 1859 and was from September 1860 included in the 1st Admin. Battalion. In March 1867 the establishment of the 2nd was increased to six companies when new personnel were recruited at Crystal Palace and Caterham. The addition of the new companies was to bring the strength of the corps up sufficiently for it to be made independent of the 1st Admin.

Redesignation as the 1st Volunteer Battalion, The Queen's (Royal West Surrey Regiment) was notified in General Order 37 of March 1883. This title was retained until April 1908 and transfer to the Territorial Force as the 4th Battalion of the regiment.

The Whitgift School of Croydon was associated with the battalion from 1874 when a cadet corps was formed from its members. The school became part of the Junior Division of the Officers Training Corps in 1908.

3RD CORPS

The 1st Admin. Battalion of Surrey Rifle Volunteers was formed in September 1860 with headquarters at Croydon and to it then or upon subsequent formation were added the following corps—

2nd Corps: Formed at Croydon on 16 June 1859. Removed from the battalion and made independent in March 1867.

4th Corps: Formed at Brixton on 10 September 1859.

8th Corps: Formed at Epsom on 21 December 1859. Moved to Carshalton in 1862.

11th Corps: Formed at Wimbledon on 11 February 1860. This corps was originally placed in the 2nd Admin. Battalion and was transferred to the 1st in July 1862.

20th Corps: Formed at Lower Norwood on 27 April 1860. Disbanded in 1863.

21st Corps: This corps was formed at Battersea on 3 May 1860 and did not join the battalion until 1863. Disbanded in 1866.

25th Corps: Formed at Epsom as the 26th Corps on 1 March 1862. Renumbered in April of the same year.

26th Corps: This was the second corps to hold this number and was formed at Lavender Hill, Clapham on 28 April 1875.

Headquarters of the battalion were moved to Wimbledon in 1862 and then to Duke Street, Southwark in 1868. Yet another move occurred in 1869 when new premises were found in Thornton Road, Clapham Park.

Upon consolidation in 1880 the battalion took on the number of its senior company and was designated as 4th Surrey Rifle Volunteer Corps. This was changed, however, to 3rd by September. The Lavender Hill Corps, 26th, was not included in the new battalion but instead was merged into the 7th Corps at Southwark. The remainder of the 1st Admin. were reorganised as follows—

'A' 'B' 'C' Companies at Brixton	Late 4th Corps
'D' Company at Carshalton	Late 8th Corps
'E' 'F' Companies at Wimbledon	Late 11th Corps
'G' Company at Epsom	Late 25th Corps

A half company was provided by the 4th Corps at Brixton.

Battalion headquarters were once again moved in 1884, this time to St George's Road in Wimbledon. Two new companies were formed in 1886 and in December of the following year redesignation as the 2nd Volunteer Battalion, The East Surrey Regiment was notified in General Order 181.

The strength of the battalion was again increased in 1900 when two new companies were formed. By 1904 various movements in company locations had taken place resulting in the following arrangment; 'A' and 'B' at Streatham, 'C' and 'D' at Sutton, 'E', 'F', 'G' and 'I' at Wimbledon with 'H' and 'K' at Epsom. A cadet corps provided by the College, Epsom had been affiliated to the battalion since formation in March 1890.

The 2nd VB transferred to the Territorial Force in 1908 as the 5th Battalion East Surreys. Epsom College became part of the Junior Division of the Officers Training Corps.

4TH CORPS

Formed in September 1860 with headquarters at Dorking the 3rd Admin. Battalion of Surrey Rifle Volunteers contained the following corps—

5th Corps: Formed at Reigate on 12 September 1859.

13th Corps: Formed at Guildford on 18 February 1860.

14th Corps: Formed as the 2nd Sub-division on 9 September 1859. Headquarters were at Dorking and redesignation as the 14th Corps appeared for the first time in the *Army List* for March 1860. Disbanded in· 1877.

17th Corps: Formed at Godstone on 23 February 1860.

18th Corps: Formed at Farnham on 6 March 1860.

22nd Corps: Formed at Albury on 16 January 1861. Disbanded in 1875.

24th Corps: Formed at Guildford as the 25th Corps on 31 January 1862. Renumbered in April of the same year.

The battalion was consolidated in 1880 as the 4th Surrey Rifle Volunteer Corps although the number of the senior corps, 5th, was used for a few months. The companies of the new corps were organised as follows—

'A' 'B' Companies at Reigate	Late 5th Corps
'C' 'D' Companies at Guildford	Late 13th Corps
'E' Company at Farnham	Late 18th Corps
'F' Company at Guildford	Late 24th Corps

A sub-division was provided by the 17th Corps at Godstone. Headquarters of the corps which under General Order 37 of March 1883 was redesignated as the 2nd Volunteer Battalion, The Queen's (Royal West Surrey Regiment) were moved from Dorking to Reigate in 1881. Ten years later yet another move was made, this time to Guildford.

Three cadet units have been associated with the battalion. The first was formed in 1873 from boys of the Charterhouse School at Godalming. Next came a corps formed in 1900 at Cranleigh School followed by one at Reigate Grammar in 1907.

In April 1908 the 2nd VB became the 5th Battalion of the Queen's (Royal West Surrey Regiment). The three cadet companies all transferred to the Junior Division of the Officers Training Corps.

5TH CORPS

The 5th Corps was formed in 1880 by the consolidation of the 2nd Surrey Admin. Battalion. Formed in September 1860 the 2nd Admin. had its first headquarters at Walton-on-Thames and included the following corps—

6th Corps: Formed at Esher on 29 October 1859.

9th Corps: Formed at Richmond as the 1st Sub-division on 2 September 1859. Increased to a full company and designated as 9th Corps in December.

11th Corps: Formed at Wimbledon on 11 February 1860 and transferred to the 1st Admin. Battalion in July 1862.

12th Corps: Formed at Kingston-on-Thames on 16 February 1860. Was removed from the battalion and made independent in 1861 after achieving a strength of four companies. Returned to battalion in 1864.

15th Corps: Formed as the 3rd Sub-division at Chertsey on 25 February 1860. Redesignated as 15th Corps the following month.

16th Corps: Formed at Egham on 2 March 1860. Disbanded 1868.

Headquarters of the battalion were moved to Kington in 1864. Upon consolidation the eight companies of the new corps were organised as follows—

'A' Company at Esher	Late 6th Corps
'B' 'C' Companies at Richmond	Late 9th Corps
'D' 'E' 'F' 'G' Companies at Kingston	Late 12th Corps
'H' Company at Chertsey	Late 15th Corps

Two new companies were formed in 1900 bringing the establishment of the corps up to ten. Also that year a cadet corps was formed by Richmond County School as did Beaumont College, Old Windsor in 1906.

The 5th Surreys were redesignated as the 3rd Volunteer Battalion of the East Surrey Regiment in December 1887, the change being notified in General Order 181. In 1908 and upon transfer to the Territorial Force the 6th Battalion of the regiment was formed. Richmond County School Cadets were eventually, in 1910, recognised by the TF and affiliated to the 6th. Beaumont College became part of the Officers Training Corps.

6TH CORPS

In February 1860 the 10th Surrey Rifle Volunteer Corps of one comapny was formed at Bermondsey. Exactly one year later the 23rd, also of one company, was raised at Rotherhithe. At first both corps remained independent and were not included in any of the County Admin. Battalions. They were, however, attached to the 19th Corps in 1863. Both the 10th and 23rd remained with the 19th until October 1868 when they were grouped together as the 4th Admin. Battalion of Surrey Rifle Volunteers. Headquarters were at first placed at Bermondsey but later, by the end of 1869, they moved to Rotherhithe.

When the 4th Admin. was consolidated as the 6th Surrey Rifle Volunteer in 1880 the establishment of the 10th Corps was of two companies. That for the 23rd was six. This gave the new corps a strength of eight companies which were organised as follows; 'A' and 'B' at Bermondsey with 'C' to 'H' at Rotherhithe.

A cadet corps was raised in Bermondsey in 1885 but this was not shown in the *Army List* after 1894. Another was formed at the Streatham Grammar School in March 1899.

The 6th Surrey RVC became the 3rd Volunteer Battalion of the Queen's (Royal Surrey Regiment) under General Order 37 of March 1883. Headquarters were moved from Rotherhithe back to Bermondsey in 1884 and in April 1908 the battalion joined the newly-formed London Regiment as its 22nd Battalion.

Although the Army Council did approve, under Army Order 297 of 1908, the transfer of Streatham Grammar School to the Officers Training Corps the company was in fact disbanded.

7TH CORPS

The 7th was one of the few Surrey Corps to attain sufficient strength not to be included in any administrative battalion. The first company was formed on 30 November 1859 followed by five others in 1860. Headquarters of the corps were in Southwark.

As previously mentioned the 26th Corps was formed at Lavender Hill, Clapham on 28 April 1875 and included in the 1st Admin. Battalion. This was also a strong corps and consisted of four companies.

In 1880 an amalgamation between the 7th and 26th took place. A new 7th Corps of ten companies was constituted with headquarters at Southwark which in December 1887 (General Order 181) became the 4th Volunteer Battalion of the East Surrey Regiment.

Shortly after the amalgamation of 1880 headquarters of the corps are given in the *Army List* as being at Upper Kennington Lane. This was changed to Clapham Junction in 1902.

A new company consisting entirely of cyclists was formed in 1900 and in 1908 the battalion became part of the London Regiment, providing its 23rd Battalion.

8TH CORPS

The 8th and last corps of the post-1880 Surrey Rifle Volunteers was originally raised as the 19th at Lambeth on 13 March 1860. The 19th was soon up to eight companies and between 1863 and 1868 had the 10th and 23rd Corps attached for drill and administration. Headquarters are given as 71 New Street, Kennington Park from 1869.

When the reorganisations were introduced in 1880 the 19th was at first numbered as 7th Corps. This was changed to 8th, however, after a few months. Redesignation as the 4th Volunteer Battalion of the Queen's (Royal West Surrey Regiment) was notified in March 1883 (General Order 37).

The establishment of the battalion was increased to ten companies in 1890 followed by a company of cyclist in 1901. A cadet corps was formed at Mayall College in Hern Hill on 29 December 1888 but in 1891 this was transferred to the care of the 22nd Middlesex Corps.

Another cadet corps to be associated with the battalion had its headquarters at the Red Cross Hall in Southwark. The corps was formed in June 1889 and within a short time consisted of four companies. In view of this it was felt that the corps could be made independent of the 4th Volunteer Battalion. Subsequently, in November 1890, they became the 1st Cadet Battalion, The Queen's (Royal Surrey Regiment).

The 4th VB transferred to the Territorial Force in April 1908 as the 24th (County of London) Battalion, The London Regiment.

Four cadet units of battalion strength were formed in Surrey between 1890 and 1908. The 1st Cadet Battalion, The Queen's (Royal West Surrey Regiment) originated in June 1889 when a cadet corps was formed for the 4th Volunteer Battalion of the regiment. The corps was to be found at the Red Cross Hall in Southwark.

The idea for the corps was first put forward in January 1889 when Captain Salmond of the 3rd Battalion, Derbyshire Regiment was asked to take charge of formation. A meeting was held, in which Lord Wolseley made a memorable speech, on 30 May at the Red Cross Hall. The following day enough recruits had come forward to complete an establishment of two companies. A third soon followed and in 1890, when a forth was formed, permission was given to form a cadet battalion. This was to be the first independent battalion of cadets formed in London and in 1891, when a strength of six companies had been reached, the battalion became the largest in England.

In 1904 headquarters were moved to Union Street, Southwark and the companies, now eight in number, were situated as follows; 'A' and 'B' at headquarters, 'C' at the Passmore Edward's Settlement, St Pancras and the Marlborough Road Board School, Chelsea, 'D' at the Haileybury Club, Stepney, 'E' at St Andrew's Institute, Westminster, 'F' at the St Peter's Institute, Pimlico, 'G' at Bethnal Green and 'H' at the Eton Mission in Hackney. The battalion continued its association with the Queen's after 1908.

The first cadet battalion to bear the title 2nd Cadet Battalion, The Queen's (Royal West Surrey Regiment) was formed in November 1890 with an establishment of four companies. Headquarters were first at Lambeth Polytechnic, Clapham. They were later moved to Kirkdale, Clapham and then to Brockwell Hall, Herne Hill. The establishment was increased to six companies in 1891 and in 1894 the battalion was redesignated as the 1st CB The King's Royal Rifle Corps.

A new 2nd Cadet Battalion was formed in October 1901 from boys of the 1st Peckham Lads Brigade which had been formed in 1894. Headquarters were at 53 Copeland Road, Peckham and the establishment was of six companies. The battalion was not recognised by the Territorial Force in 1908.

The 1st Cadet Battalion, The East Surrey Regiment was formed in 1890 with an establishment of four companies. Headquarters were at 71 Upper Kennington Lane. Interest in the battalion later declined resulting in disbandment during 1896.

SUSSEX

On 26 April 1860 three administrative battalions were formed for the County of Sussex. Not all Sussex rifle corps were to be included in the three as some became part of the 1st Cinque Ports Battalion at Hastings.

Headquarters of the 1st Admin. Battalion were at first placed at Chichester but these were moved to Worthing in 1866. Petworth was the headquarters of the 2nd Battalion, transferred to Horsham in 1869, and Brighton the home of the 3rd.

During 1863 the 3rd Admin. was broken up due to the 1st Brighton Corps being made independent. Next came the amalgamation of the 1st and 2nd Battalions in 1874 which was to bring the Sussex administration units down to one. This was designated as 1st Admin. Battalion with headquarters at Worthing.

The Sussex Rifle Volunteers prior to 1880 were—

1st Corps: Formed at Brighton on 23 November 1859. The 1st was included in the 3rd Admin. Battalion until 1863 when upon reaching a strength of six companies it was made independent.

2nd Corps: Formed at Cuckfield on 2 December 1859 and included in the 3rd Admin. Battalion. The 2nd transferred to the 1st Cinque Ports Admin. in 1863 but returned to Sussex and its 2nd Battalion in 1870.

3rd Corps: None formed.

4th Corps: Formed at Lewes on 25 January 1860 and included in the 3rd Admin. Battalion. Transferred to the 1st Cinque Ports Admin. in 1863 and in 1880 became 'D' Company of the 1st Cinque Ports Corps.

5th Corps: Formed at East Grinstead on 9 February 1860 and included in the 3rd Admin. Battalion. Transferred to the 2nd Admin. in 1862.

6th Corps: Formed at Petworth on 8 February 1860. Included in the 2nd Admin.

7th Corps: Formed as the 1st Sub-division on 29 November 1859. Became the 7th Corps in February 1860 and was later included in the 2nd Admin. Battalion. Headquarters were at Horsham.

8th Corps: Formed at Storrignton on 16 February 1860. Was at first included in the 1st Admin. but joined 2nd by the beginning of 1861. The 8th returned to the 1st Admin. in 1874 only to be disbanded in 1876.

9th Corps: Formed at Arundel on 28 February 1860. Joined the 1st Admin. Battalion.

10th Corps: Formed at Chichester on 1 March 1860. Joined the 1st Admin. Battalion.

11th Corps: Formed at Worthing on 10 March 1860. Joined the 1st Admin. Battalion.

12th Corps: Formed at Westbourne on 28 June 1860. Joined the 1st Admin. Battalion.

13th Corps: Formed at Hurstpierpoint on 14 March 1860. Joined the 2nd Admin. Battalion.

14th Corps: Formed at Crawley on 14 March 1860. Joined the 2nd Admin. Battalion and disappeared from the *Army List* in April 1863.

15th Corps: Formed at Bognor on 9 April 1860. Joined the 1st Admin. and disappeared from the *Army List* in April 1865.

16th Corps: Formed at Battle on 19 May 1860 and was at first included in the 3rd Admin. Battalion. Transferred to the 1st Cinque Ports Admin. Battalion in December 1861 and in 1876 was absorbed into the 1st Cinque Ports Corps.

17th Corps: Formed at Etchingham on 4 June 1860 and was from August shown in the *Army List* as being 'united for drill and administration' with the 37th Kent Corps. From May 1861 the 17th was attached to the

5th Kent Admin. Battalion but was yet again transferred in November this time to the 1st Cinque Ports Battalion. The 17th was aesorbed into the 1st Cinque Ports Corps in 1876.

18th Corps: Formed at Henfield on 14 June 1860 and was, by August 1861, included in the 2nd Admin. Battalion.

19th Corps: Formed at Eastbourne on 6 October 1860 and was, by August 1861, included in the 3rd Admin. Battalion. Transferred to the 1st Cinque Ports Admin. in December, 1861 and was disbanded in 1868.

20th Corps: The first corps to be numbered as 20th was formed at Billinghurst and was first seen in the *Army List* for January 1861. The corps disappeared in December having had no officers gazetted to it. The next 20th was formed at Uckfield on 27 October 1870 and was from that date included in the 1st Cinque Ports Admin. Battalion. The Corps was absorbed into the 1st Cinque Ports Corps in 1876.

As previously mentioned the 1st Corps at Brighton reached a strength of six companies in 1863. This was increased to eight in 1886 and in February of the following year (General Order 14) the 1st Corps became the 1st Volunteer Battalion of the Royal Sussex Regiment. A 9th company was raised in 1900.

In February 1880 the 1st Admin. Battalion was consolidated as the 2nd Sussex Corps. Headquarters remained at Worthing and the corps' eleven companies were organised as follows—

'A' 'B' Companies at Cuckfield	Late 2nd Corps
'C' Company at East Grinstead	Late 5th Corps
'D' Company at Petworth	Late 6th Corps
'E' Company at Horsham	Late 7th Corps
'F' Company at Arundel	Late 9th Corps
'G' Company at Chichester	Late 10th Corps
'H' Company at Worthing	Late 11th Corps
'I' Company at Westbourne	Late 12th Corps
'K' Company at Hurstpierpoint	Late 13th Corps
'L' Company at Henfield	Late 18th Corps

The 2nd Corps was redesignated as the 2nd Volunteer Battalion, The Royal Sussex Regiment under General Order 14 of February 1887 and in 1900 was increased to a strength of twelve companies.

When the Territorial Force was created in 1908 the intention was for the 1st VB to convert to an artillery roll and provide the 2nd Home Counties Brigade, RFA. The battalions officers, however, refused and were from April 1908 placed on the unattached list. This was the case until 1912 when the officers and men of the old 1st VB became the 6th (Cyclist) Battalion of the Royal Sussex Regiment. The 2nd VB, in 1908, became the 4th Battalion.

Several cadet corps were formed and affiliated to both the 1st and 2nd Volunteer Battalions. Units connected with the 1st VB were Brighton College, formed in 1900; Christ's Hospital, formed in 1904 and the Cottesmore School which was formed in 1905 and in 1907 became known as the Brighton and Preparatory Schools. In 1908 both Brighton College and Christ's Hospital became part of the

Junior Division of the Officers Training Corps. Brighton Prep did not transfer to the OTC but instead remained with the Royal Sussex Regiment and affiliated to the 4th Battalion.

The 2nd VB cadet companies were St John's College at Hurstpierpoint, formed in 1887, Lancing College at Shorham, formed in 1900 and Ardingly College, Haywards Heath, formed in 1903. All three schools transferred to the OTC in 1908.

SUTHERLAND

The following corps were formed within the county by the beginning of 1860—

1st Corps: Formed at Golspie on 2 December 1859.

2nd Corps: Formed at Dornoch on 2 December 1859.

3rd Corps: Formed at Brora on 30 January 1860.

In January 1861 the above corps plus a new company raised at Rogart that month were merged as the 1st Sutherland Rifle Volunteer Corps of four companies.

On 4 January 1864 the 1st Corps was divided and once more constituted three independent corps with the No 4 Company at Rogart now designated as 4th Corps. At the same time the 1st Orkney and Shetland and the 1st, 2nd and 3rd Caithness Corps were together with the four Sutherland companies placed into a battalion designated as the 1st Sutherland Admin. or The Sutherland Highland Rifle Volunteers.

The 4th Caithness was also included upon its formation in September 1867 as was the 5th Sutherland in 1868. The latter being formed at Bonar Bridge on 6 August.

The battalion was consolidated in 1880 as the 1st Sutherland (Sutherland Highland) Rifle Volunteer Corps. The former 1st Admin. Battalion headquarters at Golspie were retained and the ten companies organised as follows—

'A' Company at Golspie	Late 1st Sutherland Corps
'B' Company at Dornoch	Late 2nd Sutherland Corps
'C' Company at Brora	Late 3rd Sutherland Corps
'D' Company at Rogart	Late 4th Sutherland Corps
'E' Company at Bonar Bridge	Late 5th Sutherland Corps
'F' Company at Lerwick	Late 1st Orkney and Shetland Corps
'G' Company at Thurso	Late 1st Caithness Corps
'H' Company at Wick	Late 2nd Caithness Corps
'I' Company at Halkirk	Late 3rd Caithness Corps
'K' Company at Watten	Late 4th Caithness Corps

In 1884 'F' Company at Lerwick was disbanded and in its place a new 'F' was raised at Lairg in Sutherland. With this change the ten companies were then situated, six in Sutherland and four in Caithness. Things were later evened up, however, when in 1890 'L' Company was formed at Wick and in 1901 when 'M' was raised at Reay.

Since 1881 the 1st Sutherland had been a volunteer battalion of the Seaforth Highlanders. Although ranked as 2nd redesignation as such was never assumed.

The only change in title occurring in 1891 when the style 'Rifle Volunteer Corps' was changed to 'Volunteer Rifle Corps' and in 1908 when the 5th Battalion of the Seaforth Highlanders was formed upon transfer to the Territorial Force.

TOWER HAMLETS

The Tower Hamlets Rifle Volunteer Brigade was formed upon the amalgamation in 1868 of the 2nd and 4th Tower Hamlets Corps. Consisting of seven companies, 1 Hackney, 2 Dalston, 3 Bow, 4, 5, 6, Poplar and Limehouse, 7 Clapton, the 2nd Corps was formed on 6 April 1860. Headquarters were at first located in Dalston but were moved before the end of 1860 to Hackney. Two other corps of the East London Borough were, during 1861, attached to the 2nd for drill and administration. These were the 8th, who became part of the 26th Middlesex Corps in 1868 and the 9th who were transferred to the care of the 1st Tower Hamlets Admin. Battalion in 1863.

The 4th Corps was formed on 14 June 1860 and at first had its headquarters at St Leonards in Shoreditch. Five companies were soon raised by the corps which by 1862 was attached to the 6th Tower Hamlets for drill and administration. Two additional companies were formed by 1864 when the 4th was detached from the 6th and made independent. Also that year new headquarters were found at Hoxton.

Upon amalgamation in 1868 the title assumed was 1st Tower Hamlets Rifle Volunteer Corps. A 1st Corps had first appeared in the *Army List* for April 1860 and was shown as having its headquarters at Dalston. Recruiting apparently did not go well resulting in the disbandment of the corps before the end of 1860. Headquarters of the new 1st Corps were in Robert Street, Hoxton. The establishment was set at fifteen companies of which seven were provided by the 2nd corps and eight by the 4th. After a short time the 1st also assumed the title of 'The Tower Hamlets Rifle Volunteer Brigade'.

On 25 September 1860 the 6th Tower Hamlets Rifle Volunteer Corps was formed at Dalston. This corps, by the beginning of 1861, consisted of eight companies and no doubt contained members of the original 1st Corps. During 1861 headquarters were moved to Shaftesbury Street, Hoxton and the 5th and 11th Corps were attached for drill and administration. As previously mentioned the 4th Corps were also associated with the 6th and in 1862 appear in the *Army List* as 'temporarily attached for purpose of drill'.

In 1866 the strength of the 6th Corps, which had recieved the additional title of 'North East London Rifles' the previous year, stood at twelve companies. The 5th Corps ceased its affiliation upon disbandment in 1862 as did the 11th when it transferred to the 1st Admin. Battalion in 1861. The 4th became independent in 1864.

During 1873 it was decided to amalgamate the 6th with the Tower Hamlets Rifle Volunteer Brigade with effect from 1 January 1874. At this time the total strength of the two corps stood at twenty-seven companies but these, it was ordered, should merge into sixteen. The reorganisation went as follows—

'A' Company formed from 'A', 'L', 'M' and 'N' Companies' 1st Corps.
'B' Company formed from 'A' and 'L' Companies' 6th Corps.
'C' Company formed from 'B' Company's 1st Corps.
'D' Company formed from 'B' Company 6th Corps.
'E' Company formed from 'C' and 'D' Companies' 1st Corps.
'F' Company formed from 'C' and 'H' Companies' 6th Corps.
'G' Company formed from 'E' Company's 1st Corps.
'H' Company formed from 'D' Company's 6th Corps.
'J' Company formed from 'F', 'I' and 'K' Companies' 1st Corps.
'K' Company formed from 'E' Company's 6th Corps.
'L' Company formed from 'G' Company's 1st Corps.
'M' Company formed from 'F' and 'G' Companies' 6th Corps.
'N' Company formed from 'H' and 'J' Companies' 1st Corps.
'O' Company formed from 'J' Company's 6th Corps.
'P' Company formed from 'O' Company's 1st Corps.
'Q' Company formed from 'K' Company's 6th Corps.

Headquarters of the now enlarged 1st Corps were transferred to those formally used by the 6th at Shaftesbury Street.

In August 1874 the establishment of the brigade was reduced by the War Office to twelve companies. The following rearrangments in company organisation were required and were notified in Regimental Orders of 28 November 1874—

'A' Company to be formed from 'A' and 'P'
'B' Company to be formed from 'B'
'C' Company to be formed from 'O' and 'Q'
'D' Company to be formed from 'E' and 'C'
'E' Company to be formed from 'J'
'F' Company to be formed from 'F'
'G' Company to be formed from 'G'
'H' Company to be formed from 'H'
'J' Company to be formed from 'N'
'K' Company to be formed from 'K' and 'D'
'L' Company to be formed from 'L'
'M' Company to be formed from 'M'

From 1881 the 1st Tower Hamlets appear in the *Army List* as one of the volunteer battalions allotted to the Rifle Brigade. No change in title, however, was assumed. In May 1904 the corps transferred to the Royal Fusiliers and from then on were known as its 4th Volunteer Battalion. In 1908 the 4th VB became part of the London Regiment, providing its 4th (City of London) Battalion.

A cadet corps was formed during the early days of the 6th Tower Hamlets and was present at the Cadet Review held at the Crystal Palace on 11 September 1862. No mention of the unit, however, was made in the *Army List*. In 1885 a new cadet company appears and on this occasion is recorded in the *Army List* as being affiliated to the Tower Hamlets Rifle Volunteer Brigade. The commanding officer of the unit, which disappeared from the *Army List* during 1891, was commissioned on 13 November 1886.

The 1st Admin. Battalion of Tower Hamlets Rifle Volunteers was formed in May 1861 and included then or at some later date the following corps—

3rd Corps: Formed at Spitalfields on 4 May 1860. Subsequent headquarters are shown in the *Army List* as being at Great Garden Street, Whitechapel from 1865, Granby Street, Bethnal Green from 1870 and Quaker Street, Commercial Street from 1873.

7th Corps: Formed at Mile End on 13 September 1860.

9th Corps: Formed with headquarters at London Dock House on 23 November 1860. The 9th was attached to the 2nd Corps during 1861 and in 1863 became part of the 1st Admin. Battalion. Absorbed into the 26th Middlesex Rifle Volunteer Corps in 1864.

10th Corps: Formed at Goodman's Fields on 13 December 1860. Headquarters moved to Mile End Gate during 1861 to Great Garden Street, Whitechapel in 1865 to Chapel Street, Shoreditch in 1872 and to Finsbury in 1874.

11th Corps: Formed at Goodman's Fields on 21 February 1861. The 11th was attached to the 6th Corps shortly after formation but before the end of 1861 was included in the 1st Admin. Battalion. Disbanded in 1864.

12th Corps: Formed at Stoke Newington on 24 April 1861. Joined the 1st Admin. Battalion in 1863 and in 1870 was absorbed into the London Rifle Brigade.

Many members of the 3rd Corps were workers at Truman's Ltd and it was at their brewery in Spitalfields that the first headquarters of the 1st Admin. Battalion was situated. The battalion continued to share the same headquarters as the 3rd Corps.

When the battalion was consolidated in 1880 it originally took on the number of its senior corps, 3rd. This was changed to 2nd Corps, however, before the end of the year. Headquarters of the new corps were placed at Whitechapel Road and its eleven companies were organised as follows—

'A' to 'D' Companies at Quaker Street   Late 3rd Corps
'E' to 'H' Companies at Mile End   Late 7th Corps
'I', 'K', 'L' Companies at Finsbury   Late 10th Corps

In 1881 the 2nd Tower Hamlets are shown in the *Army List* as one of the volunteer battalions allotted to the Rifle Brigade. No change in title was assumed and in 1894 battalion headquarters were moved to Bow. Transfer to the Territorial Force in 1908 saw the amalgamation of the 2nd Tower Hamlets with the 15th Middlesex Corps and the formation of the 17th (County of London) Battalion of the London Regiment.

The remaining Tower Hamlets Corps were the 5th and 8th. The former was raised at Dalston on 8 August 1860 and in 1861 attached to the 6th Corps for drill and administration. That year headquarters moved to Kingsland and in 1862 the corps was disbanded. The 8th was formed at the West India Dock in Poplar on 7

November 1860. It was attached to the 2nd Corps and in 1868 absorbed into the 26th Middlesex Rifle Volunteer Corps.

On 28 May 1904 the 1st (Duke of Norfolk's Own) Cadet Battalion, The Rifle Brigade was formed in the Tower Hamlets area. Headquarters were in Mile End Road and the establishment was set at four companies. The battalion was later disbanded and disappeared from the *Army List* during 1906.

WARWICKSHIRE

In March 1860 the corps then in existence within the Birmingham area were amalgamated as the 1st Warwickshire (Birmingham) Rifle Volunteers. At this time three corps each of company strength had been formed—

1st Corps: Formed on 4 November 1859.

3rd Corps: Formed on 8 November 1859.

6th Corps: Formed on 8 February 1860.

Subsequent companies to be raised in Birmingham were from March included in the new corps.

With an establishment of twelve companies the 1st Corps became in February 1883 the 1st Volunteer Battalion of the Royal Warwickshire Regiment. The change being notified in General Order 14. In 1891 an additional four companies were sanctioned and the corps divided into two battalions; 1st Battalion 'A' to 'H' Companies, 2nd Battalion 'I' to 'Q'. Further additions to the strength of the two battalions were made in 1900 when the Cyclist Section that had been in existence since 1894 was increased to a full company. Also that year 'U' Company was formed by members of Birmingham University.

A cadet corps is shown as being part of the battalion in 1864 and according to the history of the corps was formed by 'the Grammar School'. No mention of the unit was made in the *Army List* after 1866. Another cadet corps appeared in 1883 but had disappeared by the end of the following year having had no officers appointed. Next came the company forced by the Solihull Grammar School in October 1904 which was followed three years later by one from King Edward's School.

In April 1908 the 1st VB transferred to the Territorial Force as the 5th and 6th Battalions of the Royal Warwicks. The University Company, however, became part of the Officers Training corps. The two cadet units, Solihull and King Edward's, also joined the OTC.

In May 1860 the remaining Warwickshire corps were placed into an administrative battalion which until April 1861 appeared in the *Army List* as 2nd. In this month the battalion is shown as 1st and as having its headquarters at Coventry. The corps to be included were as follows—

2nd Corps: Formed at Coventry on 8 November 1859 and in 1862 absorbed the 6th and 7th Corps who were also at Coventry.

3rd Corps: Formed as 4th Corps at Rugby on 26 November 1859. Redesignated as 3rd Corps in May 1861 and in 1868 absorbed the 12th Corps, also at Rugby, as No 2 Company. Much of the 3rd Corps was recruited from Rugby School which in 1873 also provided a cadet corps.

4th Corps: Formed as 5th Corps at Warwick on 13 February 1860. Renumbered as 4th in May 1861.

5th Corps: Formed as 7th Corps at Stratford-on-Avon on 9 February 1860. Became 5th in May 1861.

6th Corps: Formed as 8th Corps at Coventry on 15 June 1860. Became 6th in May 1861 and in June of the following year was absorbed into the 2nd Corps.

7th Corps: Formed as 9th Corps at Coventry on 31 October 1860. Became 7th in May 1861 and like the 6th Corps was absorbed into the 2nd in 1862.

8th Corps: Formed as 10th Corps at Nuneaton on 1 December 1860. Became 8th in May 1861.

9th Corps: Formed on 29 June 1861. Headquarters of the corps are given in the *Army List* as Saltley but in the *London Gazette* dated 5 July 1861 they are recorded as being at the Saltley Training College.

10th Corps: Formed at Leamington on 15 July 1861 and in 1862 absorbed the 11th Corps.

11th Corps: Formed at Leamington on 3 April 1862. Absorbed into the 10th Corps in 1862.

12th Corps: Formed at Rugby on 22 May 1868. Became No 2 Company of the 3rd Corps by the end of the year.

In March 1880 the 1st Admin. Battalion was consolidated as the 2nd Warwickshire Rifle Volunteers. Headquarters remained at Coventry and the corps' twelve companies were organised as follows—

'A' 'B' 'C' 'D' Companies at Coventry	Late 2nd Corps
'E' 'F' Companies at Rugby	Late 3rd Corps
'G' Company at Warwick	Late 4th Corps
'H' Company at Stratford-on-Avon	Late 5th Corps
'I' Company at Nuneaton	Late 8th Corps
'K' Company at Saltley	Late 9th Corps
'L' 'M' Companies at Leamington	Late 10th Corps

The corps was redesignated yet again when in 1883 and under General Order 14 of February it became the 2nd Volunteer Battalion, The Royal Warwickshire Regiment. The establishment of the battalion was increased to thirteen companies in 1900 but this was reduced to eleven by the end of the following year.

As previously mentioned a cadet corps was formed for the 3rd Corps by Rugby School in 1873. This was to continue service with the 2nd Corps after 1880 and then with the 2nd VB from 1883. Other cadet units to be associated with the battalion were the King's Grammar School at Warwick, formed in 1885, Leamington College, formed 1900 and the King's County School, Warwick whose cadet corps was formed in 1905. King's Grammar was, in 1894, designated simply as Warwick School and was not seen in the *Army List* after 1906. Interest in the Leamington College Corps was slight and the unit desappeared after a few months having had no officer gazetted to it.

Upon transfer to the Territorial Force in 1908 the 2nd VB provided the 7th Battalion of the Warwickshire Regiment. Both Rugby and King's County Schools became part of the Junior Division on the Officers Training Corps.

The first cadet battalion to appear in the *Army List* was that raised in Birmingham in June 1886. It was designated as the 1st Cadet Battalion, The Royal Warwickshire Regiment and had an establishment of four companies. Interest later fell off resulting in disbandment in 1893.

WESTMORLAND

The 1st Admin. Battalion of Westmorland Rifle Volunteers was formed in May 1860. Headquarters were at first placed at Kirkby Lonsdale but these were moved to Kendal in 1861.

1st Corps: Formed at Lonsdale on 29 February 1860.

2nd Corps: A 2nd Corps first appeared in the *Army List* for April 1860 and showed an officer with a commission dated 6 March 1860. No location was given for the company which was removed from the *Army List* in September and shown as having been absorbed into the 3rd Corps at Kendal. A new 2nd Corps, this time with headquarters at Appleby, was formed on 7 August 1878.

3rd Corps: Formed at Kendal on 28 February 1860.

4th Corps: Formed at Windermere on 29 February 1860.

5th Corps: Formed at Ambleside on 28 February 1860.

6th Corps: Formed at Grasmere on 17 April 1860.

The 1st Admin. Battalion was consolidated as the 1st Westmorland Corps in February 1880. Headquarters remained at Kendal and the corps' nine companies were organised as follows—

'A' Company at Kirkby Lonsdale	Late 1st Corps
'B' Company at Appleby	Late 2nd Corps
'C' 'D' 'E' Companies at Kendal	Late 3rd Corps
'F' Company at Stavely	Newly-formed
'G' Company at Windermere	Late 4th Corps
'H' Company at Ambleside	Late 5th Corps
'J' Company at Grasmere	Late 6th Corps

The 1st Corps was redesignated as the 2nd (Westmorland) Volunteer Battalion of the Border Regiment in 1887, the change being notified in General Order 181 of December. Upon the transfer in 1908 to the Territorial Force the 2nd and 4th Volunteer Battalions of the Border Regiment were amalgamated as the regiments' 4th Battalion.

Two cadet units have been associated with the 2nd VB. The first was formed in 1901 by Sedbergh School which in 1908 became part of the Junior Division of the Officers Training Corps. Next came a unit known as the Kirkby Lonsdale Cadet Company which was raised in April 1902 and in 1908 became affiliated to the new 4th Battalion.

WIGTOWNSHIRE

Included in the administrative battalion created on 30 June 1860 and designated as 'The Galloway' were the 1st to 5th Kirkcudbrightshire Corps, a 6th was formed in 1869, and those then in existence or subsequently formed in Wigtownshire. In all five corps were formed—

1st Corps: Formed at Wigtown on 24 February 1860. Absorbed into the 3rd Corps in 1874.

2nd Corps: Formed at Stranraer on 16 March 1860.

3rd Corps: Formed at Newton-Stewart on 22 March 1860. Absorbed the 1st Corps in 1874.

4th Corps: Formed at Whithorn on 11 April 1860. Disbanded in 1874.

5th Corps: Formed at Drumore on 23 November 1860. Disbanded in 1866.

In 1880 the battalion was consolidated as the Galloway Rifle Volunteer Corps. The former admin. battalion headquarters at Newton-Stewart were retained and the eight company establishment was organised as follows—

'A' Company at Kirkcudbright	Late 1st Kirkcudbright Corps
'B' Company at Castle-Douglas	Late 2nd Kirkcudbright Corps
'C' Company at Stranraer	Late 2nd Wigtown Corps
'D' Company at Newton-Stewart	Late 3rd Wigtown Corps
'E' Company at New Galloway	Late 3rd Kirkcudbright Corps
'F' Company at Maxwelltown	Late 5th Kirkcudbright Corps
'G' Company at Maxwelltown	Late 5th Kirkcudbright Corps
'H' Company at Dalbeattie	Late 6th Kirkcudbright Corps

The Galloway Rifles joined the Royal Scots Fusiliers as one of its allotted volunteer battalions in 1881. No change in title was assumed and in 1899, Army Order 65, the corps transferred to the King's Own Scottish Borderers taking up the position of 4th in the Volunteer line-up. Again no change in designation was assumed.

Headquarters of the battalion were moved to Castle-Douglas in 1885 and then in 1904 to Maxwelltown. In April 1908 the Galloway Rifles transferred to the Territorial Force, providing four companies, three in Kirkcudbrightshire and one in Wigtownshire, of the 5th Battalion, the King's Own Scottish Borderers and one company, Wigtownshire, of the 5th Battalion, the Royal Scots Fusiliers.

WILTSHIRE

The 1st Admin. Battalion of Wiltshire Rifle Volunteers was formed with headquarters at Salisbury on 8 March 1861. The corps included in the battalion were as follows—

1st Corps: Formed at Salisbury on 10 August 1859.

2nd Corps: Formed at Trowbridge on 16 February 1860.

6th Corps: Formed at Maiden Bradley on 2 April 1860 and in July 1861 absorbed the 1st Wilts Mounted Rifle Volunteer Corps. The 6th was later disbanded and was last seen in the *Army List* for January 1873.

8th Corps: Formed at Mere on 1 May 1860 and was disbanded in 1875.

9th Corps: Formed at Bradford on 17 May 1860.

10th Corps: Formed at Warminster on 5 March 1860.

13th Corps: Formed at Westbury on 12 March 1860.

14th Corps: Formed at Wilton on 1 May 1860.

Headquarters of the battalion were moved to Warminster in 1879 and the following year the 1st Admin. was consolidated as the 1st Corps. The new corps consisted of eight companies organised as follows—

'A' 'B' Companies at Salisbury	Late 1st Corps
'C' 'D' Companies at Trowbridge	Late 2nd Corps
'E' Company at Bradford	Late 9th Corps
'F' Company at Warminster	Late 10th Corps
'G' Company at Westbury	Late 13th Corps
'H' Company at Wilton	Late 14th Corps

In 1881 the 1st Wiltshires joined the Wiltshire Regiment as one of its allotted volunteer battalions but although ranked as 1st no change in designation was assumed.

A new company, 'I', was formed in 1892 from around the Tisbury and Mere areas. This was followed in 1900 by a cyclist company designated as 'K' and formed at Bradford. A cadet corps with headquarters at Salisbury was raised in 1890 but this had disappeared from the *Army List* by the end of 1897.

The 2nd Admin. Battalion of the county had its first headquarters at Swindon but these were moved to Chippenham in 1864. The battalion was formed on 8 March 1861 and included the following corps—

3rd Corps: Formed at Malmesbury on 28 January 1860.

4th Corps: Formed at Chippenham on 16 February 1860.

5th Corps: Formed at Devizes on 3 March 1860.

7th Corps: Formed at Market Lavington on 2 March 1860.

11th Corps: Formed at Swindon on 31 March 1860.

12th Corps: Formed at Melksham on 1 March 1860.

15th Corps: Formed at Wootton Bassett on 18 June 1860.

16th Corps: Formed at Old Swindon on 13 July 1860.

17th Corps: Formed at Marlborough on 27 July 1860. Many of the corps members were from Marlborough College.

18th Corps: Formed at Highworth on 24 November 1860.

The battalion was consolidated in April 1880 as the 3rd Corps but by July had been renumbered as 2nd. Headquarters remained at Chippenham and the corps' twelve companies were organised as follows—

'A' Company at Malmesbury	Late 3rd Corps
'B' Company at Chippenham	Late 4th Corps
'C' 'D' Companies at Devizes	Late 5th Corps
'E' Company at Market Lavington	Late 7th Corps
'F' 'G' Companies at Swindon	Late 11th Corps
'H' Company at Melksham	Late 12th Corps
'I' Company at Wootton Bassett	Late 15th Corps
'K' Company at Swindon	Late 16th Corps
'L' Company at Marlborough	Late 17th Corps
'M' Company at Highworth	Late 18th Corps

There was also a sub-division at Calne.

A reduction was made to eleven companies in 1882 and in 1887 the 2nd Corps was designated as the 2nd Volunteer Battalion of the Wiltshire Regiment under General Order 181 of December.

In 1908 and upon transfer to the Territorial Force the 1st Wiltshire VRC and the 2nd VB were amalgamated as the 4th Battalion, The Duke of Edinburgh's (Wiltshire Regiment). The 1st Wiltshires provided HQ and five companies while the 2nd VB supplied three.

As previously mentioned the 17th Corps contained many recruits from Marlborough College. In 1870 a cadet corps was formed by the College and affiliated to the 2nd Admin. Battalion. The corps continued its association with the 2nd Wiltshires and later the 2nd VB. In 1908 it became part of the Junior Division of the Officers Training Corps.

WORCESTERSHIRE

The 1st Admin. Battalion of Worcestershire Rifle Volunteers was formed on 24 April 1860. Headquarters were at Hagley and the corps included were as follows—

1st Corps: Formed at Wolverley on 1 November 1859.

2nd Corps: Formed at Tenbury on 18 November 1859.

3rd Corps: Formed at Kidderminster on 17 January 1860. Headquarters of this corps are given in the *Army List* as Franche House, Kidderminster from 1861.

4th Corps: Formed at Kidderminster on 24 January 1860.

5th Corps: Formed at Bewdley on 2 March 1860.

6th Corps: Formed at Halesowen on 2 March 1860.

7th Corps: Formed at Dudley on 2 March 1860.

8th Corps: Formed at Stourport on 2 March 1860.

9th Corps: Formed at Stourbridge on 2 March 1860.

16th Corps: Formed at Oldbury on 13 April 1860.

20th Corps: Formed at Kidderminster on 16 November 1860. Headquarters are given as Greatfield House, Kidderminster from 1861.

The 10th Corps was shown in the *Army List* as being part of the 1st Admin. until September 1860 when it was included in the 2nd.

The battalion was consolidated as the 1st Worcestershire Rifle Volunteer Corps in 1880. Headquarters remained at Hagley and the corps' eleven companies were organised as follows—

'A' Company at Wolverley	Late 1st Corps
'B' Company at Tenbury	Late 2nd Corps
'C' Company at Kidderminster	Late 3rd Corps
'D' Company at Kidderminster	Late 4th Corps
'E' Company at Bewdley	Late 5th Corps
'F' Company at Halesowen	Late 6th Corps
'G' Company at Dudley	Late 7th Corps
'H' Company at Stourport	Late 8th Corps
'I' Company at Stourbridge	Late 9th Corps
'K' Company at Oldbury	Late 16th Corps
'L' Company at Kidderminster	Late 20th Corps

In 1882 a new company was raised at Dudley and the following year the corps was designated as the 1st Volunteer Battalion, The Worcestershire Regiment under General Order 80 of June.

Headquarters of the battalion were moved to Kidderminster in 1891 and by 1908 those of 'A' Company were located at Dudley.

In 1908 and upon transfer to the Territorial Force the 1st VB became the 7th Battalion, The Worcestershire Regiment.

Worcester was the headquarters of the county's 2nd Admin. Battalion. Formed on 17 August 1860 the 2nd Admin. contained the following corps—

10th Corps: Formed at Pershore on 13 March 1860. The 10th was shown in the *Army List* until August 1860 as being included in the 1st Admin. Battalion.

11th Corps: Formed at Gt Malvern on 9 March 1860.

12th Corps: Formed at Evesham on 13 March 1860.

13th Corps: Formed at Worcester on 10 April 1860.

14th Corps: Formed at Worcester on 13 April 1860.

15th Corps: Formed at Ombersley on 13 April 1860. This corps was disbanded in 1868.

17th Corps: Formed at Redditch on 4 May 1860.

18th Corps: Formed at Droitwich on 15 June 1860.

19th Corps: Formed at Upton-on-Severn on 6 November 1860.

21st Corps: Formed at Bromsgrove on 20 August 1861.

The 2nd Admin. was consolidated in February 1880 as the 10th Worcestershire Rifle Volunteer Corps but by July had been renumbered as 2nd. The corps' eight companies were organised as follows—

'A' Company at Worcester	Late 13th Corps
'B' Company at Worcester	Late 14th Corps
'C' Company at Gt Malvern and Upton-on-Severn	Late 11th and 19th Corps
'D' Company at Evesham	Late 12th Corps
'E' Company at Droitwich	Late 18th Corps
'F' Company at Pershore	Late 10th Corps
'G' Company at Bromsgrove	Late 21st Corps
'H' Company at Redditch	Late 17th Corps

The 2nd Corps was redesignated as the 2nd Volunteer Battalion, The Worcestershire Regiment under General Order 80 of June 1883. The next change was in 1908 when the 2nd provided the Worcester's 8th Territorial Battalion.

A company of cadets was formed by the Victoria Institute at Worcester in 1903 but these were not seen in the *Army List* after 1908.

YORKSHIRE (EAST RIDING)

It was originally intended to group the corps formed in the Hull area into an administrative battalion designated as 1st. Such a battalion did appear in the *Army List* but was gone by March 1861. The Hull volunteers were in fact merged into one corps by the beginning of 1861.

1st Corps: Formed at Hull on 9 November 1859. Absorbed the 2nd and 3rd Corps in March 1860 and the 9th Corps in October.

2nd Corps: Formed at Hull on 24 November 1859 and absorbed into the 1st Corps in March 1860.

3rd Corps: Formed at Hull on 12 January 1860 and absorbed into the 1st Corps in March.

4th Corps: Formed at Hull on 5 January 1860 and absorbed into the 1st Corps by January 1861.

9th Corps: A 9th Corps, no headquarters given, is shown in the *Army List* with its officers' commissions dated 12 May 1860. Absorbed into the 1st Corps in October 1860.

The amalgamated Hull corps was designated as the 1st Yorkshire (East Riding) Rifle Volunteers and in 1883, under General Order 63 of May, became the 1st Volunteer Battalion of the East Yorkshire Regiment. A cadet corps was formed for the battalion by Hymers College in July 1900.

In 1908 the 1st VB provided the 4th Battalion, East Yorkshires and the cadet corps became part of the Junior Division of the Officers Training Corps.

The 2nd Admin. Battalion of East Yorkshire was formed in May 1860 with headquarters at Beverley. Renumbered as 1st in February 1861 the battalion contained the following corps—

3rd Corps: Formed at Howden on 28 March 1860.

5th Corps: Formed at Bridlington on 3 March 1860.

6th Corps: Formed at Beverley on 28 February 1860.

8th Corps: Formed at Driffield on 3 March 1860 and appeared in the *Army List* as 7th Corps until October 1860.

9th Corps: Formed at Market Weighton on 11 May 1860 and was shown as 8th Corps until October 1860. In the January 1861 *Army List* the corps is shown as the 9th Sub-division but it is once again included as 9th Corps by May.

10th Corps: Formed at Hedon on 3 August 1861 and disappeared from the *Army List* in late 1876.

11th Corps: Formed at Pocklington on 8 August 1868.

The 1st Admin. was consolidated as the 3rd Corps in 1880 but this was changed to 2nd within a few months. Headquarters remained at Beverley and the corps' six companies were lettered 'A' to 'F' and formed in order of seniority by the remaining six corps of the battalion.

Under General Order 63 of May 1883 the 2nd became the 2nd Volunteer Battalion of the East Yorkshire Regiment. In 1908 the battalion provided four companies of the 5th Battalion Yorkshire Regiment.

YORKSHIRE (NORTH RIDING)

In July 1860 the existing Yorkshire North Riding Rifle Corps were placed into two administrative battalions. All subsequent units raised were also included until 1877 and the formation of the 21st Corps at Middlesbrough. This corps was formed on 13 October and from that date was included in the 4th Admin. Battalion of Durham Rifle Volunteers. The 21st remained with that battalion until 1880 and its consolidation as the 1st Durham Rifle Volunteer Corps. The Middlesbrough Corps providing 'G' and 'H' Companies.

Headquarters of the 1st Admin. Battalion were at Richmond and the corps included were as follows—

2nd Corps: Formed at Swaledale on 18 February 1860. Disbanded in December 1863.

4th Corps: Formed at Leyburn on 29 February 1860. Absorbed the 12th Corps in 1874.

5th Corps: The original 5th Corps was formed at Forcett on 23 February 1860 and disbanded in May 1871. On the nineteenth of the following month a new 5th Corps was formed from the No 3 Company of the 15th Corps. This unit had been raised at Gilling on 28 December 1865. The new 5th was to last until 1875 when it too was disbanded.

7th Corps: Formed at Startforth on 29 February 1860. In November 1863 the corps was transferred to the 4th Durham Admin. Battalion. By the end of December the 7th had been transferred to Durham's 2nd Admin. and redesignated as the 21st Durham Corps. Headquarters were at this time moved to Barnard Castle.

8th Corps: Formed at Bedale on 19 March 1860.

9th Corps: Formed at Stokesley on 6 March 1860.

11th Corps: Formed at Masham on 17 March 1860. Disappeared from the *Army List* in October 1866.

12th Corps: Formed at Carperby on 10 March 1860. Moved to Thornton Rust in 1869 and absorbed into the 4th Corps in 1874.

14th Corps: Formed at Catterick on 19 April 1860.

15th Corps: Formed at Richmond on 16 April 1860. A 2nd Company was formed at Reeth on 9 March 1865 followed by a 3rd at Gilling on 28 December. A 4th was raised in February 1868 but in June 1871 the Gilling Company was made independent and designated as 5th Corps.

18th Corps: Formed at Skelton on 30 May 1860.

19th Corps: Formed at Northallerton on 20 August 1860.

20th Corps: A 20th Corps was to be formed at Whitby but this disappeared from the *Army List* in April 1861 having had no officers gazetted to it. A new 20th was formed at Guisborough on 3 February 1863.

Upon consolidation in 1880 the battalion at first took on the number of its senior corps, 4th. This, however, was changed to 1st after a few months. As the 1st Yorkshire (North Riding) Rifle Volunteer Corps the battalion retained its head-quarters at Richmond. The establishment was set at nine companies which were organised as follows—

'A' Company at Thornton Rust	Late 4th Corps
'B' Company at Bedale	Late 8th Corps
'C' Company at Stokesley	Late 9th Corps
'D' Company at Catterick	Late 14th Corps
'E' Company at Richmond	Late 15th Corps
'F' Company at Reeth	Late 15th Corps
'G' Company at Skelton	Late 18th Corps
'H' Company at Northallerton	Late 19th Corps
'K' Company at Guisborough	Late 20th Corps

In 1883 headquarters of the corps were moved to Northallerton and under General Order 14 of February the designation 1st Volunteer Battalion, The Princess of Wales's Own (Yorkshire Regiment) was assumed.

An additional company was formed in 1900 and in April 1908 the 1st VB became the 4th Battalion of the Yorkshire Regt. At this time the ten companies were located at Bedale, Eston, Stokesley, Catterick, Richmond, Redcar, Skelton, Northallerton, Thirsk and Guisborough.

The original headquarters of the 2nd Admin. Battalion were at Malton but in 1876 a move was made to Scarborough. The corps contained were—

1st Corps: Formed at Malton on 18 February 1860.

3rd Corps: Formed at Hovingham on 10 February 1860.

6th Corps: Formed at Scarborough on 28 February 1860.

10th Corps: Formed at Helmsley-in-Ryedale on 9 March 1860.

13th Corps: Formed at Thirsk on 27 March 1860. Disappeared from the *Army List* in May 1868.

16th Corps: Formed at Pickering Lythe on 4 May 1860.

17th Corps: Formed at Pickering Lythe East on 28 April 1860. Moved to Wydale Brompton, York in 1861 and was last seen in the *Army List* for December 1865.

When the battalion was consolidated in March 1880 it was at first designated as 1st Corps. This, however, was changed to 2nd in the following June. Headquarters remained at Scarborough and the seven companies of the new corps organised as follows—

'A' Company at Malton	Late 1st Corps
'B' 'C' Companies at Hovingham	Late 3rd Corps
'D' 'E' Companies at Scarborough	Late 6th Corps
'F' Company at Helmsley-in-Ryedale	Late 10th Corps
'G' Company at Pickering	Late 16th Corps

Under General Order 14 of February 1883 the 2nd Corps became the 2nd Volunteer Battalion of the Princess of Wales's Own (Yorkshire Regiment). The regiment's 5th Battalion was formed in April 1908 upon the amalgamation of the 2nd VB with the 2nd VB of the East Yorkshire Regiment. The North Yorkshire battalion providing headquarters and four companies.

YORKSHIRE (WEST RIDING)

During 1880 the existing rifle corps of the West Riding of Yorkshire were organised into nine independent units. These new formations were numbered as 1st to 9th Corps and were later to provide the volunteer battalions of the West Yorkshire, Duke of Wellington's, King's Own Yorkshire Light Infantry and York and Lancaster Regiments. Previous to 1880 the Riding had raised corps numbered to 45th. Companies formed in the areas of Sheffield, Bradford, Halifax and Leeds were, from a very early date, merged into corps of battalion strength while those situated in rural districts were placed into one or other of the five administrative battalions created.

Details of the various corps raised have been recorded, in the following, under the post-1880 series of numbers.

1ST CORPS

The senior corps of the West Riding was created in 1880 by the consolidation of the 1st Admin. Battalion. Formed at York in May 1860, the 1st Admin. contained the following corps—

1st Corps: The services of the 1st Corps, headquarters York, were accepted on 5 September 1859. Four companies were soon formed, the last of which was raised by members of St Peter's School.

16th Corps: Formed at Harrogate on 21 February 1860.

17th Corps: Formed at Knaresborough on 27 February 1860.

27th Corps: Formed at Ripon on 13 April 1860.

31st Corps: A 31st Corps, headquarters Tadcaster, first appeared in the *Army List* for July 1860. Officers were appointed but their commissions were not issued until 16 February 1864. Did not join the battalion until September.

33rd Corps: The first commissions issued to this corps were dated 24 December 1860. It was not shown in the *Army List*, however, until December 1861. The 33rd was subsequently broken up in 1863 having had its headquarters at Wetherby.

38th Corps: Formed at Selby on 1 January 1861 the 38th was originally included in the 3rd Admin. Battalion. Transfer to the 1st was in December 1863.

Headquarters of the new 1st Corps remained at York and the eleven companies were organised as follows—

'A' to 'E' Companies at York	Late 1st Corps
'F' Company at Harrogate	Late 16th Corps
'G' Company at Knaresborough	Late 17th Corps
'H' 'J' Companies at Ripon	Late 27th Corps
'K' Company at Tadcaster	Late 31st Corps
'L' Company at Selby	Late 38th Corps

Under General Order 181 of December 1887 the 1st Corps became the 1st Volunteer Battalion of the West Yorkshire Regiment. An additional company was raised in 1900 and in 1908 the 5th Battalion West Yorkshire Regiment was formed upon transfer to the Territorial Force. At this time company locations were; York (5), Harrogate (2), Knaresborough (1), Ripon (2), Pateley Bridge (1), Selby (1).

2ND CORPS

According to Bartholomew's *Survey Gazetteer of the British Isles*, Hallamshire is an 'ancient lordship of the West Riding of Yorkshire'. It is mentioned in the *Domesday Book* and is represented by the parishes of Sheffield and Ecclesfield. It was in Sheffield, on 30 September 1859, that three companies of rifle volunteers were formed and designated as the 2nd, 3rd and 4th Yorkshire West Riding Corps.

It was soon decided that the City of Sheffield would be better served by a corps of battalion strength and in December 1859 amalgamation of the three companies plus one newly-raised was proposed. The merger took place under the title of 'The

Hallamshire Rifle Volunteer Corps' but the official designation '2nd Yorkshire West Riding (Hallamshire)' was conferred by February 1860. The four company strength was later increased to five when a company was raised from employees of the Atlas Works. This was followed by two more and by the end of 1861 the establishment of the battalion stood at seven companies.

Redesignation as the 1st (Hallamshire) Volunteer Battalion of the York and Lancaster Regiment was notified in General Order 14 of February 1883. In 1908 the 1st VB provided the regiment's 4th Battalion.

3RD CORPS

On 27 September 1859 two companies of rifle volunteers were formed in Bradford and designated as the 5th and 6th West Riding Corps. In February of the following year the two corps, together with other Bradford Companies, hitherto unnumbered, were merged as 5th Corps. By April 1860 the Bradford Corps had been re-numbered as 3rd and in October its strength was increased to five companies upon amalgamation with the 24th Corps at Eccleshill. The 24th had been formed on 27 February 1860.

Another corps to be associated with the 3rd was the 39th which was attached for drill and administration in 1862. With headquarters at Bingley the 39th was formed on 8 April 1861. It moved to Saltaire in 1871 and was disbanded in April 1875.

In 1887, and under General Order 181 of December, the 3rd became the 2nd Volunteer Battalion of the West Yorkshire Regiment. The regiment's 6th Battalion was formed upon transfer to the Territorial Force in April 1908.

4TH CORPS

The original 7th and 8th Corps were formed at Halifax on 13 October 1859. These were shortly followed by the 13th and 14th, also at Halifax, and on 24 February 1860 the four companies were amalgamated as 7th. Re-numbering as 4th Corps took place on 27 April 1860. A 5th company was formed at Sowerby in 1861 which was followed by units at Brighouse, Hebden Bridge and Upper Shibden Hall.

With an establishment of six companies the 4th Corps became the 1st Volunteer Battalion of the Duke of Wellington's Regiment in 1883. The change being notified in General Order 14 of February. In 1908 the 1st VB provided the regiment's 4th Battalion, the company locations at that time being: Halifax (4), Brighouse (1), Checkheaton (1).

5TH CORPS

The 3rd Admin. Battalion of Yorkshire West Riding Rifle Volunteers was formed in June 1860 and contained the following corps—

5th Corps: Formed as the 9th Corps at Wakefield on 17 November 1859. Re-numbered as 5th in July, of the following year. The corps soon consisted of three companies, the 1st being formed by tradesmen, the 2nd by clerks and the 3rd by working men.

28th Corps: Formed at Goole on 2 May 1860.

29th Corps: Formed at Dewsbury on 3 May 1860. In 1867 the strength of the 29th reached six companies enabling it to become indepentent of the 3rd Admin. Battalion. A reduction in strength to three companies occurred in 1873 and the corps was once again included in the battalion.

30th Corps: Formed at Birstal on 1 September 1860. This corps disappeared from the *Army List* in October 1873.

37th Corps: Formed at Barnsley on 2 November 1860. This corps remained independent until March 1862 when it joined the 3rd Admin. Battalion. Transfer to the 4th Admin. occurred in April 1863.

38th Corps: Formed at Selby on 1 January 1861 and transferred to the 1st Admin. Battalion in December 1863.

43rd Corps: The services of the 43rd were accepted on 22 June 1867. Headquarters were at Batley.

In 1880 the battalion, whose headquarters were at Wakefield, was consolidated as the 5th Corps. Company organisation went as follows—

'A' to 'D' Companies at Wakefield	Late 5th Corps
'E' Company at Goole	Late 28th Corps
'F' to 'H' Companies at Dewsbury	Late 29th Corps
'J' 'K' Companies at Batley	Late 43rd Corps

Under General Order 14 of February 1883 the 5th Yorkshire (West Riding) Rifle Volunteer Corps became the 1st Volunteer Battalion of the King's Own Light Infantry (South Yorkshire Regiment).

Although the ten company establishment was retained, several changes in organisation took place. By 1908 the battalion was located as follows; Wakefield (3 companies), Normanton (1), Goole (1), Dewsbury (2), Ossett (1) and Batley (2).

Upon transfer to the Territorial Force in 1908 the 1st VB provided both TF battalions of the King's Own. The 4th was formed by the Wakefield, Dewsbury, Ossett and Batley Companies while the 5th was created by the Normanton and Goole personnel. The remainder of this battalion was found by elements of the 2nd VB York and Lancaster Regiment.

6TH CORPS

The last of the West Riding Admin. Battalions, the 5th, was formed on 18 September 1862. Headquarters were placed in Huddersfield and the corps included then or at some later date were—

6th Corps: The services of a corps of rifle volunteers raised in Huddersfield were accepted on 3 November 1859. The number received by the corps was 10th although this had originally been intended for the company raised at North Craven (see 9th Corps). Redesignation as the 6th Corps occurred in July 1860 and on 25 January 1868 the additional title 'The Huddersfield' was sanctioned. By March 1860 the establishment of the corps had reached four companies. A 5th was added in 1864 and in 1868 additional personnel were added at Outlane, four miles north-west of Huddersfield, providing No 6

Company. Also that year No 7 Company was formed at Lindley being mainly recruited from employees of the several manufacturing firms of the area.

32nd Corps: Formed at Holmfirth on 26 May 1860.

34th Corps: This corps was formed at Saddleworth on 10 September 1860 and was, in April 1862, permitted to include '(Saddleworth)' in its full title. By 1869 a strength of eight companies had been attained. These were located at Saddleworth, Delph, Lydgate, Slaithwaite, Marsden, Golcar, Woodsome and Kirkburton. In 1877, however, a reduction to four companies occurred and from that year the 34th became part of the 5th Admin. Battalion.

41st Corps: Formed at Mirfield on 15 November 1864.

44th Corps: Formed at Meltham on 10 July 1868. This corps was disbanded on 11 January 1876.

The 5th Admin. Battalion was consolidated as the 6th Corps in June 1880. Headquarters remained at Huddersfield and the ten companies were organised as follows—

'A' to 'D' Companies at Huddersfield	Late 6th Corps
'E' Company at Holmfirth	Late 32nd Corps
'F' to 'J' Companies at Saddleworth	Late 34th Corps
'K' Company at Mirfield	Late 41st Corps

By 1908 the strength of the battalion stood at eleven companies which upon transfer to the Territorial Force provided both the 5th and 7th Battalions of the Duke of Wellington's Regiment. The 6th Corps had become the 2nd Volunteer Battalion of the regiment under General Order 14 of February 1883.

7TH CORPS

On 17 November 1859 the first company of Leeds Rifle Volunteers was formed within the city. This was numbered as the 11th Corps which by March 1860 consisted of five companies. In May 1860 the 22nd Corps, raised in Leeds on 29 February 1860, was absorbed into the 11th, but this brought about no increase in establishment. By 1861, however, an additional four companies had been raised. Of these No 6 was provided by the Monkbridge Steel Company, No 7 by the Wellington Foundry, No 8 by Messrs Greenwood & Batley and No 9 by Messrs Joshua Tetley's Brewery. The last company to be formed was in August 1875. This was to bring the establishment up to ten companies which remained the strength of the corps until 1908.

As a result of the amalgamation during the early part of 1860 between the Halifax Corps the 7th position in the West Riding list became vacant. This was filled by the 11th Corps on 3 July. In 1864 the additional title '(Leeds)' was added to the full designation of the corps. The next change, which was notified in General Order 181 of December 1887, saw the 7th styled as the 3rd Volunteer Battalion of the West Yorkshire Regiment. This was followed in April 1908 by the transfer of the 3rd VB to the Territorial Force as the 7th and 8th Battalions of the regiment.

8TH CORPS

Doncaster was the headquarters of the West Riding's 4th Admin. Battalion. This was formed in August 1860 and contained then, or upon formation, the following corps—

18th Corps: Formed at Pontefract on 3 March 1860.

19th Corps: Formed at Rotherham on 29 February 1860.

20th Corps: Formed at Doncaster on 5 March 1860.

21st Corps: Formed at Doncaster on 5 March 1860.

36th Corps: Formed at Rotherham on 19 October 1860. This corps was not included in the battalion until the latter part of 1862.

37th Corps: Formed at Barnsley on 2 November 1860. Remained independent until March 1862 when it joined the 3rd Admin. Battalion. Transfer to the 4th was in April 1863.

40th Corps: Formed at Hoyland Nether on 19 March 1863. Headquarters moved to Wath-upon-Dearne in 1866.

Upon consolidation in 1880 the original number adopted was 18th, this being the position of the senior company. After a few months, however, this was changed to 8th. Headquarters of the new corps remained at Doncaster and its nine companies organised as follows—

'A' Company at Pontefract	Late 18th Corps
'B' Company at Rotherham	Late 19th Corps
'C' Company at Doncaster	Late 20th Corps
'D' Company at Doncaster	Late 21st Corps
'E' Company at Rotherham	Late 19th Corps
'F' Company at Barnsley	Late 37th Corps
'G' Company at Wath-upon-Dearne	Late 40th Corps
'H' Company at Barnsley	Late 37th Corps
'J' Company at Rotherham	Late 36th Corps

The 8th Corps became the 2nd Volunteer Battalion of the York and Lancaster Regiment in 1883 the change being notitied in General Order 14 of February.

In 1894 a cadet corps was formed at Rotherham and affiliated to the battalion. This, however, disappeared from the *Army List* during 1899. An additional company was formed by the battalion in 1884 followed by two more in 1900. By 1908 company locations were; Pontefract (1), Rotherham (3), Doncaster (5), Barnsley (2) and Wath-upon-Dearne (1).

When the Territorial Force was created in 1908 the 2nd VB York and Lancasters were split. The Rotherham, Barnsley and Wath-upon-Dearne personnel remained with the regiment and provided its 5th Battalion while the men from Doncaster and Pontefract formed the 5th Battalion of the King's Own (Yorkshire Light Infantry).

9TH CORPS

The 2nd Admin. Battalion of Yorkshire (West Riding) Rifle Volunteers was formed with headquarters at Skipton-in-Craven during June 1860. The corps included then or at some later date were—

12th Corps: Formed at Skipton on 8 February 1860. Shown in the *Army List* as Skipton-in-Craven from 1865.

15th Corps: In the *Army List* for October 1859 a 10th Yorkshire (West Riding) Corps is shown as existing at North Craven. In that for December, however, the 10th position is given as being held by Huddersfield while North Craven appears as the 1st Sub-division. The strength of the North Craven corps was, by March 1860, increased to that of a full company but by this time only the precedence number 15th could be allocated. Headquarters of the corps were moved to Settle in 1871.

23rd Corps: Formed at Burley on 20 February 1860.

25th Corps: Formed at Guiseley on 5 March 1860 but disbanded in August 1876.

26th Corps: Formed at Ingleton on 21 March 1860. This corps was later broken up and is last seen in the *Army List* for January 1874.

35th Corps: Formed at Keighley on 27 October 1860 and remained independent until 1862 when attached to the 3rd Corps. The corps joined the 2nd Admin. in 1865 and in 1867 '(Airedale)' appears in the *Army List* as part of its full designation. Airedale is the name given to the Valley area of the River Aire.

42nd Corps: Formed at Haworth on 9 April 1866.

45th Corps: This corps was formed at Bingley on 30 June 1875 largely from members of the recently disbanded 39th Corps.

As was the custom the number of the senior corps, 12th, was adopted upon consolidation in 1880. This, however, was changed to 9th after a few months. Headquarters remained at Skipton-in-Craven and the eight companies of the new corps were organised as follows—

'A' Company at Skipton-in-Craven	Late 12th Corps
'B' Company at Settle	Late 15th Corps
'C' Company at Burley	Late 23rd Corps
'D' to 'F' Companies at Keighley	Late 35th Corps
'G' Company at Haworth	Late 42nd Corps
'H' Company at Bingley	Late 45th Corps

Redesignation as the 3rd Volunteer Battalion of the Duke of Wellington's Regiment was notified in General Order 14 of February 1883. Additional companies were raised in 1884 and 1900 and in 1908 the 3rd VB became the 6th Battalion of the regiment.

Postcard sent by a member of 'L'
Company, 1st VB Worcestershire Regt
from Brigade camp, Porthcawl 1907.

page 172

BIBLIOGRAPHY

Monthly Army Lists 1859–1908.
London Gazettes 1859–1908.
The Lambeth and Southwark Volunteers by J. M. A. Tamplin.
History of the Cambridge University OTC by Hew Strachan.
Lineage Book of the British Army by J. B. M. Frederick.
Records of the Scottish Volunteer Force by Lt-Gen Sir James Moncrieff Grierson.
Hertfordshire's Soldiers by J. D. Sainsbury.
Records of the 3rd Middlesex Rifle Volunteers by E. T. Evans.
HM Territorial Army by W. Richards.
The Volunteer Service Magazine 6 vols, May 1892 – June 1898.
Territorial Year Book 1909.
West Yorkshire Rifle Volunteers, 1859–1887 by K. D. Pickup.
History of the Volunteer Infantry by Robert Potter Berry.
The History of the Prince of Wales' Own Civil Service Rifles.
The O.T.C. and the Great War by A. R. Haig-Brown.
History of the Royal Hampshire Regiment, Vol 1 by C. T. Atkinson.
Cinque Ports Battalion by Col E. A. C. Fazan.
History of the Corps of the KSLI Vol IV by G. Archer Parfitt.
Historical Records of the Herefordshire LI by G. Archer Parfitt.
Volunteers in Suffolk by Major E. R. Cooper.
Short History of the 4/6th Bn Royal Berkshire Regt.
The Tower Hamlets Rifle Volunteer Brigade by Col E. T. Rodney Wilde.
History of the Rugby School Corps 1860–1960 by Lt-Col H. J. Harris.
History of the 1st VB, The Royal Warwickshire Regt by Col C. J. Hart.
The Story of the Rye Volunteers by L. A. Vidler.
Faithful, The Story of the DLI by S. G. P. Ward.
History of the KOYLI 1755 to 1914 by Col H. C. Wylly.
The King's Own, The Story of a Royal Regiment, Vol II by Col L. I. Cowper.
The Horncastle Detachment, 4th Bn Royal Lincolnshire Regt by H. R. Tweed.
Regimental Records of the 24th Middlesex RV 1868–1896.
History of the 1st VB Hampshire Regt by Col Sturmy Cave.

Printed at Picton Print
keyboarding Veronica Pinniger
page make-up Lyn Burton
negatives Liz Wilkins
platemaking Mike Simmonds
machining Neville Fox